BIG BEND &
WEST TEXAS

BIG BEND & WEST TEXAS

ERIC O'KEEFE

Lone Star Books®
An imprint of Gulf Publishing Company
Houston, Texas

LONE STAR GUIDES:
BIG BEND & WEST TEXAS

Lone Star Books®
An imprint of Gulf Publishing Company
P.O. Box 2608 ☐ Houston, Texas 77252-2608

10   9   8   7   6   5   4   3   2   1

Library of Congress Cataloging-in-Publication Data

O'Keefe, Eric.
    Lone Star guide. Big Bend and West Texas / Eric O'Keefe.
        p.   cm.
    Includes index.
    ISBN 0-89123-037-8 (alk. paper)
        1. Big Bend Region (Tex.)—Guidebooks.   2. Texas, West—
    Guidebooks.   I. Title.   II. Title: Big Bend and West Texas.
    F392.B54054   1999
    917.64′90453—dc21   99-29206
                                                          CIP

Printed in the United States of America.
Printed on acid-free paper (∞).

*Front cover photo of Big Bend National Park, Pine Canyon, © Charles E. Schmidt,
Unicorn Stock Photos.*

*Back cover photo of Big Bend National Park, "The Window," © Andre Jenny,
Unicorn Stock Photos, and photo of Palo Duro Canyon © Wyman Meinzer.*

Cover design by Laura A. Dion.

Dedicated to the memory
of two legendary West Texans,
Gene Hendryx
and
Barton Warnock

CONTENTS

FOREWORD

Texas is a place where we develop a love affair with the outdoors early and stay committed for a lifetime. When I think of West Texas, I think of camping and canoe trips and those precious moments when I get the chance to get down to the river and back to a place that puts the frustrations of life into perspective. From the brilliant red cliffs of Big Bend National Park to the vastness of the Panhandle Plains, traveling out West is sort of a Texas right of passage.

Yet the West Texas frontier brings to mind much more than natural beauty. It is the everlasting stage of Texas history. From the revolutionary battles of a fledgling Republic to the swirling song and dance of Indian ceremony, West Texas has served as the backdrop for the events that defined our heritage and shaped our lives. West Texas remains a place of wonder and adventure, where legends and heroes are larger than life and Texas history is as vivid as the stars in a midnight sky.

With *Big Bend & West Texas* as your guide, you'll experience the beauty of West Texas in grand style. Eric O'Keefe has done an outstanding job collecting the sights and stories that make West Texas the heart and soul of God's country.

Ann W. Richards
Governor of Texas
(Jan. 1991–Jan. 1995)

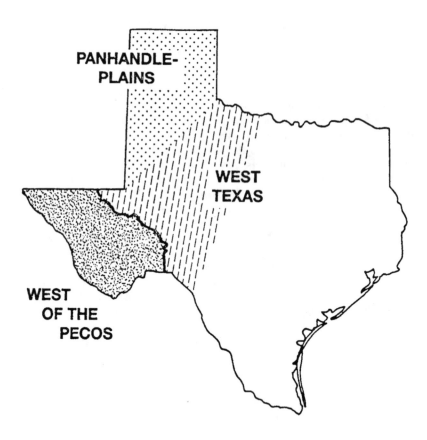

PANHANDLE-
PLAINS

WEST
TEXAS

WEST
OF THE
PECOS

INTRODUCTION

Just once during your visit to West Texas, follow these simple directions and you'll learn more about this country than any guidebook offers. One evening right after sunset, pull safely off whatever byway you're traveling and cut the engine. Step outside. It'll take a moment for your ears and eyes to adjust.

If you're like most people, you'll quickly find yourself hoping that you didn't lock yourself out of the car and praying that it starts once you get back in because most of us aren't fit to be out here on our own.

It's too big. It's too rugged. It's that authentic. Just a century ago, buffalo roamed, cavalry patrolled, and renegades haunted this last frontier. The few towns in West Texas that existed then were American attempts to settle country that Spain and Mexico had given up on centuries before. Thousands of square miles north of the Rio Grande remained unsettled, even unexplored, dating back to the 1500s. The best lands had been home to North America's great horsemen—the Comanche. Up in the hills, the Apache lived—high in the Guadalupe, Davis, and Chisos Mountains. The conquistadors had a name for the rest of the land—*despoblado*—unpeopled. The term described barren flats, rugged canyons, and distant mesas prone to flash floods and plagued by lethal reptiles and spiny cacti.

Tear up a few highways, board up a few towns, roll up the barbed wire, and you're back in the country Cabeza de Vaca crossed nearly five centuries ago. The millions of acres that stretch from the Rio Grande to New Mexico and Oklahoma are full of national and state parks, as well as ranches and farms—where city lights and city ways aren't a part of life but visitors are always welcome.

LISTINGS

West Texas is comprised of a wide array of geological, biological, political, and historical regions. In the organization of this guidebook, three well-known ones are utilized: West of the Pecos, the Panhandle-

Plains, and West Texas. Only one region, the Trans-Pecos, is so distinct that few will find fault with its limits: the Mexican border to the south and west, the New Mexican border to the north, and the Pecos River to the east. The second one, the Panhandle-Plains, has clear boundaries along its northern and western reaches: Oklahoma and New Mexico. Along its southern and eastern edges, however, several criteria limit its range such as the Permian Basin and the Rolling Plains. The third grouping is referred to as West Texas. A more specific term is inappropriate because this region includes portions of the Edwards Plateau, the Chihuahuan Desert, the Rolling Plains, and the Permian Basin.

Immediately following a brief introduction to each region begins an alphabetical listing of cities and the larger parks. All descriptions start with the county name, the most recent population figures, and the area code. All these major listings include some or all of the following criteria:

TOURIST SERVICES

Most are not-for-profit organizations whose mission includes assisting visitors either planning trips or just in town. Examples include the National Park Service and local chambers of commerce or visitor bureaus. When appropriate, for profit guides or shuttle services are also included.

GUIDEBOOKS AND PUBLICATIONS

In addition to local visitor guides, magazines and newspapers published weekly or less frequently are listed. Less likely to clutter your mailbox, they often cater to out of town readers.

BIRD'S-EYE VIEW

Sometimes it's the top of the county courthouse (Marfa); sometimes it's a view from a prominent city park (El Paso); or it might even be the top of Texas (Guadalupe Mountains National Park).

MUSEUMS

In the major metropolitan areas, count on museums to operate according to posted schedules. Many smaller historical societies don't have the personnel or funding to cover all shifts or, in some cases, even regular shifts. If you are making a special trip to a specific small town museum, call in advance. They'll appreciate the courtesy and you'll be happy to see someone there.

HISTORIC PLACES

Ruins, ranch houses, abandoned mining operations, and other historic sites are included under this heading. For a listing of Texas historical roadside markers, pick up a copy of *Why Stop?* by Betty Dooley Awbrey and Claude Dooley (Houston: Gulf Publishing Co.).

OTHER POINTS OF INTEREST

Look for zoos, observatories, research centers, and most state parks under the Other Points of Interest headings.

SPORTS AND ACTIVITIES

A generous helping of participant and spectator sports and activities are included. Many are free.

COLLEGES AND UNIVERSITIES

Every institution of higher education surveyed welcomes visitors even if just for a guided tour. Almost all of them sponsor activities open to the public, ranging from NCAA football games featuring nationally ranked teams to rodeos, concerts, art shows, and seminars. Many have facilities covered elsewhere in the book, like museums and galleries.

PERFORMING ARTS

A partial listing includes world-class musicals like *TEXAS* (performed each summer in Palo Duro Canyon State Park), concerts, dramas, operas, and dance. The telephone number listed offers the best opportunity to nail down specific times, dates, and prices.

SHOPPING

The objective is to offer products or services that you either don't find at home or don't find this cheap. Many of the shops, or *tiendas*, make up for their poor or downright shabby decor by offering the real McCoy: *ristras* (strings of onions or garlic) from nearby fields, or rare rock samples right off the ranch. Major shopping centers are included in case you end up far from home without one of life's many accessories.

SIDE TRIPS

You won't bump into these places in the city, town, or park being featured. They're often out of state, usually out-of-the-way, and always well worth the time.

ANNUAL EVENTS

Listings range from nationally known events like the Terlingua Chili Cook-Off or El Paso's Sun Bowl to the not-so-well-known. With few exceptions, all are well established and regularly held. Each event lists a contact phone number. Often it rings at the local chamber of commerce or the visitor bureau. Times, dates, fees, entertainers, and venues are all subject to change. Quite often the person giving you information can also offer updates on hotels and availability.

RESTAURANTS

The purpose of this guide is to spread the word about good places you haven't been to before, i.e., chains and franchises are not included. What are included are local favorites, restaurants of note, and any other establishment that delivered what was promised or better. Bad food, poor service, and irregular hours were the principal factors in any omissions. The pricing guide for dining is a simple one: cheap, moderate, and pricey dinner entrées:

($ = Under $7.50, $$ = Under $15, $$$ = $15+ plus tax & tip)

Using this scheme, add your choice of beverage as well as taxes and tip to estimate your dinner tab (or lunch if dinner is not served). At the end of most listings, as well as in the CLUBS AND BARS section, is a reference to the alcohol served. "Bar" refers to a full liquor license (which means hard liquor, as well as beer and wine). The "Beer and wine" designation excludes mixed drinks.

The following abbreviations are listed after the pricing symbol and indicate which, if any, credit cards are accepted.

AE	American Express
D	Discover
DC	Diners Club
MC	Master Card
V	Visa
Cr	All major credit cards accepted

ACCOMMODATIONS

Covering hotels, motels, bed and breakfasts, and youth hostels, the pricing guidelines below are for rack rates, i.e., a standard room without any discounts, and are based on double occupancy.

$ = Under $40, $$ = $40–$75, $$$ = $75–$100, $$$$ = Over $100

The exorbitant combination of city, county, state, and hotel and motel occupancy taxes may also be listed and is added to your bill.

No discounts or surcharges are factored in. Plenty exist. Some of the more obvious ones are membership in organizations like AARP or AAA, attendance at special events, a business-related stay, and off-season rates (when occupancy levels tend to slump).

Almost all of the toll-free numbers listed are to central reservations centers, not to the properties themselves. Personnel at the property are better versed in pricing changes, more likely to offer discounts, and much more accountable when you arrive (always get a name).

WHEELCHAIR ACCESSIBILITY SYMBOLS

Most public buildings and many private ones maintain reserved parking, and an increasing number offer handicapped facilities with no more than two steps to a wide entrance. Symbols used are:

No symbol	Inconvenient or no access.
W	Wheelchair accessible but not to areas like restrooms.
W+	All major areas including restrooms are accessible.
W+ but not all areas	Accessible and with restroom facilities, however, some areas are inaccessible.

GETTING AROUND

DRIVING IN WEST TEXAS

Call the Texas Department of Transportation's Travel Information Center at 800-452-9292 for information on road conditions, weather delays, construction schedules, even foliage updates. Its phone lines are open seven days a week from 8 a.m. to 9 p.m. Interstate speed limits have a legal ceiling of 70 mph, with some state and county roads 55 mph. After jetting across Far West Texas, New Mexico, or Chihuahua, take care in El Paso along Interstate 10 where curving concrete canyons are notorious speed traps with numerous blind spots to shield EPPD's radar.

Don't be surprised to encounter Border Patrol checkpoints as you leave areas like El Paso, the Big Bend, and Del Rio. As a rule the most courteous of federal officers, Border Patrol agents are looking for illegal aliens and/or contraband and usually ask for a verbal declaration of citizenship and perhaps where you've been or your final destination. Compared to Customs, they'll seem like the welcome wagon.

Thank Lyndon Johnson for the many roadside stops you'll encounter during your drive across West Texas. As the Lone Star State's director for the National Youth Administration in the 1930s, he kept thousands of Texans at work during the Depression building the nation's largest system of roadside parks. Many have vending machines, restrooms, and phones; others are quite spartan and offer just picnic tables and a trash bin.

GOING INTO MEXICO

Keep in mind that all regulations are subject to change, particularly to and from Mexico. For Americans and Canadians, no permits or passports are required to cross over and back. Deeper forays into Mexico incur a $15 fee and require a tourist card (free), which can be picked up at the port of entry or at a Mexican consulate in the United States. Border cities like Juarez are best enjoyed for short trips to sightsee and shop or to dine and dance. Most merchants and restaurateurs welcome U.S. dollars.

To reenter, a verbal declaration of citizenship or the presentation of an alien registration card is typically all that is required. The American government allows U.S. residents to bring back without duty items for personal or household use with a value up to $400.00 (retail) every 31 days. In addition, U.S. residents may bring from Mexico into the U.S. once every 31 days up to one quart of liquor per person 21 or older and/or one carton of cigarettes or 100 cigars (not Cuban). The U.S. Department of Agriculture has strict guidelines on bringing fruits, vegetables, plants, bulbs, seeds, and cuttings back to the States. Don't forget the State of Texas, whose Alcoholic Beverage Commission levies a minor charge on any alcohol brought back from Mexico.

WEST OF THE PECOS

Despoblado. It means unpopulated, and it describes the region west of the Pecos and north of the Rio Grande as accurately in the twenty-first century as when conquistadors arrived in the sixteenth. This massive territory shapes the lives of its citizens and the tours of its visitors in every respect. Here's an example: Like kids everywhere, school children from Candelaria take the bus to school. The only difference is the Presidio Independent School District sees fit to send six-, eight-, and ten-year-olds 50 miles each way. That's every morning and every afternoon. Keep distances of that sort in mind during any visit west of the Pecos. Convenient it is not. Try spectacular, historic, *despoblado.*

Governments local, national, and international have designated the arid Trans-Pecos and its mix of mountains, deserts, waterways, and caverns a treasure for all mankind. Once you arrive (an accomplishment in itself), you'll begin to see how the parts fit together: an enormous expanse of Chihuahuan Desert atop geologic formations 30 million years old, 300 million years old, even Precambrian.

Rocky Mountain rivers set this country apart from neighboring terrain and distinguish it from other American deserts like the Mojave, the Sonoran, and the Great Basin. Surrounding it all, the Rio Grande and the Pecos rivers (with some help from Mexico's Rio Conchos) turn some of America's most inhospitable country into some of its most dramatic.

ALPINE

BREWSTER COUNTY SEAT • 5,637 • (915)

The commercial center of the Big Bend, Alpine has been a stopover for conquistadors, Comanches, and, most recently, thousands of Sul Ross State University students. Ranching and the railroad gave birth to

WEST OF THE PECOS

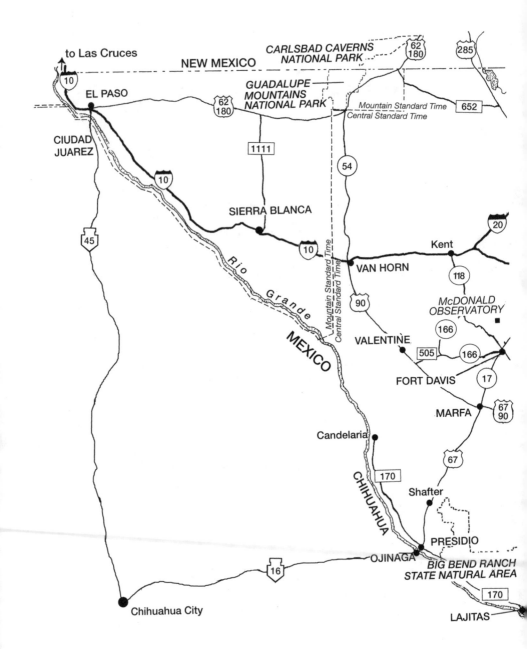

to Las Cruces

NEW MEXICO

CARLSBAD CAVERNS
NATIONAL PARK

62
180

285

10

EL PASO

62
180

GUADALUPE
MOUNTAINS
NATIONAL PARK

Mountain Standard Time
Central Standard Time

652

CIUDAD
JUAREZ

1111

54

10

45

SIERRA BLANCA

Rio

10

Kent

20

VAN HORN

118

Grande

90

McDONALD
OBSERVATORY

MEXICO

VALENTINE

166

505

166

FORT DAVIS

17

MARFA

67
90

Candelaria

67

CHIHUAHUA

170

Shafter

PRESIDIO

OJINAGA

BIG BEND RANCH
STATE NATURAL AREA

16

170

Chihuahua City

LAJITAS

Alpine over a century ago (1883) and are key elements of an economy that also relies on the university, tourism, and burgeoning federal and state payrolls in this border hub. One of the best ways to arrive in the Big Bend and the only stop that Amtrak's *Sunset Limited* and *Texas Eagle* make between Del Rio and El Paso is in Alpine (800-872-7245).

TOURIST SERVICES

ALPINE CHAMBER OF COMMERCE

203 N. 3rd St • 79830 • Monday–Friday 9–12 and 1–5
800-561-3735 • www.alpinetexas.com • www.travelbigbend.com

Alpine serves as the crossroads and refueling stop for many visits to the Big Bend and has numerous restaurants in addition to the area's largest bed base. Information on accommodations, attractions, and transportation services is available, and the Chamber of Commerce is the best resource for updates and schedules on events such as the **Cowboy Rendezvous and Chuckwagon Cook-off**, the **Balloon Rally**, and the **Taste of Texas.**

FIRST NATIONAL BANK IN ALPINE

Intersection of Highway 118 N. and Highway 90 W.
915-837-3375

Participating systems include Cirrus, Pulse, Plus, Discover, Service Card, and Texas Cash.

MUSEUMS

MUSEUM OF THE BIG BEND

Lawrence Hall • SRSU campus • 915-837-8143 • Free • W
Tuesday–Saturday 9–5 • Sunday 1–5 • Closed Monday
www.sulross.edu/~museum/

This museum chronicles millions of years of natural history and the thousands of years that man has traversed and inhabited the Big Bend. The contributions of American Indian, Spanish, Mexican, and Anglo-American cultures are examined including numerous artifacts and mementos (many from pioneering Big Bend families). If you pass through during late February or early March, stop by to view the Trappings of Texas exhibit, which is presented in conjunction with the Texas Cowboy Poetry Gathering.

SPORTS AND ACTIVITIES

Baseball

KOKERNOT FIELD
Loop Road • 915-837-8226 (SRSU Athletic Department) • W

If you time your visit right, the Sul Ross State University Lobos or the Alpine High Fighting Bucks will be taking practice or playing a game at this, America's finest small-town baseball field. Built after World War II at a cost of $1,250,000 by local rancher and team owner Herbert Kokernot Jr., this park has no equal. Its field compares with and often exceeds major league dimensions. The centerfield wall, known as the Green Monster, is 430 feet from the batter's box to the longest home run in the Lone Star State. The wrought-iron lanterns, the manicured infield, and the red base paths (originally Georgia clay) bespeak a tradition of play that includes legendary names like Norm Cash, Jim Fregosi, Satchel Paige, and Gaylord Perry.

Hunting

For starters, consider both Black Gap Wildlife Management Area (*see* **BIG BEND NATIONAL PARK**) and Elephant Mountain Wildlife Management Area (*see* **SIDE TRIPS**). Both of these tracts are owned and administered by the State of Texas specifically for breeding and maintenance of indigenous species like del Carmen white-tailed and mule deer, javelina, quail, and dove. Most other hunts are on private property. The Alpine Chamber of Commerce, at 800-561-3735, has general information about prices, seasons, and availability.

Rodeo

Alpine is the home of National Intercollegiate Rodeo, and Sul Ross hosts a rodeo the first weekend in October for the Southwest Region featuring teams from Texas and New Mexico (*see* **ANNUAL EVENTS**). Several others to consider are the Old Timers Rodeo in Marfa and the Prude Ranch rodeos in Fort Davis.

COLLEGES AND UNIVERSITIES

SUL ROSS STATE UNIVERSITY
915-837-8011 • www.sulross.edu • W+ but not all areas

Sul Ross serves an enormous expanse of Far West Texas and also draws students from across Texas, nationwide, and internationally.

Founded to train teachers in 1917, the teacher education program is the university's largest. Given the outstanding research opportunities throughout the Trans-Pecos, biology, geology, and the Range Animal Science program enjoy excellent reputations.

With the rise of the *maquiladora* and the ongoing interest in the North American Free Trade Agreement, the SRSU MBA program has strengthened its reputation in international trade. Like Range Animal Science, the MBA has developed ties with the University of Chihuahua, and students from both universities take studies across the border.

The Theatre of the Big Bend is well into its third decade, and concerts, performances, and pageants are regularly scheduled in the Marshall Auditorium. The Archives of the Big Bend catalog much of the history of the region—and the state. In intercollegiate athletics, Sul Ross has had several notable campaigns, including a Tangerine Bowl appearance and an NAIA baseball crown. The greatest claim to fame has been the SRSU Rodeo Club. Much as Notre Dame and USC are farm clubs for the ranks of professional football, Sul Ross has had more than its share of alumni on the pro rodeo circuit including El Paso native Tuff Hedeman. In addition to being a three-time world champion, Hedeman passed the $1 million mark in career bull riding earnings and is easily the all-time money winner in that category.

PERFORMING ARTS

THEATRE OF THE BIG BEND
Outdoor Theatre by Kokernot Lodge • 915-837-8218
Thursday–Sunday from early July to 2nd weekend of August
Admission • W

For over 25 years, this repertory company has brought Broadway to West Texas. Sponsored by the Sul Ross State University Fine Arts and Communications Department, each summer's program alternates nightly with a musical and a drama. Recent performances include *Arsenic and Old Lace, Cinderella, Gypsy, Little Shop of Horrors, Once Upon a Mattress, Pippin, Reckless,* and *Tintypes.*

SHOPPING

APACHE TRADING POST
1.5 miles west of Alpine on Highway 90 • 915-837-5506
Monday–Saturday 9–6 • Sunday 1–6 • W

This log cabin just west of Alpine is a must for visitors to the Big Bend. Purchase topographic, geologic, and hiking maps of Big Bend National Park, Big Bend Ranch State Park, and the Davis Mountain region, as well as books and videos on local history, natural sciences, and the Marfa Lights, which are viewed about 15 minutes farther west on Highway 90. Other items include Indian jewelry, rugs, and pottery.

BIG BEND SADDLERY

E. Highway 90 • 915-837-5551 or 800-634-4502
Monday–Friday 8–5:30 • Saturday 8–5

The lion's share of business comes from the local ranching community. Saddles and tack along with authentic cowboy accessories like hats and jackets have kept the doors open since 1905. Cowboy cookery—cast iron skillets and the like—as well as tents and bed rolls help out during nights on the open range. Specialty items range from hand-tooled leather goods like belts, notebooks, and checkbooks to hand-crafted silver bracelets and earrings. Plenty of kid stuff, too.

COWBOYS N CADILLACS

101 W. Holland right across from Amtrak • 915-837-7486
Monday–Saturday 10–6 • W

Stop in and you'll understand why some Amtrak passengers have missed their trains while browsing. Over 100 different artists, artisans, craftsmen, and other exhibitors have booths, counters, corners, even nooks with their wares. At the high end of the price scale are antiques, sterling, china, and cowboy memorabilia. Also running into the thousands are amethysts, geodes, and quartz clusters as well as player pianos and roll top desks. On the less expensive side are books, antique bottles, brainteasers, livestock brands, hand-blown crystal, gourmet food products, paintings, photos, and pottery. There's even a year-round Christmas booth.

FRONT STREET BOOKS

121 East Holland Ave. • 915-837-3360 • 800-597-3360
www.fsbooks.com • Monday–Saturday 9–6 • Sunday 1–6

Despite all the mergers and consolidations in the publishing world, small independent booksellers like Front Street are still thriving, thanks to superior service and the advent of the Internet. Specializing in new, used, and antiquarian books, the success of Front Street's two locations prompted a February 1999 profile in *Biblio.* (The second store is in Marathon.)

J. DAVIS STUDIO/PORTABLE ART

510 W. Holland • 915-837-3812 • Monday–Friday 10–5

Inlaid stoneware vessels with a Far West Texas influence are John Davis's forte. The advantages of stopping by his studio and seeing his wares locally are numerous: lower prices than what you'll pay at Joan Cawley's Gallery in Santa Fe, a broader selection, and the opportunity to view his wife Robin Brown's Portable Art. Her hand-dyed and block-printed fashions are available nationally at the Smithsonian Museum Shop, Nordstrom's, and Jane Smith's in Aspen and Santa Fe. Just blocks from her factory, you can buy Portable Art by Robin Brown for all ages, sizes, and sexes.

IVEY'S EMPORIUM

116 North Fifth St. • 915-837-7474 • ghostown@overland.net
Monday–Saturday 10–5:30 • Closed Sunday

Once a seasonal shop open during the Christmas holiday season, this interesting gift and decorating emporium is now open full time. The same proprietors own the Terlingua Trading Co. in the Terlingua Ghost Town, so the gift selection is always interesting and varied. Ivey's Emporium is the only place in town to find hand-dipped chocolate truffles, and they also carry their own label of gourmet coffees.

KIOWA GALLERY

105 E. Holland Ave. • 915-837-3067
Tuesday–Friday 10–5 • Saturday 10–3

The success of the Kiowa parallels the rise of the Big Bend as a haven for artists and artisans from this region working in sculpture, bronze, pottery, furniture, watercolor, pen and ink, and oil. Easy to find, the gallery's west wall features a 17' × 81' Stylle Read mural of Milton Faver crossing the Rio Grande in 1873.

OCOTILLO ENTERPRISES

205 N. Fifth St. • 915-837-5353 or 800-642-0427
Monday–Saturday 9–6 • Sunday 10–6

Owner Judith Brueske wrote a 50-page study on the Marfa Lights that is a bestseller locally. Pick up a copy at her shop and browse through books on area and regional travel; cultural, natural, and historical topics; westerns; books for kids; and an extensive selection of periodicals. Ocotillo always offers a wide assortment of rocks and other geologic items.

SIDE TRIPS

ELEPHANT MOUNTAIN WILDLIFE MANAGEMENT AREA

26 miles south of Alpine on Highway 118 • 915-364-2228
Call for list of scheduled tours • Hunting by permit • W

The old Nevill Ranch is now one of several sites in West Texas where bighorn sheep have been reintroduced by Texas Parks & Wildlife. Starting in February 1987 with ten rams and ten ewes and with a later addition of three young rams, the herd now numbers above 40.

The best way, the only way, to view this species at Elephant Mountain is by calling in advance and getting listed on one of the regularly scheduled tours for Texas Conservation Passport holders. The tours are two to four hours long; bring your own supplies like binoculars, camera, and lunch. Elephant Mountain also offers hunting for dove, quail, deer, and javelina. For more information on species, permits, and seasons, contact the Austin office of Texas Parks & Wildlife toll free at 800-792-1112.

WOODWARD RANCH

Take Highway 118 18 miles south of Alpine • 915-364-2271
Daily 8 a.m. until dark • Full RV hookups • Camping • W

Mention the Woodward Ranch to any serious rock collector, and "red plume agate" is the response. Naturally occurring mineral formations have drawn rock hounds to Brewster County from around the world. Agates of all kinds, including red plume and flower garden, can be hunted, discovered, graded, weighed, and purchased at 50¢ a pound (if you do the hunting) or right off the shelf at the rock shop for prices that approach $200 for museum quality pieces. Others include calcite, garnet, obsidian, selenite, and plenty of turquoise. Precious stones, including blue opal with purple fire and labradorite, are also found on the ranch.

The rock shop also books tours to a variety of different mines in nearby Mexico: Boquillas and the Puerto Rico silver mine (including a candelilla wax camp tour) or San Carlos and its gorgeous agate mine featuring purple moss agate and sagenite.

Mountain bikers can ride on-road and off-road, birders can stalk beside two running streams, and picnickers have thousands of acres to choose from. RV hookups and camping sites are available.

ANNUAL EVENTS

February–March

TEXAS COWBOY POETRY GATHERING

Sul Ross State University • 915-837-8191
Last weekend of February or first weekend of March

This gathering was established to help preserve and promote the heritage of the American West. It kicks off Friday with open sessions, iron-bending demonstrations, and the well-attended chuckwagon supper ($) complete with coffee, cobbler, and impromptu presentations. Remember, you'll be out past sundown and the mountains around you are more than a mile high, so bring a warm jacket and some blankets. Saturday features the Gear Auction at the Museum of the Big Bend and the bulk of the sessions on the Sul Ross State University campus. Presented simultaneously is the Trappings of Texas exhibit at the Museum of the Big Bend featuring examples of western craftsmanship.

April

GEM & MINERAL SHOW

Alpine Civic Center • 915-837-5353 (Ocotillo Enterprises)
Third weekend of the month • Admission and field trip fees

Every April, aficionados gather at the Alpine Civic Center to browse, buy and sell, and barter with demonstrating dealers. Mineral and fossil samples, gemstone faceting, and wire wrapping are some of the many exhibits. Field trips to private ranches and into Mexico are scheduled the weeks before and after the show and require pre-registration.

July

PAISANO BAPTIST ENCAMPMENT
10 miles west of Alpine on Highway 90 • 915-837-3074
Begins on fourth Sunday of the month • Donations accepted

Just before World War I, several prominent West Texans gathered beneath Paisano Mountain and founded this renowned Baptist encampment. Most were familiar with the non-denominational Skillman Grove Camp Meeting (*see* **BLOYS CAMP MEETING in FORT DAVIS**) and favored a Baptist encampment that would augment, not compete with, the older camp meeting.

Since the early 1920s, Paisano has evolved into a West Texas tradition and serves as a testament to the vision of Brother L. R. Millican, a man whose considerable talents included preaching, cattle raising, and co-founding Hudspeth County. Paisano makes a point of offering something for the whole family. Newborns and infants are cared for in the nursery, a day camp is held for youngsters, and young adults enjoy a full youth program. Count on strong attendance at the daily services and at all meals, where everyone enjoys authentic cowboy cooking prepared under the direction of the 06 Ranch since 1922. Limited housing and 48 RV hookups are available.

October

SUL ROSS NATIONAL INTERCOLLEGIATE RODEO
SRSU Rodeo Arena just off East Highway 90 • 915-837-8200

Alpine is the birthplace of the National Intercollegiate Rodeo Association (NIRA), and, for half a century, the Sul Ross Rodeo Club and a large portion of the community have teamed up to host this event.

November

GALLERY NIGHT
Downtown • 915-837-3067

A new tradition to West Texas, Gallery Night is a collaborative effort hosted by a variety of Alpine galleries, artisans, and merchants. Typically held the Saturday night before Thanksgiving, this wonderful evening attracts visitors from across the country, as well as press coverage by state and national publications.

RESTAURANTS

($ = Under $7.50, $$ = Under $15, $$$ = $15+ plus tax & tip)

KATE

209 West Holland in the Holland Hotel • 915-837-2001
Lunch Monday–Saturday • Dinner Thursday–Saturday • MC V • W

The restored original lobby of the "hysterical" Holland Hotel, as this eclectic hotel is known to locals (*see* **ACCOMMODATIONS**), is the new home of ever-popular Kate. If roughing it out in the Big Bend includes cappuccino and espresso, this is where you need to be. Lunch features homemade soups, salads, sandwiches, and gourmet deli fare. The eclectic dinner menu ranges from veggie stir-fry to steaks. Beer and wine.

LA CASITA

1104 East Ave. H • 915-837-2842 • Daily • Lunch and dinner • $

The Ramos family continues to serve up some of the Big Bend's best Mexican food, and one indication of their success is the line of latecomers who show up after 12 for lunch—all waiting for a table. The beef enchiladas, the carne asada, the soft flour taco plate—*¡que bueno!* Beer.

LITTLE MEXICO CAFE

204 W. Murphy Ave. • 915-837-2855 • Monday–Saturday
Lunch and dinner • $ • Discount for seniors and college students

Several generations of Valenzualas are portrayed in photos along the walls of this popular, family-owned and operated one-room Mexican restaurant. Frequently ordered favorites range from the Mexican plate to the deluxe *campechanas* (best attempted as a half order). The Chaparral Burger is a meal in itself, and goes best with guacamole instead of ketchup. Save room for the sopapillas with some butter and honey. Beer.

ORIENTAL EXPRESS

3000 West Hwy 90 • 915-837-1159
Lunch and dinner • Closed Sunday • $–$$ • Cr • W

Buffet lunch and dinner are served at the only Chinese restaurant for hundreds of miles. High praise for the chef's shrimp special and the spicy pork. The drunken chicken (not on the menu) makes a great appetizer. Allowances are made for patrons who aren't keen on Chinese food; several American entrées are included on the menu. No MSG. Beer and plum wine.

OUTBACK BAR & GRILL

103 South Phelps • 915-837-5074
Daily • Lunch and dinner • $–$$ • Cr • W

The menu here covers a little bit of everything and all ably prepared, including a soup and salad bar, sandwiches, Mexican food, seafood, and burgers. Beer and wine.

PONDEROSA

East Highway 90 • 915-837-3321
Breakfast, lunch, and dinner • $ • W

The Ponderosa is back on track since chef Lewis Gordon returned to the kitchen. Locals are partial to the luncheon specials. An early morning visit is worthwhile just for the breakfast burrito. This monster is stuffed with potatoes, chorizo, beans, and cheese.

REATA

203 N. Fifth • 915-837-9232
Closed Sunday • Lunch and dinner • $$–$$$ • Cr

Located in a late nineteenth-century Territorial adobe, order yourself fish, fowl, or beef at this exceptional eatery which *Cowboys & Indians* magazine listed as the in spot for a taste of *haute* Texas. Wild game and a well-stocked bar are two of the high points as is rustic decor reminiscent of area ranches. Bar.

CLUBS AND BARS

CRYSTAL BAR

410 E. Holland Ave. • 915-837-2819 • Daily except Sunday

Right across the street from Furr's supermarket stands a nondescript building graced by a Stylle Read mural of a horseman, his mount, and Cathedral Mountain. Inside, grimy "gimme" caps and gas station signs set the tone. Stop by in the late afternoon for a game of "42" or darts with the locals. After sundown, the youngsters show up. Occasional bands and an able jukebox. Beer and wine.

RAILROAD BLUES

504 West Holland Ave. • 915-837-3103
Monday–Friday 4–12 • Saturday 4–1 • Closed Sunday

Over the last five years, Richard Fallon and R. C. Toler have turned the Blues into a mandatory stop for musicians heading to or coming from the West Coast—luring in the likes of Alejandro Escovedo, Joe King Carrasco, Arlo Guthrie, Ray Wylie Hubbard, Canned Heat, James McMurtry, Toni Price, and even old Jerry Jeff. Count on bands most Friday and Saturday nights. Over 100 beers and twentysomething wines.

ACCOMMODATIONS

($ = Under $40, $$ = $40–$75, $$$ = $75–$100, $$$$ = Over $100)

ALPINE CLASSIC INN

East Highway 90 • 915-837-1530 or 800-528-1234 • $$

This Best Western property has 64 smoking and non-smoking rooms and offers a free continental breakfast, cable TV, and an outdoor unheated pool. Free parking. Pets with deposit.

ALPINE INN

East Highway 90 • 915-837-3417 • $

A single-story motel located just east of Alpine along Highway 90, the Days Inn has 40 smoking and non-smoking rooms all with room phones (free local calls) and cable TV (HBO). The popular Ponderosa Restaurant is right in the middle of the property by the outdoor unheated pool. Free parking. Pets OK.

HIGHLAND INN

1404 East Highway 90 • 915-837-5811 • $–$$

This two-story motel is located directly across Highway 90 from Sul Ross State University and has 44 units, including suites and non-smoking rooms with cable TV and room phones (free local calls). Amenities include a hotel restaurant, an outdoor spring-fed pool, and free parking. Please register pets. AAA, AARP, corporate, government, and military rates available.

HOLLAND HOTEL

209 West Holland Ave • 915-837-3844 or 800-535-8040 • $–$$

Built in 1928 and fondly referred to as the "hysterical" Holland by locals, this eclectic establishment is the only hotel in Alpine that is a registered Texas landmark. It boasts 16 rooms and suites, all with private baths. Guests enjoy an in-room complimentary continental breakfast and have access to free local phone service. Deluxe rooms feature antiques, marble wet bars, refrigerators, and microwaves. **Kate** (*see* **RESTAURANTS**) is located in the lobby, and the top floor penthouse has its own deck and panoramic views from Alpine's tallest building. Smoking and non-smoking rooms available.

RAMADA LIMITED

West Highway 90 • 915-837-1100 or 800-272-6232 • $–$$$

This 61-room property overlooks Alpine from its western edge and offers an excellent view of the city, Hancock Hill, and the Glass Mountains. Among the amenities included are free local calls, handicapped rooms/facilities, meeting/banquet facilities, modem lines in room, cable television, on-site coin-operated laundry, and a deluxe complimentary continental breakfast.

BALMORHEA

REEVES COUNTY   •   765   •   (915)

Situated beside a lonely stretch of Interstate 10, verdant Balmorhea is an ideal break on any trans-Texas trip. Every day over 26 million gallons of spring water from beneath the Davis Mountains course through the State Recreation Area, the town, and out into thousands of acres of cultivated farmland. Soak up some yourself; it's hours in almost every direction to the next stop.

POINTS OF INTEREST

BALMORHEA LAKE

Two miles south of town • 915-375-2308 (Balmorhea Lake Store) $3 daily per person over 14 • W but not all areas

If you want to swim, head to the State Recreation Area. The lake is strictly for fishing: bigmouth, littlemouth, black and striped bass, carp, catfish, and crappie. Full and partial RV hookups are available. Late night arrivals pay the next day.

BALMORHEA STATE PARK

Highway 17 four miles southwest of Balmorhea • 915-375-2370 Pool open year-round • Admission: $3 • W www.tpwd.state.tx.us/park/balmorhe/balmorhe.htm

Balmorhea is as close to a beach as West Texas offers. The surface of the pool covers almost two acres, its depth exceeds 20 feet, and it holds over three million gallons of water. Spring fed, the water is crystal clear and refreshing: San Solomon Spring maintains a constant temperature range of 72 to 76 degrees. A concession stand opens from Memorial Day weekend through Labor Day and serves burgers, cokes, and chips. Inner tube rentals are made on a first-come-first-served basis. Lifeguards patrol during the summer months.

ACCOMMODATIONS

($ = Under $40, $$ = $40–$75, $$$ = $75–$100, $$$$ = Over $100)

SAN SOLOMON COURTS

Balmorhea State Recreation Area • 915-375-2370 • $–$$

There are 18 adobe units at the State Recreation Area; all are within walking distance of the pool. Each has central heat and air and cable TV, and some come with kitchenettes. Bring your own cooking utensils. Campsites are available with electricity ($10 per night) and without ($7 per night).

BIG BEND NATIONAL PARK

BREWSTER COUNTY • (915)

Unlike many Texas boasts, the Big Bend will never be referred to as the biggest or the tallest. To many, it's in the running for the most out-of-the-way. Just over 300,000 visit it each year. That's not even one-tenth the visitation at Grand Canyon National Park. Yet, while a visitor to the Seventh Wonder of the World spends on average seven minutes actually looking at that great gorge, a three-day stay is the norm for Big Bend.

Big Bend stands at the intersection of desert, river, and mountain, a mix of plant and animal, heat and breeze, where northern Mexican ecosystems blend with the southern extension of the Rockies. Within the park's boundaries are found such a unique diversity of life forms that the United Nations has designated Big Bend National Park a U.S. Biosphere Reserve.

From a low point along the Rio Grande of 1,800 feet (550 meters) above sea level, the elevation rises almost a mile to the top of Emory Peak, at 7,825 feet (2,400 meters). Away from the river, saltcedars and reed grass give way to cactus and creosote bush. Higher up, the Chisos Mountains offer shade and protection to plants, animals, and man, and though prickly pears persist, so do maidenhair ferns and aspens.

This section is meant to get you on your way. You will find enough guidance to see many of the contrasting life forms; however, the intent is not to be a primary source but to facilitate and enhance your trip. Big Bend National Park has hundreds of sights. Some of the better known are listed below.

Specialized guidebooks are available on all aspects of the park including birds and wildlife, plants, geology, and history. Naturalists, guides, and other specialists are available to guide you down the Rio Grande, up in the Chisos Mountains, or out in Dagger Flat. Some charge a fee, others work for the National Park Service, and many just volunteer. Some of their names are listed under **TOURIST SERVICES**, and throughout this section are listed many books, publications, and other resources. Make use of them each time you're lucky enough to come back.

ACCESS

There is no public transportation to or through the park. Alpine (about 100 miles north) offers regularly scheduled train service on Amtrak's *Sunset Limited* or *Texas Eagle* (800-872-7245), and bus service via Greyhound (800-231-2222). Auto rental and shuttle information is available from the Alpine Chamber of Commerce (800-561-3735 or www.travelbigbend.com) and the Brewster County Tourism Board (915-424-3220 or www.visitbigbend.com).

BIG BEND NATIONAL PARK

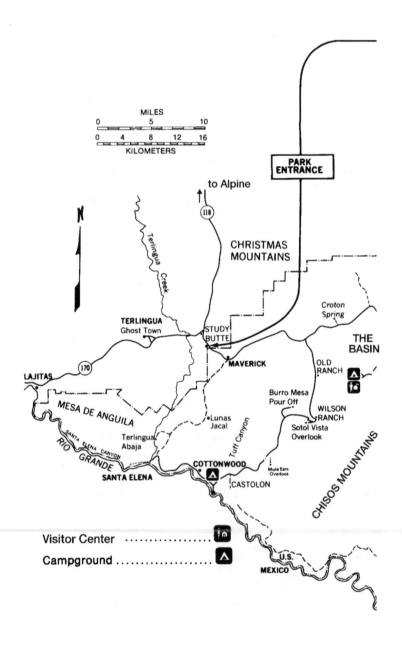

MILES
0   5   10

0   4   8   12   16
KILOMETERS

PARK
ENTRANCE

to Alpine

118

CHRISTMAS
MOUNTAINS

Croton
Spring

TERLINGUA
Ghost Town

STUDY
BUTTE

THE
BASIN

170

MAVERICK

OLD
RANCH

LAJITAS

MESA DE ANGUILA

Burro Mesa
Pour Off

WILSON
RANCH

Lunas
Jacal

Sotol Vista
Overlook

Terlingua
Abaja

Tuff Canyon

SANTA ELENA CANYON

RIO GRANDE

COTTONWOOD

Mule Ears
Overlook

CHISOS MOUNTAINS

SANTA ELENA

CASTOLON

Visitor Center ....

Campground ....

U.S.
MEXICO

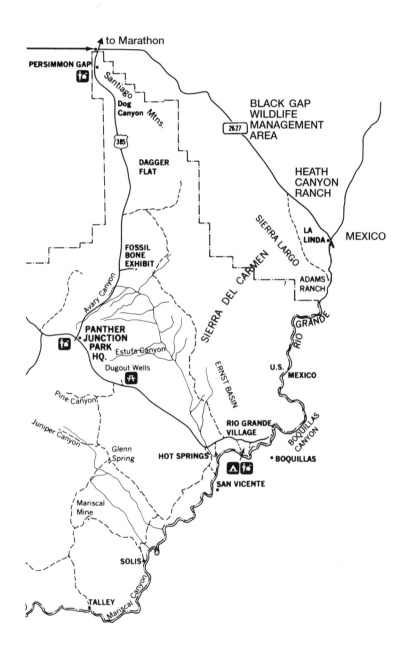

to Marathon

PERSIMMON GAP

Santiago Mtns.

Dog
Canyon

385

DAGGER
FLAT

BLACK GAP
WILDLIFE
MANAGEMENT
AREA

2627

HEATH
CANYON
RANCH

LA
LINDA

MEXICO

SIERRA LARGO

FOSSIL
BONE
EXHIBIT

Avary Canyon

SIERRA DEL CARMEN

ADAMS
RANCH

PANTHER
JUNCTION
PARK
HQ.

Estufa Canyon

Dugout Wells

RIO GRANDE

U.S. MEXICO

Pine Canyon

ERNST BASIN

Juniper Canyon

Glenn
Spring

RIO GRANDE
VILLAGE

BOQUILLAS CANYON

HOT SPRINGS

SAN VICENTE

BOQUILLAS

Mariscal
Mine

SOLIS

TALLEY

Mariscal Canyon

The major carriers including American (800-433-7300), Continental (800-525-0280), Delta (800-221-1212), and Southwest (800-435-9792) come as close as Midland (230 miles) or El Paso (325 miles). Car rentals are available from the major agencies at both airports. Two shuttle companies serve park visitors: Big Bend Shuttle Service (800-729-2860) and Scott Shuttle Service (915-386-4574).

Alpine is also the closest city to the western edge of the park via Highway 118 and offers the quickest access for those driving in from the west. Travelers departing El Paso, Carlsbad Caverns, or Guadalupe Mountains national parks can detour south at Marfa on Highway 67 to enjoy *el Camino del Rio* (the River Road—FM 170), which follows the Rio Grande from Presidio through the Big Bend Ranch State Park to Lajitas and then on to Big Bend National Park.

Visitors driving in from Houston or San Antonio can take Interstate 10 to Fort Stockton and then south on US 385 through Marathon to the park or Highway 90 west from San Antonio to Marathon and then head south on US 385 to the park's north entrance.

The closest airstrips are at Lajitas (4,777-foot, paved), the Terlingua Ranch (4,800-foot, gravel) and Alpine (6,000-foot, paved). The following distances to the park are based on the shortest routes to park headquarters. Adjust drive time for speed limits, time of day through major cities, and slower night driving to avoid cattle and wildlife close to the park.

Distances from Big Bend National Park Headquarters

Starting Point	Distance miles/kilometers
Alpine	100 miles/161 km
Big Bend Ranch (Warnock Center)	41 miles/66 km
Big Bend Ranch (Fort Leaton)	100 miles/161 km
Carlsbad Caverns NP	307 miles/495 km
Dallas	559 miles/902 km
Del Rio	253 miles/408 km
El Paso Airport	323 miles/521 km
Fort Stockton	127 miles/205 km
Guadalupe Mountains NP	265 miles/428 km
Houston	603 miles/973 km
Lubbock	360 miles/580 km
Midland Airport	232 miles/374 km
San Antonio	406 miles/655 km
Van Horn	200 miles/323 km

TOURIST SERVICES

Park entrance fee: $10 per vehicle or $5 per person not in car

There are several ways to enjoy the park: on your own, through the programs, facilities, employees, and volunteers of the National Park Service or the Big Bend Natural History Association, and with the services of a guide. The Big Bend Natural History Association, a non-profit organization, serves to support and augment the Park Service particularly with regard to educating visitors. Local guides include a talented assortment of individuals with varied backgrounds, educational levels, specialties, and fees. Most live west of the park in Study Butte, Terlingua, or Lajitas and are available to enhance your trip to the Big Bend area.

BIG BEND NATIONAL PARK

Superintendent • 79834 • 915-477-2251 • www.nps.gov/bibe/

The majority of park visitors pass through Persimmon Gap on US 385 south of Marathon. The Persimmon Gap Visitor Center serves as an appropriate introduction to the park and the National Park Service: it has the most up-to-date displays, materials, and news on campground occupancy. The National Park Service staffs this and three other visitor centers including one high in the mountains at the Chisos Basin, one at Rio Grande Village, and the centrally located headquarters at Panther Junction. There is also a ranger station at Castolon. Look for schedules of park naturalist programs, including nature walks, workshops, and slide shows, at no charge posted throughout the park. A word of caution: The park service does not operate any emergency wrecker service. The two service stations located in the park—Panther Junction (gasoline, diesel, oil, and minor repairs) and Rio Grande Village (gasoline and oil)—are private concessions. **For wrecker service in the park, call 915-477-2291.**

BIG BEND NATURAL HISTORY ASSOCIATION

P.O. Box 196 • Big Bend National Park • 79834 • 915-477-2236

A wealth of information—books, maps, and seminars—is available through this private, non-profit organization which provides visitors to Big Bend National Park a more comprehensive understanding than government funding allows. The well-informed staffers, the self-guided trail booklets, and the award-winning *Big Bend Paisano* are all examples of how the Big Bend Natural History Association makes the park more accessible to visitors. Call or write for their lengthy catalog of books, guides, audio/visual materials, and schedule of seminars. For phone orders, Discover, MasterCard and Visa are accepted and second-day delivery is available.

PRIVATE GUIDES

The following entities offer step-on tour guides: Big Bend Touring Society (915-371-2548); Big Bend Birding Expeditions (888-531-2223), and Far Flung Adventures (800-359-4138). The National Park Service does not provide these services. Expect to pay about $100 per day per group. Some charge more, and a few charge per person. For additional information, contact the Brewster County Tourism Board (915-424-3220 or www.visitbigbend.com).

GUIDEBOOKS AND PUBLICATIONS

BIG BEND: THE OFFICIAL NATIONAL PARK HANDBOOK

It's no surprise that the park bookstores have trouble keeping up with the demand for this well-written and superbly photographed 128-page paperback ($5.95). It's the best general overview available on the Big Bend. Key sections include the most important aspects of the park, like biology, geology, and history, as well as lucid summaries by park experts on birding, hiking, running the river, and other activities.

THE BIG BEND PAISANO

National Park Service & Big Bend Natural History Association
P.O. Box 196 • Big Bend National Park • 79834 • 915-477-2236

Published four times annually, this award-winning publication is free at the park, or send four dollars for a year's subscription. Each 16-page issue packs a load of pertinent information on park updates, trail openings and closures, notes on natural science, and Big Bend history.

BIRD'S-EYE VIEW

THE LOST MINE TRAIL
Trailhead starts at Panther Pass on the Basin Road

The views along this route are superb, regardless of whether you take a 30-minute hike or go the full 4.8 miles (round trip). Park your car at the trailhead, spend a quarter for the self-guiding booklet, and hit the trail. It starts at 5,600 feet and goes up to 6,850 feet. Views of Casa Grande, the Sierra del Carmens, and Juniper and Pine canyons make it unforgettable. Best of all, the walk back is downhill (unlike the Window Trail).

HISTORIC PLACES

The streams and springs, as well as the Rio Grande itself, nourished the plentiful game that attracted Paleo-Indians to the Big Bend thousands of years ago. It wasn't until the 16th century that the wanderings of Cabeza de Vaca brought a European through the Big Bend (1535), and it was almost two more centuries (1727) before subjugating the Native Americans emerged on Spain's political agenda. Much history has transpired since the Big Bend was ruled by Spanish and Mexican governors. Several historic structures, listed below, stand from those times.

CASTOLON

Via Ross Maxwell Drive (paved road)

Tremors from the Mexican Revolution were felt along the Rio Grande, and the U.S. Cavalry responded by establishing a tiny cavalry post at Castolon. Barracks, officers' quarters, and other structures were completed by 1920 but never used for military purposes. Today, the barracks houses a trading post and the officers' quarters serve park personnel. Remnants of the Big Bend's only cotton gin stand outside the trading post.

GLENN SPRING

Almost nine miles from the north end of Glenn Spring Rd. (unimproved) • Check with park personnel for road conditions and exact directions

A steady supply of water made Glenn Spring an important stop on the Comanche Trail and for early settlers including H. E. Glenn, a Big Bend pioneer and Indian fatality. During World War I, Glenn Spring grew to its height and also made national headlines. In 1914, a candelilla wax camp began operation. Soon, American troops were posted along the Mexican border at points including Castolon and Glenn Spring. In 1916, Mexican renegades attacked a nine-man contingent from the Fourteenth Cavalry on May 5th (Cinco de Mayo). Three soldiers, one civilian, and an unknown number of attackers were killed. Several other attacks were staged simultaneously, and the Eighth Cavalry trailed the banditos into Mexico.

MARISCAL MINE

Almost 20 miles from the east end of River Road • Accessible by high clearance or four-wheel-drive vehicles only • Check with park personnel for road conditions and exact directions

The Big Bend area abounds in mineral deposits. The Presidio Mine near Shafter (on the far side of the Big Bend Ranch State Park) produced more silver and gold than any mine in Texas history. Multinational Companies like DuPont and Dow ran fluorspar operations in Mexico just east of the park. And the Chisos Mine near Terlingua was a national leader in cinnabar (quicksilver) production. The Mariscal Mine also produced cinnabar and was the only commercial mine within the bounds of what is now the park. The mining facilities have been designated a National Register Historic District. In addition to dilapidated commercial buildings and rock houses, the most visible remnants are a Scott furnace and a concrete condenser.

OTHER POINTS OF INTEREST

HOT SPRINGS

From near the Rio Grande Village, drive two miles down the improved dirt road to the Hot Springs parking lot. Park and then hike a quarter of a mile to the springs. RVs and oversized vehicles must be parked about three-quarters of a mile from the springs.

J. O. Langford left Alpine in 1909 looking for better health and bringing his wife and daughter, Lovie, to these hot springs. The abandoned buildings that stand today hardly convey their story, but Langford committed it to paper in *Big Bend: A Homesteader's Story* (University of Texas Press), co-authored by Fred Gipson. The springs spew over 250,000 gallons of 105-degree water daily, and you don't have to pay the dime he charged to enjoy them.

SANTA ELENA CANYON

Via Ross Maxwell Drive

If you don't have the opportunity to float the canyon (*see* **SPORTS AND ACTIVITIES**), be sure to either stop at the parking lot to enjoy the vista or hike the two-mile self-guided trail into the canyon's mouth. At 1,500 feet high, the sheer walls are not quickly forgotten. Neither is the silence. The first part of the hike crosses Terlingua Creek (occasionally muddy). Concrete stairs switchback into the canyon before descending to the river.

THE WINDOW

Chisos Basin

The Window is the sole drainage for the Basin and regularly offers unforgettable sunsets in addition to a pleasant hike. It can be reached on foot via the Window Trail (2.8 miles) or on horseback. To hike down to the smooth pour off, pick up a copy of the park service brochure on the Window Trail at the Basin Visitors Center. Don't forget that it's all uphill on the way back. An excellent way to enjoy the view is the short Window View Trail (three-tenths of a mile round trip). This trail is paved, wheelchair accessible, and begins at the Chisos Basin Trailhead and leads to bench seats for prime sunset views.

SPORTS AND ACTIVITIES

Birding

Because of its location on the north-south flyway and its position along the dividing line between Eastern and Western species, Big Bend offers more species of birds than any other national park. At last count, nearly 450 species had been identified including the only U.S. sightings of the Colima Warbler. More fly through, but about 100 species or so actually nest.

The top birding spot is the Rio Grande Village, with the Basin a close second. Springtime is best. To avoid the imposing mountains immediately east of the park (the Sierra del Carmens), northbound lowland and mountain birds fly along the southern flank of the del Carmens right through the Big Bend, with most continuing through. During their fall migration, many of these same birds take the opposite tack and veer east of the del Carmens, thereby avoiding the park and leaving a smaller group to pass through the park.

Driving Tours

Two excellent (and inexpensive) guides have been produced by the Big Bend Natural History Association in conjunction with the National Park Service for on-road and off-road touring: *A Road Guide to Paved and Improved Dirt Roads of Big Bend National Park* and *A Road Guide to Backcountry Dirt Roads of Big Bend National Park.* A complete list of routes, points of interest, and guidelines is provided. Check your vehicle before any backroad trips. Keep in mind that the maximum driving speed in the park is 45 mph (72 kph), and that park rangers are authorized to give tickets. Point of fact: If ticketed, you either pay the fine or appear before a U.S. Magistrate. There's no way out. An excellent first tour is the 30-mile Ross Maxwell Scenic Drive (paved). This route includes views of the Basin (framed by the Window) and Mule Ears Peaks and stops at historic Castolon and the Santa Elena Canyon overlook and Nature Trail.

Fishing

No fishing license is required within the park, and the free permit can be obtained at any park visitor center. Over 30 species have been recorded including carp, freshwater drum, gizzard shad, and longnose gar. Catfish is most common, and a large yellow is the park record at 100 pounds.

Hiking/Backpacking/Camping

Though Texans have historically chosen New Mexico and Colorado for hiking and backpacking, a dedicated cadre has been making the ten-hour pilgrimage from Houston or Dallas to enjoy the Big Bend's 210 miles of trails and an unequaled amount of roadless terrain. Another attraction is the dramatic change in elevation: from less than 2,000 feet above sea level along the Rio Grande to almost 8,000 feet on top of Emory Peak.

Only overnight trips require a backcountry permit (free of charge and available at any visitor center). Get a copy of the Big Bend Natural History Association's *Hiker's Guide to the Trails of Big Bend National Park* ($1.25). This 28-page booklet includes 36 hikes of all distances and in all parts of the park. Some require sneakers, others call for full back-packing regalia.

As you survey the different choices, keep one thought in mind: **stay out of the Basin during the spring.** Spring break and Easter are perfect examples of the 80/20 Rule: Twenty percent of the park's trails get eighty percent of the hikers. Wait till fall and early winter to hike the Chisos.

An additional reason is that some of the most rewarding hikes—the southeast Rim, for instance—are forbidden from February 1 until July 15 to protect nesting peregrine falcons. During the high season (spring-time), get more out of your visit by choosing a less trafficked portion of the park. Spring is the best time for desert hiking: Avoid the heat and enjoy the foliage. When things slow down and you can really enjoy the Basin, drop 50¢ and pick up *Chisos Mountains Trails Map* (Big Bend Natural History Association), which lists trails, distances, campsites, and tips for travel in the mountains.

Horseback Riding

Only personally owned horses may be used within the park. There is plenty of fine print on bringing your own mount to the park, including cleanup, restricted paths, and sanitation. Contact park headquarters and ask for the park's *Regulations and Information Regarding Use of Personal Horses* (915-477-2251). Another option is to leave Trigger at home and make use of one of the off-park riding companies.

BIG BEND STABLES
Study Butte • 915-371-2212

Just west of the park in Study Butte, these wranglers offer hourly, half- and full-day trips, and overnighters. Among the most popular excursions are the saddle/paddle combo trips, which are offered in conjunction with local rafting companies.

Mountain Biking/Cycling

The longtime locals at Desert Sports in Terlingua are the only way to go when it comes to biking the Big Bend (888-989-6900 or www.desertsportstx.com). These folks know their stuff: Each February they put on the highly competitive Chihuahuan Desert Challenge Mountain Bike Race and Festival. They offer equipment rentals (bikes, rafts, canoes), customized mountain bike tours, float trips, guide services, and even hike/bike/boat packages.

River Rafting

There's a lot more to the park than piñon pines and dusty roads. A great way to escape the blazing heat, as well as see an entirely different portion of the Big Bend, is to ride the river. A 1978 Act of Congress designated the southeastern 69 miles of the national park—literally, the

Big Bend—and an additional stretch downstream the "Rio Grande Wild and Scenic River" (www.nps.gov/rigr/).

The most common float trips in order of length and with approximate times are Black Rock Canyon (half day), Colorado Canyon (full day with lunch stop), Santa Elena Canyon (at least one and up to three days), Mariscal Canyon (at least one and up to three days), Boquillas Canyon (three days), and the Lower Canyons (a week). There are three ways to ride the river:

- Bring your own equipment
- Rent equipment
- Hire a guide service

By far the most common way to run the river is with one of the local guide services. The ones listed below are all licensed and fully insured, take care of shuttles to and from the trip, handle backcountry permitting (a requirement for all river runners), and depending on the length of the trip offer snacks, refreshments, meals, entertainment, even seminars. All offer similar packages for roughly the same cost, and each has creative programs featuring artists, entertainers, and chefs:

Big Bend River Tours (Lajitas) 800-545-4240
Desert Sports (Terlingua) 888-989-6900
Far Flung Adventures (Terlingua) 800-359-4138
Texas River and Jeep Expeditions (Terlingua) 800-839-7238

If you plan on running the river on your own, you should still call one of the tour companies. All are outgoing and willing to tell you how the river is running and other details that only a local knows. A backcountry use permit is required for any river excursion. Backcountry use permits are free and are available at all Big Bend National Park Visitor Centers— Persimmon Gap, Panther Junction, Rio Grande Village—as well as at the self-permit stations at Lajitas and the Stillwell Store en route to the Lower Canyons put-in at Heath Canyon across from La Linda.

If you're going to float the Lower Canyons, Heath Canyon is the last put-in (though you can start as far upstream as you wish). The most common take-out is Dryden Crossing, 83 miles downstream. Advice gleaned from knowledgeable guides and the following booklets listed will certainly enhance any Lower Canyon trip.

Once you've secured a permit and you have the necessary equipment, then you're off. If you need to rent rafting equipment, contact Desert Sports (888-989-6900) or Rio Grande Adventures (800-343-1640). Equipment runs about $15 per person per day, and the staff can help with routes and itineraries, put-ins and take-outs. Contact the Big Bend Shuttle Service (800-729-2860) to arrange to be dropped off, met, or maybe just to have your vehicles shuttled to your final take-out.

For serious river rats, a series of four guides to the Rio Grande has been produced by the Big Bend Natural History Association in conjunction with the National Park Service. The series is entitled *River Guide to the Rio Grande*. *General Information* includes regulations, safety, and ethics, and the others are for different stretches of the river: *Colorado Canyon through Santa Elena Canyon, Mariscal Canyon through Boquillas Canyon,* and *The Lower Canyons*. All are available through the Big Bend Natural History Association.

Rock Climbing

Think again. The igneous rock throughout the entire Big Bend/Davis Mountains region makes for treacherous climbing at best. The only suitable climbing in the region is at Hueco Tanks (*see* **EL PASO**).

SHOPPING

NATIONAL PARK CONCESSIONS
Basin • 915-477-2291 • 9–8:45 (summer)
Castolon • 10–1 & 1:30–6
Panther Junction • 7–7
Rio Grande Village • 9–6 June–Feb; 9–8 March–May

Each store stocks essentials you were sure you brought. The Rio Grande Village Store caters to the RV campground and offers a coin laundry and showers in addition to groceries and general merchandise. The Basin store has the widest selection, including meats, fruits, canned goods, and hiking supplies.

STUDY BUTTE STORE
Study Butte • 915-371-2231 • Daily 7–9 • Cr

For over half a century, the Study Butte Store has been the mercantile headquarters of the Big Bend. Ages ago, the store's clientele was cinnabar miners. Now the trade is locals and tourists. A sampling of the inventory includes cold beer, shotgun shells, aspirin, antacids, band aids, Dramamine, fresh produce, meats, canned vegetables and other groceries, videos, and pesticides. For motorists, there are jumper cables, gas, diesel, motor oil, transmission fluid, and fuel cans.

SIDE TRIPS

BOQUILLAS CANYON & BOQUILLAS, COAHUILA, MEXICO
Park at Boquillas Canyon parking lot for the trail to the canyon. Park at the Boquillas Crossing parking area for Boquillas, Mexico. The canyon walk is entirely on the U.S. side and gets off to a boring begin-

ning. The rewards come twenty minutes into the hike, and the canyon itself is memorable. Budget at least 45 minutes each way. To go over to Mexico, walk to the river's edge and the ferryman will fetch you. He charges a couple of dollars per person round trip. After you cross, either walk or ride a burro to town (additional charge). Crossing over to this little *pueblito* is park tradition, and no visit to Boquillas is complete without stopping in on the Falcon family for burritos, a Coke, or a cold beer.

BLACK GAP WILDLIFE MANAGEMENT AREA

Take US 385 just north from Persimmon Gap and go east on FM 2627 15 miles • 915-376-2216 • Scheduled tours only; call in advance • Hunting by permit only

If you're not familiar with wildlife management areas, this is the state's largest. Unlike state parks, which are administered by the Public Lands Division of Texas Parks & Wildlife, wildlife management areas fall principally under the control of the Fisheries and Wildlife Division. Over 100,000 acres at Black Gap are devoted to developing and maintaining mule deer, javelina, dove, and quail (among others).

With substantial Rio Grande frontage, it's not surprising that the fishing is excellent and uncrowded. If hunting or fishing is not part of your plans, call in advance to be listed on a scheduled tour, available only to Texas Conservation Passport holders. About ten tours are offered annually. They take a full day and the longer one requires two. Bring everything with you: lunch, drinks, sunscreen, cameras, film, toilet paper. Other than hunting and fishing permits, nothing is sold at the wildlife management area, and once the tour leaves headquarters the only restroom available is the great wide open.

These tours are an opportunity to visit parts of Texas that few folks have ever heard of and even less will ever see. If your timing is off and no tours are available, consider the Maravillas Canyon Tour offered at Stillwell's (*see* **HALLIE'S HALL OF FAME MUSEUM**).

Because the primary mission of a wildlife management area is wildlife research and demonstration, this area does not offer the kinds of interpretive centers, amenities, or other facilities that visitors (non-hunters and non-fishers) might expect. Woe to those who journey out to the headquarters who have not called, are not listed for a tour, or are not registered to hunt or fish. Given the remote setting of Black Gap, this is more than a minor inconvenience. Even worse is to simply hike or camp on your own (state officials consider this is trespassing).

Hunting or fishing without registering or possessing an annual permit is a more serious criminal offense. For information about hunting seasons, the differing permits, and registration, as well as weather and conditions, contact Black Gap Wildlife Management Area Headquarters at 915-376-2216.

HALLIE'S HALL OF FAME MUSEUM

At US 385 just north of Persimmon Gap, go east on FM 2627 six miles • Big Bend Route Box 430 • Alpine • 79830 • Open daily No admission (donations accepted) • 915-376-2244

The life of Hallie Stillwell is commemorated in this museum, designed by her great-nephew, David Busey, who ably rendered Hallie's original abode (a small corner of the present museum) as well as the rest of the museum, which is filled with family and historical treasures. Hallie's story, and that of her pioneering ranch family, has drawn admirers from across Texas as well as nationwide. Letters and photos from Texas governors ranging from John Connally to Ann Richards are interspersed with notes from notable Texans such as Walter Cronkite.

The varied memorabilia includes some of Hallie's many crowns as Queen of the Terlingua Chili Cook-Off (where she reigned without challenge for twenty-odd years), to pistols, saddle guns, rifles, and shotguns that Hallie and her kin used since the early days. Also on display are antique farm and ranch equipment and the remnants of a candelilla wax camp, which the Stillwell Ranch operated during the drought in the early 1950s.

The Stillwell Trailer Park has complete hookups for RVs as well as camping sites, a washateria, showers, a grocery store, and gasoline. If you're interested in a first-rate tour of the Northern Chihuahuan Desert, sign up for the **Maravillas Canyon Tour** at the store. Your destination is the scenic canyon; your chariot is four-wheel drive.

En route, you'll view Indian pictographs, unusual geological formations and desert flora and fauna. Bring your lunch, some binoculars, and a camera, and be prepared to get going early. The tour runs a considerate five hours, requires little hiking, and wraps up before the heat of the day. The cost is $30 per adult and $15 per child.

HEATH CANYON GUEST RANCH

Take US 385 just north from Persimmon Gap and go east on FM 2627 28 miles • P.O. Box 386 • Marathon • 79842 915-376-2235 • $ • Checks accepted

Twenty-three miles past Hallie's Hall of Fame, where the pavement ends and the now closed Gerstacker Bridge crosses the Rio Grande to La Linda, Heath Canyon Guest Ranch sits on your right (river runners note that downstream to your left on the Texas side is the put-in/take-out point at Heath Crossing).

Homesteaded over a century ago by Tom Heath, the present quarters come with your choice of bunkhouse rooms or campsites and offer four thousand feet of frontage along the Rio Grande as well as miles of border with Black Gap Wildlife Management Area.

The ranch is reached by boat from the Rio Grande at the Heath Crossing put-in/take-out which has vehicle access, by car from Big

Bend National Park or Marathon via Highway 385 and FM 2627, and by plane on the 2,900-foot paved airstrip.

Once you make it to the ranch, the opportunities are endless. Get a Texas fishing license and hit the river. Whip out your binoculars for prime birding; this country sits right in the center of a north-south flyway. Bring your own raft or rent one from Desert Sports (888-989-6900) or Rio Grande Adventures (800-343-1640). Hike in and around the ranch or head over into Mexico—it's literally a stone's throw away. Bring your horse and some feed; you can use owner Andy Kurie's corral. Pets are welcome, too, as long as they're supervised.

Owner Kurie first came across the ranch during his tenure as a geologist at nearby fluorspar mines, *Aguachile* and *Cuatro Palmas*. Fluorspar, once valued for its use in aerosol and freon, is in little demand these days. That's why La Linda supports only two families, the church is unused, and the town has no baseball team. As the mining slowed down, Kurie's interest didn't. When DuPont moved out, he moved in. His house stands directly across from the bunkhouse and always seems to welcome new friends.

Camping rates include water. With a full kitchen (bring your own groceries), living room, and dining room, the bunkhouse is not as primitive as it may sound, especially once the air conditioner starts to cool off the Mexican tile floors and encourages you to wrap up in a handmade bedspread.

SANTA ELENA, CHIHUAHUA
Located across the Rio Grande from Castolon.

Located downstream from its namesake canyon, Santa Elena is a typical Mexican town of less than 300 people and comes complete with a plaza, church, and school. Originally settled as an *ejido* by a group of 30 families from Juarez (1935), droughts, crop failures, and insects ended all hopes of cotton farming, and by the late 1950s Santa Elena became the ranching community it is today. Avoid the heat of the day and cross later in the afternoon. It's not only cooler but gives you the opportunity to savor some of the fine cooking from one of the three local restaurants.

ANNUAL EVENTS

October

INTERNATIONAL GOOD NEIGHBOR DAY FIESTA
Rio Grande Village • 915-477-2251 • Free

Organized by the Interpretation Division of the Big Bend National Park, this day-long event is held on the third Saturday of the month and celebrates the distinctive culture of the borderlands. Cultural demonstrations and entertainment that reflect traditional themes and

customs of border folk are highlighted from noon till sundown. Color-
fully costumed entertainers from both sides of the river perform traditional American and Mexican folk dances, musical programs, and
authentic Mexican ballads. The Kid's Fiesta featuring games and educational activities is always popular. Concessionaires offer burgers, barbecue, Mexican delicacies, and cowboy cooking along with drinks and
handcrafted items.

RESTAURANTS

($ = Under $7.50, $$ = Under $15, $$$ = $15+ plus tax & tip)

BIG BEND MOTOR INN RESTAURANT & STORE
Study Butte • 915-371-2483
Daily • Breakfast, lunch, and dinner • $–$$ • Cr

The main reason to stop here for a burger, some Mexican food, or a
chicken-fried steak is because it's 80 miles to Alpine and 30 miles to Big
Bend National Park. Breakfast includes eggs, hot cakes, breakfast burritos, and cereal. The Roadrunner Deli has a better kitchen but closes
mid-afternoon.

CHISOS BASIN LODGE RESTAURANT
Daily • Breakfast, lunch, and dinner • 915-477-2291
$–$$ • Cr • W

The dining room is only open for meals and serves better-than-average
burgers, as well as steaks and a good chef's salad. The coffee shop stays
open all day long making sandwiches, malts, milk shakes, and the like.

HEATH CANYON
Heath Canyon Ranch • 915-376-2235
Just north of Persimmon Gap, take FM 2627 all the
way to the Mexican border • Dinner • $–$$ • Checks

Call in advance just to make sure this out-of-the-way eatery is serving when you show up. Any size table is welcome, but groups larger
than 10 should give several days notice. Special arrangements can be
made for lunch or other catering.

ROADRUNNER DELI
By the Study Butte Store • 915-371-2364
Daily • Breakfast and lunch • $

Plenty of fresh coffee, hearty sandwiches, and delicious cheesecake.
You can't go wrong at breakfast: good omelets, breakfast sandwiches,
muffins, and scones. Call or stop by to order a picnic basket for two or
twenty. They also offer the only cappuccino and espresso down south.

ACCOMMODATIONS

($ = Under $40, $$ = $40–$75, $$$ = $75–$100)

BIG BEND MOTOR INN/MISSION LODGE

Study Butte • 915-371-2218 or 800-848-2363 • $$

These spartan, single-story inns are located on opposite sides of the intersection of Highway 118 and FM 170 three miles north of the western entrance to Big Bend National Park. There are 76 smoking and non-smoking units including six suites. All rooms have phones and satellite TV featuring the major networks, and some come with microwaves and refrigerators. Also on the property are a restaurant, convenience store, service station, and a 75-unit RV park with full hookups. All guests have access to the outdoor unheated pool. Small pets OK.

CHISOS MOUNTAIN LODGE

Chisos Basin • Big Bend National Park • 915-477-2291 • $$

The only lodging in the park is located in the heart of the Chisos Mountains. There are 72 units including six stone cottages with bath and three double beds and the newer Casa Grande Lodge which has non-smoking rooms and handicap access. Amenities include the Chisos Mountain Lodge Dining Room, a gift and curio shop, and free parking. Pets are welcome, but the maid staff doesn't service rooms with pets inside. The property runs 100 percent occupancy during the high seasons—October to New Year's and during Spring Break.

LONGHORN RANCH MOTEL

15 miles north of the west entrance to BBNP • 915-371-2541 • $$

A one-story motel, the Longhorn Ranch sits alone in the desert surrounded by mountains on Highway 118 about 12 miles north of Study Butte going toward Alpine. There are 24 smoking and non-smoking rooms, all with two double beds and satellite TV featuring the major networks. An outdoor unheated swimming pool, a pay phone, and El Matterhorn restaurant are all located on the property. El Matterhorn is open daily except Monday and has no liquor license, but it does permit patrons to bring in their own alcoholic beverages. AAA and summer rates are available.

TERLINGUA RANCH

From Study Butte, take Highway 118 17 miles north to the ranch entrance and head east 16 miles to the property • 915-371-2416 • $

One of the most solitary settings in America, for many the Terlingua Ranch is heaven. Head north from Study Butte or south from Alpine to the well-marked turnoff or ignore the directions and use the 4,800-foot gravel strip. Eight wooden buildings with three or four units make up the 31-room complex. None are designated smoking or non-smoking, and none have TV or telephone. The hotel restaurant serves seven days a week from 8 a.m. to 9 p.m. and has a beer and wine license. Also on the property are about 20 RV hookups (12 of which are full ones), campsites, an outdoor unheated pool, a gift shop, and a coin-operated laundry. Pets OK.

Recreational Vehicles

With the exception of Green Gulch (which leads up to the Chisos Basin), most paved roads in Big Bend National Park are suitable for RVs. Steer clear of all dirt roads. The only campground with hookups in the park is at the Rio Grande Village (915-477-2293). Operated on a first-come, first-served basis, there are 25 sites with electric, water, and sewer connections. Full hookup capability is required. Register at the Rio Grande Village Store from 9 a.m. to 6 p.m. year-round except when they stay open longer during Spring Break. Other locations with RV hookups include the Stillwell RV Park (915-376-2244) by the park's east entrance (*see* **SIDE TRIPS**), the Big Bend Motor Inn (915-371-2218) in Study Butte (*see* above), the Terlingua Ranch (915-371-2416) north of Study Butte (*see* above), the Big Bend Travel Park (915-371-2250), and the Lajitas RV Park (915-424-3471) at Lajitas on the Rio Grande (*see* **LAJITAS**).

BIG BEND RANCH STATE PARK

PRESIDIO AND BREWSTER COUNTIES • (915)

At close to 300,000 acres, the State Natural Area is the largest component of the Parks & Wildlife Department of the State of Texas. Acquired in 1988 after years of negotiation, it is meant to be the showpiece of the state's park system. Because of its unique archaeologic, biologic, geologic, and historic resources, Parks & Wildlife has committed substantial funds, personnel, and time in preparation for its presentation to Texans and the world.

To protect its primitive nature, catalog its resources, and develop a master plan, access to the State Natural Area has been limited until recently. Also, policies to protect the many private parcels adjacent to or surrounded by the Natural Area had to be developed. During the past few years, the public was limited to two visitor centers, 30 miles of hiking trails, guided bus trips into the ranch, and three put-in points along the Rio Grande.

Long awaited changes are now being implemented at the Big Bend Ranch. TP&W is tripling the amount of hiking trails from 30 to 100 miles. Activities other than hiking, rafting, camping, and bus tours will be permitted including mountain biking, horseback riding, car camping, ecotours, and tours by private guides in buses, vans, and four-wheel-drive vehicles. This includes several innovative programs that Parks & Wildlife now sponsors (see **SPORTS AND ACTIVITIES**).

One element that hasn't changed is getting to the Big Bend Ranch State Park. A single thoroughfare, Farm-to-Market Road 170, offers access to the park's eastern and western gateways, and a 28-mile dirt road leads to the old headquarters, Sauceda. It parallels the Rio Grande from Lajitas (east) to Presidio (west) and is easy to get to from Big Bend National Park, Alpine, and Marfa. Known as *el Camino del Rio* (the River Road), it serves both visitor centers and offers unmatched views of the Rio Grande, several of its canyons, the Big Bend Ranch, and Mexico.

Drive carefully. The combination of the beautiful views and the treacherous terrain makes for trouble. Among the many hazards are plenty of loose livestock, grades in excess of 15 percent, sharp curves with limited sight distance, poor shoulders, and numerous low-water crossings.

TOURIST SERVICES

FORT LEATON STATE HISTORICAL PARK

Three miles east of Presidio along FM 170 • 915-229-3613
Park Superintendent • P.O. Box 1180 • Presidio • 79845
Daily 8–4:30 • $6 per person per day
www.tpwd.state.tx.us/park/bigbend/bigbend.htm

Fort Leaton serves as the western gateway to the Big Bend Ranch State Park and stands almost 60 miles west of the Warnock Center along FM 170. A complete description of its history is included under the **PRESIDIO & OJINAGA** listing. Tours of Fort Leaton are also available (fee) and include 25 of the fort's 40 rooms with exhibits and programs detailing the history of the Spanish, Mexican, Texan, and American colonizers.

BARTON WARNOCK ENVIRONMENTAL EDUCATION CENTER

HCR 70, Box 375 • Lajitas • 79852 • 915-424-3327
www.tpwd.state.tx.us/park/barton/barton.htm
Daily 8–4:30

The Warnock Center sits several hundred yards east of Lajitas. Named for the distinguished Sul Ross professor emeritus, it is the eastern gateway to the park. Well-staffed, its gift shop offers numerous titles on the Big Bend and Trans-Pecos as well as maps and other items. Bus tours of the Big Bend Ranch leave here and travel 136 miles round trip compared with the 74-mile tour from Fort Leaton. The additional mileage along the River Road is quite spectacular and allows for commentary, question and answers—and naps.

BIG BEND RANCH STATE PARK

Management Plan for Expanded Public Use

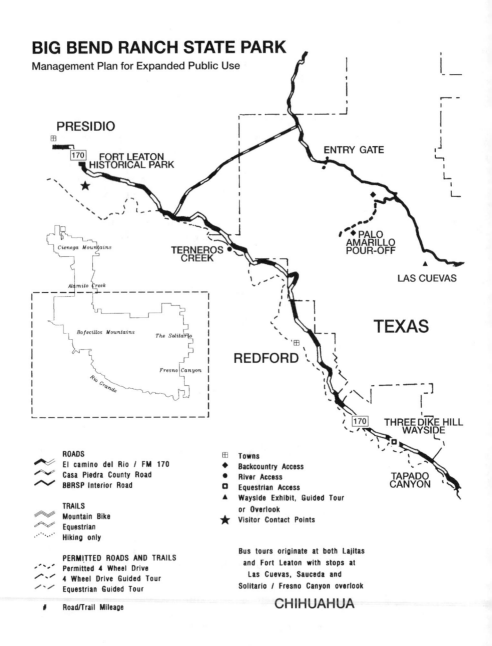

PRESIDIO

FORT LEATON
HISTORICAL PARK

ENTRY GATE

PALO
AMARILLO
POUR-OFF

LAS CUEVAS

Cienega Mountains

Alamito Creek

Bofecillos Mountains

The Solitario

Rio Grande

Fresno Canyon

TERNEROS
CREEK

TEXAS

REDFORD

THREE DIKE HILL
WAYSIDE

TAPADO
CANYON

ROADS
~ El camino del Rio / FM 170
~ Casa Piedra County Road
~ BBRSP Interior Road

TRAILS
~ Mountain Bike
~ Equestrian
··· Hiking only

PERMITTED ROADS AND TRAILS
-·- Permitted 4 Wheel Drive
~ 4 Wheel Drive Guided Tour
/~/ Equestrian Guided Tour

Road/Trail Mileage

⊞   Towns
◆   Backcountry Access
●   River Access
▢   Equestrian Access
▲   Wayside Exhibit, Guided Tour
    or Overlook
★   Visitor Contact Points

Bus tours originate at both Lajitas
and Fort Leaton with stops at
Las Cuevas, Sauceda and
Solitario / Fresno Canyon overlook

CHIHUAHUA

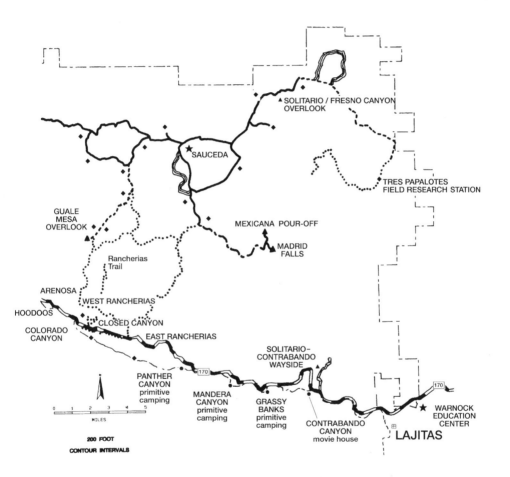

SOLITARIO / FRESNO CANYON
OVERLOOK

SAUCEDA

TRES PAPALOTES
FIELD RESEARCH STATION

GUALE
MESA
OVERLOOK

MEXICANA POUR-OFF

MADRID
FALLS

Rancherias
Trail

ARENOSA

WEST RANCHERIAS

HOODOOS

CLOSED CANYON

COLORADO
CANYON

EAST RANCHERIAS

SOLITARIO–
CONTRABANDO
WAYSIDE

170

PANTHER
CANYON
primitive
camping

MANDERA
CANYON
primitive
camping

GRASSY
BANKS
primitive
camping

CONTRABANDO
CANYON
movie house

170

WARNOCK
EDUCATION
CENTER

LAJITAS

0 1 2 3 4 5
MILES

200 FOOT
CONTOUR INTERVALS

Map courtesy of Texas Parks & Wildlife Department.

OTHER POINTS OF INTEREST

SOLITARIO

This classic geologic dome was uplifted by an intrusive igneous body and runs about eight miles east to west and nine miles north to south. The sides or rim of the Solitario are composed of Cretaceous limestone and have been tilted to a near vertical position. For decades, geologists thought that the Paleozoic formations at the center of the Solitario were exposed by erosion, but the most recent studies indicate that the Solitario actually erupted, taking off the dome's crest. This makes it one of the world's few lacco-calderas. Contact the Warnock Center or Fort Leaton for information on tours and access.

SPORTS AND ACTIVITIES

Bus Tours

The most popular way to see most of the park is via one of the two bus tours operated by Texas Parks & Wildlife. Tours depart the first and third Saturdays of the month on air-conditioned, battle-tested buses complete with restroom. Reservations and a deposit are required. Contact TP&W central reservations at 512-389-8900.

A discount is available to Texas Conservation Passport holders. Each tour begins at 8:00 a.m.; show up early to check in and take care of any loose ends (like paying). Departures alternate from the Warnock Center (915-424-3327) and Fort Leaton (915-229-3613). Both are excellent tours. The one that departs Fort Leaton ventures farther into the interior of the State Natural Area and includes a view of the Solitario. The one that departs the Warnock Center goes into the heart of the Big Bend Ranch as far as the park headquarters but spends more time on the River Road, rated by *National Geographic* (in its June 1985 issue) as perhaps the prettiest drive in America. All trips are guided, have plenty of rest breaks including iced beverages, and include lunch at Sauceda, the ranch headquarters.

Fishing

Fishing along the Rio Grande is allowed. Unlike the national park, however, a fishing license and a park permit are required. Trotline and jug fishing are discouraged.

Hiking and Camping

The expansion of the State Natural Area's trail system is underway. As new trails are developed they will be incorporated into future editions of the *Big Bend Ranch State Park Trail Guide*, produced by the Texas Parks & Wildlife Department and available at the Warnock Center or Fort Leaton. Used in conjunction with a separately available trail map and a compass, the guide is easily the best resource for the trails and includes suggested itineraries. It also has a complete list of guidelines about water usage, critical management zones, private property, and other topics. **Portions of all trails include areas subject to flash flooding.** None of the routes are improved or marked with signs, only rock cairns. Routes can vary from old wagon roads to modern jeep trails and animal paths—wild, as well as livestock.

The Closed Canyon Trail (1.4 miles round trip) is a good trek for families with older kids. It follows a narrow, shaded drainage carved through Santana tuff to a series of impassable pour-offs overlooking the Rio Grande. With its steep walls, smooth sides and sandy bottom, it's an ideal escape from the heat of the day.

The entire trail is in the bottom of this water-worn canyon and **highly susceptible to flash floods.** So, too, is the Rancherías Canyon Trail (9.6 miles round trip). A full day's hike, the route passes remnants of ancient lava flows 20 and 30 million years old and terminates at the fourth highest waterfall in Texas, Rancherías Falls.

The Rancherías Loop Trail (19 miles from trailhead to trailhead) makes an ideal three-day hike with two nights out on the trail. It can be accessed via two trailheads, the East and West Rancherías Trailheads, and travels through three different canyon systems. It is best enjoyed beginning at the east trailhead and hiking through to the west one.

About three miles along FM 170 separates both trailheads, so try to set up a shuttle or ride before you hit the trail. Numerous arroyos and canyon bottoms form major portions of the trail. Like the other two trails, **beware of flash flooding.** Both suggested camps are convenient to natural water sources, but bring your own and don't get caught dry. Budget about a gallon a day per person (one gallon weighs approximately eight pounds), and be prepared to purify any water you gather.

River Rafting

Refer to **River Trips** under **BIG BEND NATIONAL PARK** for a complete listing of guide services, trips, and suggestions. As in Big Bend National Park, you can run the river on your own or with a commercial service. Within the State Natural Area, access is offered at seven points. Heading west from the Warnock Center, they are, in order, Contrabando Canyon, Grassy Banks, Madera Canyon, Panther Canyon, Colorado Canyon, Arenosa, and the Hoodoos. Each of these is right off of FM 170 and is marked on maps available at the Big Bend Ranch State Park. Some have primitive campsites with self-composting outhouses, but none offer potable water, electricity, or much shade.

Seminars

Seminars at the Big Bend Ranch typically last two or three days, cost around two to three hundred dollars, and range from desert survival to rock art to useful plants of the Chihuahuan Desert. Call 915-424-3327 or fax 915-424-3404 for more information. Keep in mind that Texas Conservation Passport holders enjoy discounted seminar rates.

SIDE TRIPS

COPPER CANYON, MEXICO
See separate listing under **PRESIDIO & OJINAGA.**

RESTAURANTS & ACCOMMODATIONS

See separate listings under **BIG BEND NATIONAL PARK, LAJITAS, PRESIDIO & OJINAGA,** *and* **TERLINGUA.**

CANDELARIA & RUIDOSA

PRESIDIO COUNTY • A few hardy souls • (915)

FM 170 winds its way north and west from Presidio on the south side of the Chinatis for close to 50 miles. For many visitors (and more than a few locals), this remote stretch of borderland is as close to the Big Bend of old as can be found in this day and age (without crossing into old Mexico). At about the 36-mile mark, Ruidosa comes into view.

RUIDOSA AND CANDELARIA, TEXAS
36 and 48 miles west of Presidio via FM 170 (paved)
Ruidosa Store • 8 a.m. to whenever • 915-229-4534

Lajitas sits 50 miles east of Presidio along FM 170. Head west on that same road and you'll end up in two of the most remote outposts in Texas today. Ruidosa and Candelaria serve area cattle ranches in remote Presidio County and Chihuahua as well as curious tourists. The Pancho Villa-era cavalry post is a short stroll from the mercantile as is the town of San Antonio. This clean little cowtown of several hundred *mexicanos* is conveniently reached by a footbridge across the rio or your own four-wheel-drive vehicle.

SPORTS AND ACTIVITIES

Hot Springs

CHINATI HOT SPRINGS
Take FM 170 .5 miles past Ruidosa towards Candelaria • Turn right at the Hot Springs sign and follow the gravel road for 7 miles 915-229-4165 • hotsprings@brooksdata.net

This wonderful, quiet lovely place is the real McCoy: an oasis in the desert. Who knows how long travelers have sought refuge here, but you can enjoy the baths for a day fee of $10, hike the grounds, and go birding along Hot Springs Creek, which flows from a separate cold spring. Overnight camping costs $10 per person. A limited number of cabins is available by reservation ($–$$).

SHOPPING

LA JUNTA GENERAL STORE
Ruidosa • 915-229-4534 • Daily 8–8

After an hour or two cooped in your car, the two benches that Celia Hill keeps out front of her store make just about everyone who drives up this way stop and sit a while. Of course, that's after you've stopped inside and bought a coke or some chips or maybe a cold beer. There's ice for your cooler, and ice cream for the kids. She also stocks a few staples that you may need if you're on your way to the Hot Springs.

CLUBS AND BARS

BEN'S LOUNGE
Ruidosa • 915-229-4715 • Hours: whenever Ben wants

Ben Benavidez opened this joint a few years ago and usually shows up in the afternoon to unlock the door. Come sundown, he calls it quits, so if it's open at night, that means Janet Hinds is behind the big L-shaped bar. Besides the interesting paint scheme and the various items from Ben's ranch on the walls, the lounge has the only pool table in the south part of the county, satellite TV for the NASCAR races, and a jukebox stocked with country songs, Hispanic *exitos*, and a few *corridos*. Ben proudly serves Texas beers such as Lone Star and Pearl. If you're so inclined, the usual Yankee beers are available like Bud, Bud Light, Coors, Coors Light. Chips, snacks, and cokes.

ACCOMMODATIONS

($ = Under $40, $$ = $40–$75, $$$ = $75–$100, $$$$ = Over $100)

CASA DE LOS SANTOS
P.O. Box 187 • Marfa • 79834 • 915-229-3597
lossantos@brooksdata.net • $–$$

This historic hacienda dates back to the late 1880s. At various times a barracks, a cantina, judicial offices, and a store, the hundred-year-old adobe is now available for guests. Many come here to enjoy birding, bike riding, and hiking. Horseback riding costs $30 per half day, not including a $25 guide fee. Casa de los Santos has a well-deserved reputation for extended overnight horse treks on both sides of the border.

Many guests prefer just to enjoy the solitude and quiet of the picturesque posada. The rate of $40 per person ($20 for children under 12) includes dinner and breakfast. Special rates and accommodations are available for artists and writers interested in extended stays over a week. Prepared meals and specialized tours are available by prior arrangement as are lunches and dinners for those not staying overnight. Guests can also make use of a full kitchen to fix their own meals.

CARLSBAD CAVERNS NATIONAL PARK

EDDY COUNTY, NEW MEXICO
MOUNTAIN TIME • (505)

Nearly a century ago, a lone cowboy became intrigued by the nightly flight of hundreds of thousands of Mexican free-tail bats from the mouth of the caverns. Jim White's curiosity led to years of pioneering exploration and ultimately the designation of the caverns as a national monument (1923) and a national park (1930). Carlsbad Caverns National Park continues to be a fascinating subterranean wilderness with more than 86 caves in the park. Recent discoveries within the Caverns include the Bifrost Room and Storm Cloud Chamber (1982), the Rim Room (1984), and Chocolate High (1992). In 1986, a collapsed opening in Lechugilla Cave was cleared, and exploration began on what has become the deepest cave in America (1,567 feet) and the fifth longest cave in the world (100 miles).

TOURIST SERVICES

SUPERINTENDENT, CARLSBAD CAVERNS NATIONAL PARK
3225 National Parks Highway • Carlsbad, NM • 88220
505-785-2232 or 505-785-2107 (recorded info line)

The most visible aspect of the National Park Service is the Visitor Center through which all cavern tours depart. Located seven miles west of White's City, New Mexico, and 27 miles southwest of Carlsbad, New Mexico, it includes kennels for pets, a gift shop with an extensive collection of books and cavern items, and a restaurant.

GUIDEBOOKS AND PUBLICATIONS

CARLSBAD CAVERNS NATIONAL PARK:
SILENT CHAMBERS, TIMELESS BEAUTY

By John Barnett
Carlsbad Caverns/Guadalupe Mountains Association • $3.00

This 32-page magazine-style piece includes simplified explanations of cavern formation and superb photos of the caverns and the surrounding Chihuahuan Desert.

STORIES FROM STONES:
THE GEOLOGY OF THE GUADALUPE MOUNTAINS
By David H. Jagnow and Rebecca Rohwer Jagnow
Carlsbad Caverns/Guadalupe Mountains Association

Guadalupe Mountains and Carlsbad Caverns national parks are the best known natural legacies of the Permian era. Many, however, know the Permian name because of the enormous oil fields that initially formed during this period. This booklet provides a detailed explanation of the unique geological conditions that led to the formation of the Permian reef and a better understanding of modern geography as well as subsurface mechanics. Available at both parks and through the Carlsbad Caverns/Guadalupe Mountains Association at 505-785-2318.

SPORTS AND ACTIVITIES

Cavern Tours

Daily except Christmas • Admission: Adults $6, under 16 $3

The National Park Service has done a great job of facilitating access to the caverns. Visitors can either walk from the Visitor Center to the cave's natural entrance and descend by foot (the Natural Entrance Tour) or take an elevator to a point 750 feet below the Visitor Center and begin in the heart of the caverns (the Big Room Tour). A third option is the King's Palace Tour, which is guided.

All three tours are about a mile long and take roughly an hour. All tours exit via elevator. The paths, including the walk into the cave, are on paved trails that are well lighted. Plenty of handrails and rock benches are available for safety and comfort. Park rangers are available to answer questions, offer explanations, and render assistance. Wear a light jacket or sweater; the caverns maintain a temperature of 56 degrees all year long.

It would be a catastrophic mistake to not spend three bucks to rent a CD-ROM headset at the visitor center. It picks up low-level transmissions at different points in the cave and broadcasts explanations of the cave's history and exploration, the geology of the caverns, and the nature of the different formations. These audio guides are available for adults in English or Spanish.

Cavern Hours

	Summer	Non-Summer
Visitor Center Opens	8:00 a.m.	8:00 a.m.
Visitor Center Closes	7:00 p.m.	5:30 p.m.
Natural Entrance Route Opens	8:30 a.m.	8:30 a.m.
Natural Entrance Route Closes	3:30 p.m.	2:00 p.m.
Big Room Route Opens	8:30 a.m.	8:30 a.m.
Big Room Route Closes	5:00 p.m.	3:30 p.m.
King's Palace Guided Tours	Call Park	Call Park
Last King's Palace Guided Tour	Call Park	3:00 p.m.
Last Elevator to Surface	6:30 p.m.	5:00 p.m.
Bat Flight	Call Park	Go to Mexico

King's Palace Guided Tours are scheduled four times daily during the summer months: 9:00 a.m., 11:00 a.m., 1:00 p.m., and 3:00 p.m.

SLAUGHTER CANYON CAVE OR NEW CAVE TOURS
Admission: Adults $15, under 16 $7.50, under 6 not allowed

Slaughter Canyon Cave is new in the sense that it was discovered after the Caverns in 1937. Tours are available by reservation only (800-967-2283) and are offered daily from June through August and on weekends the rest of the year. All tours are guided, and several require-ments are made of the participants, including one flashlight per person, good walking shoes or hiking boots, drinking water, and transportation to the cave parking lot at the mouth of Slaughter Canyon.

A much more strenuous venture than the Caverns, only the physical-ly fit should consider the 1.25-mile tour, which lasts about 2.5 hours. The most taxing part of the entire trip is the thirty-minute hike from the parking lot to the cave, which is where your guide awaits you, the tour begins, and actual tour distances are calculated.

All tour times are scheduled from the cave entrance and not the park-ing lot. To reach the parking lot at the mouth of Slaughter Canyon, drive five miles southwest of White's City on US 62-180 (toward Texas and Guadalupe Mountains National Park). The Slaughter Canyon turnoff to the west is clearly marked. Eleven miles down this road is the parking lot. Once you leave your vehicle, budget 3 to 4 hours for the hike up, the tour, and the hike back. Cave temperature is 62 degrees, humidity is 90 percent, and photography is permitted (no tripods).

Hiking and Camping

About 750,000 people visit the park, and almost all go not a single step beyond the Visitor Center and the Caverns themselves. The 30 miles of primitive backcountry trails and 33,125 acres of designated

wilderness that lie west of the Visitor Center are completely overlooked. They are rugged, formidable, even unforgiving, and never
crowded. A backcountry permit is required (no charge), and a topographic map is essential. Both are available at the Visitor Center. Bring
plenty of water—none is available on the trail. Because these trails are
completely ignored, you'll find park personnel more than willing to
suggest itineraries and to discuss possible hazards like summer storms,
winter lows, flash floods, and the parched conditions.

Scenic Drive

At just under ten miles, the Walnut Canyon Desert Drive offers
ample opportunity to enjoy a backcountry excursion including views of
Rattlesnake Canyon and upper Walnut Canyon. The gravel, one-way
loop is fine for passenger cars but not recommended for trailers or
motor homes. Stop by the Visitor Center for a self-guiding booklet.
The drive begins just west of the Visitor Center.

OTHER POINTS OF INTEREST

BAT FLIGHT
**Outdoor Amphitheater at the cave's natural entrance behind the
Visitor Center • Late May to October just before sunset**

During the warmer half of the year, sundown signals feeding time for
thousands of Mexican free-tail bats. This nocturnal procession led to
the discovery of the caverns by Jim White in 1901. The bats winter in
Mexico and summer at the caverns. About 30 minutes before they
emerge, a park ranger makes a brief presentation on the bats including
their prey, their migratory habits, and their highly developed sonar system known as echolocation. *Bats of Carlsbad Caverns National Park* is a brief
and colorful 32-page guide available at the gift shop.

SIDE TRIPS

LIVING DESERT STATE PARK
**P.O. Box 100 • Carlsbad NM • 88220 • 505-887-5516
22 miles north of White's City and 2 miles north of Carlsbad
via US 285 • Daily except major holidays • Admission**

Atop the Ocotillo Hills, Living Desert is an 1,120-acre botanical and
zoological collection featuring native Chihuahuan Desert species. The
Visitor Center offers detailed explanations of species and the ecosys-
tem, and the Desert Arboretum houses more than 300 different succulents from around the world as well as the desert southwest. The 1.3-
mile self-guided trail takes about 90 minutes.

RESTAURANTS & ACCOMMODATIONS

($ = Under $40, $$ = $40–$75, $$$ = $75–$100)
Room Tax 11%

After touring the Caverns, everyone assumes that White's City was named for or started by Cavern discoverer Jim White. It actually was founded in 1927 by a friend of Jim's, C. L. White, who forecasted the park's popularity. By 1936, White had developed a 13-unit lodge, ran a Texaco station, and was the lone resident. Fifty years later, the Texaco station is still in place as are three lodges with a combined 132 rooms—as well as two restaurants, several gift shops, a museum, and year-round population of 27.

White's City sits astride the entrance to the National Park; you literally have to drive through it to go the last seven miles to the Caverns. Reasons to stay here include the close proximity to the caverns, the variety of facilities and range of prices (from campsites to RV hookups to rooms), and your alternatives. Carlsbad, New Mexico, is half an hour north and Van Horn, Texas, is more than an hour and a half south. Gas, gift shops, and groceries are all within walking distance of the town's several properties.

BEST WESTERN CAVERN INN
White's City • 800-CAVERNS • $$–$$$

This two-story inn has 63 smoking and non-smoking rooms with satellite TV (HBO), phones with free local calls to Carlsbad, and thermocuzzis in some. There are two restaurants: Fast Jacks, and the Velvet Garter Restaurant and Saloon. There are also two pools—an Olympic-sized unheated one and a smaller heated one, two hot tubs, an arcade on the boardwalk, a tennis court and a basketball court, several gift shops, a laundry room, and plenty of free parking. The melodrama theater runs from May through September and by special appointment. A shuttle runs to the Caverns (fee). No pets. AAA, AARP, and military rates offered.

BEST WESTERN GUADALUPE INN
White's City • 800-CAVERNS • $$–$$$

Right across the street from the Cavern Inn, the Guadalupe Inn offers 42 non-smoking rooms. All amenities are similar. No pets.

Recreational Vehicles and Other Accommodations

PARK ENTRANCE RV AND CAMPERS PARK
White's City • AAA approved • 800-CAVERNS

Pull-through hookups (water, sewer, and electric). Bathrooms and showers surrounded by a grassy picnic area with tables and barbecue pits. Controlled access via coded gate (changed daily). Access to the pools, hot tub, and laundry at the other facilities.

The city of Carlsbad, with its hundreds of hotel rooms and restaurants, is 27 miles northwest of the Caverns via Highway 62–180. The Carlsbad Chamber of Commerce (505-887-6516) offers a complete listing of hotels/motels as well as other attractions. Resources include the *New Mexico Vacation Guide* produced by *New Mexico* magazine in cooperation with the New Mexico Department of Tourism (800-545-2040).

EL PASO & JUAREZ

EL PASO COUNTY SEAT • 700,000 • (915)
STATE OF CHIHUAHUA • 2,000,000+ • (011 52 16)

When people's thoughts turn to El Paso, a Marty Robbins ballad comes to mind. It's about a West Texas town whose *cantinas* are full of gunfighters and beautiful *señoritas*, and to millions *El Paso* is a catchy tune. But when you belly up to the bar at the L&J Cafe and listen as the proprietor tells you about Texas Rangers raiding his grandfather's cantina, the hitching post that used to be out front, and the gravesite across the street of a preacher's son who killed thirty men, keep in mind that Robbins sang a ballad and not a song.

El Paso has more than its share of beautiful señoritas (including a recent Miss USA), enjoys the most convenient snow skiing for Texans (three hours away), and serves as the home of the Scudbuster (Fort Bliss). El Paso and Juarez retain the crown as Mexican food capital of the world, and bullfights are just a cab ride away. But there's a lot more to the fourth largest city in Texas than most people (including some locals) give it credit for.

El Paso is commonly referred to as a Texas city. Though its origin dates back to 1598, it wasn't until the Compromise of 1850 that El Paso was located within the bounds of the state of Texas. For almost two centuries, El Paso was administered as a part of New Mexico (first by Spain and then by Mexico).

Its location and orientation are still closer to the capitals of Arizona, Chihuahua, and New Mexico than to Austin. Notice how regional news and weather from Las Cruces or Tucson replace talk about Texas in the *El Paso Times*. The Pacific coast is closer than Galveston Bay, and the El Paso perspective refocuses accordingly. Unlike Houston, Dallas, or even San Antonio, El Paso blends its Spanish heritage, Mexican legacy, and thoroughly western orientation to produce an outlook and a visit found nowhere else in Texas.

Locals and savvy travelers rarely stay put in "the Pass." When you take for granted crisscrossing El Paso to get to old Mexico, to New

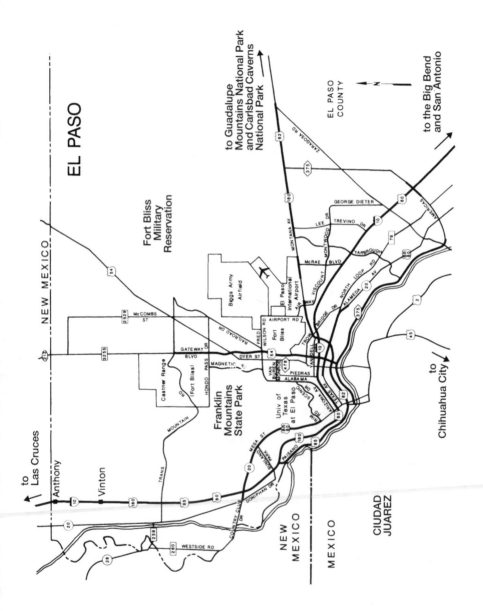

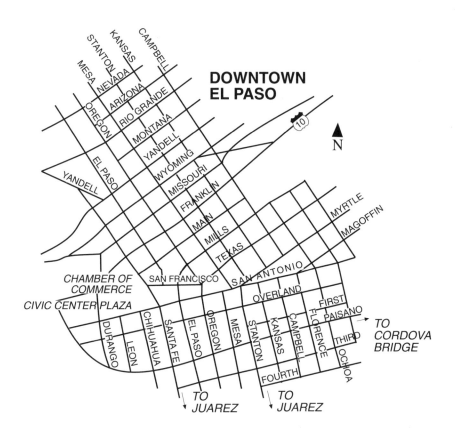

DOWNTOWN EL PASO

N

MESA
STANTON
KANSAS
NEVADA
CAMPBELL
ARIZONA
OREGON
RIO GRANDE
MONTANA
YANDELL
EL PASO
YANDELL
WYOMING
MISSOURI
FRANKLIN
MAIN
MILLS
TEXAS
MYRTLE
MAGOFFIN

CHAMBER OF
COMMERCE

SAN FRANCISCO

SAN ANTONIO

CIVIC CENTER PLAZA

OVERLAND

FIRST
PAISANO

TO
CORDOVA
BRIDGE

DURANGO
LEON
CHIHUAHUA
SANTA FE
EL PASO
OREGON
MESA
STANTON
KANSAS
CAMPBELL
FLORENCE
THIRD
OCHOA

FOURTH

TO
JUAREZ

TO
JUAREZ

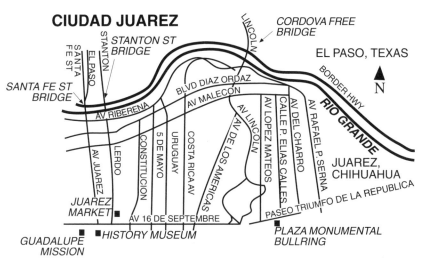

CIUDAD JUAREZ

CORDOVA FREE
BRIDGE

EL PASO, TEXAS

N

STANTON ST
BRIDGE

LINCOLN

SANTA FE ST
BRIDGE

SANTA FE ST
STANTON
EL PASO

BLVD DIAZ ORDAZ

AV MALECON

BORDER HWY

RIO GRANDE

AV RIBERENA

AV JUAREZ
LERDO
CONSTITUCION
5 DE MAYO
URUGUAY
COSTA RICA AV
AV DE LOS AMERICAS
AV LINCOLN
AV LOPEZ MATEOS
CALLE P. ELIAS CALLES
AV DEL CHARRO
AV RAFAEL P. SERNA

JUAREZ,
CHIHUAHUA

PASEO TRIUMFO DE LA REPUBLICA

JUAREZ
MARKET

AV 16 DE SEPTEMBRE

PLAZA MONUMENTAL
BULLRING

GUADALUPE
MISSION

HISTORY MUSEUM

Mexico, as well as around town, you'll begin to enjoy El Paso. Stay in the heart of the downtown, and a bullfight and dinner in Juarez are closer than a baseball game and hot dogs at Cohen Stadium. If the west side is your base, a day at the Sunland Park Racetrack and Casino playing the ponies and the gaming machines is far more convenient than a tour along the Mission Trail. This natural mix of cultures and function as a crossroads is the hallmark of historic El Paso as well as its future.

El Paso's origin centers on *el Camino Real* and the imperial goals of conquest and spreading the faith, not on dry goods or real estate speculation. The Royal Road wound its way from Mexico City via Chihuahua City to the most northerly outpost of the Spanish Empire— Santa Fe. Traversing nearly two thousand miles, *el Camino* was among the longest conquest and trade routes in North America, with branches forking off through the Big Bend and Davis Mountains to San Antonio and on to the Gulf of Mexico. Much of Interstate 10 and Interstate 25 north of El Paso follows its course.

Nearly four centuries ago (1598), Spanish colonization of the American Southwest advanced significantly when Juan de Oñate led a colonizing expedition across the Chihuahuan Desert of what is now northern Mexico to the Rio Grande, trailblazing the route for *el Camino*.

Where the Rio Grande sliced through the Franklin Mountains, he named this crossing *El Paso del Rio del Norte*. Half a century later, another Spaniard, Fray Garcia de San Francisco y Zuniga, built the Mission of Our Lady of Guadalupe and founded a fledgling settlement (1659). This landmark is typical of El Paso; the construction of Our Lady of Guadalupe is recognized as the founding of the 24th largest city in the United States, even though the site of the mission is the main square of Juarez.

Across the river on what is now American soil, only small and scattered settlements like Coon's Ranch, Concordia, Franklin, and Magoffinsville existed as late as the American Civil War. During its early years, El Paso was often overlooked as a commercial or political hub. When El Paso County was organized (1850), more established communities like San Elizario and Ysleta vied for the county seat. It wasn't until the railroads reached west to El Paso that the focus of the valley shifted upriver. Soon El Paso boasted five rail lines. This combination of interstate and international arteries made El Paso as natural a choice as a distribution center in the nineteenth century as it does today.

Many of the economic forces that propelled El Paso into the twentieth century are now permanent elements of the community. Mineral deposits in Mexico, New Mexico, and Arizona led to the founding of the State School of Mines and Metallurgy (known today as the University of Texas at El Paso). Centuries of cotton farming along the Rio Grande created a textile industry that produces millions of garments for American and global markets. Fort Bliss, once the headquarters of America's southern flank, has evolved into America's air defense headquarters.

Here is a quick look at things to come. Individually, both El Paso and Juarez are the largest border cities in the United States and Mexico. Together, they have no match from Brownsville to San Diego and stand to be catapulted economically into the twenty-first century. *Maquiladoras* are the engine of this growth. The *maquiladoras* utilize factories in Mexico where components produced elsewhere are assembled using less expensive Mexican labor. The finished goods are then shipped to another plant for final assembly.

Juarez has no equal in Mexico when it comes to the number of *maquiladoras* or the number of people employed by *maquilas*. The list of *maquilas* in Juarez numbers about 400, the number of employees approaches 200,000, and the roll call of American and international companies in Juarez includes companies like A.C. Nielsen, Briggs and Stratton, Honeywell, Murata, Proctor-Silex, Sylvania, and TDK. Eighty percent are American-owned.

Both El Paso and Juarez will be important components of the success of free trade on a broader scale. Already, the spillover from the *maquila* program affects numerous facets of El Paso today: increased employment and housing starts, the development of new businesses, and higher enrollment at local universities. But the most fortunate by-product from the standpoint of this book has been that as prospects for El Paso's future have brightened, awareness of the unique attributes of this region and renewed interest in cultural attractions like the historic Mission Trail grows stronger among locals and visitors like yourself.

Going Across

A roadtrip to Juarez is easier than driving around parts of Dallas these days. For you it might be the first time, but going over to shop or grab a bite has been a way of life out here for centuries. Stroll across or take a shuttle (*see* **TOURIST SERVICES**). Driving is not a bad idea, it's just not the best one if you are unfamiliar with Mexico's largest border city. Why put up with the hassle of directions, roundabouts, and the Mexican penchant for demolition-derby driving when someone else will do it for small change?

Walking Across. Park your car at one of the lots by the Santa Fe Street Bridge. An attendant collects the $3 to $5 per day fee. Hoof it over and pay the quarter toll. Stroll down Avenida Juarez with its hundreds of shops, restaurants, bistros, and bars heading south from the base of the Santa Fe Bridge. The intersection with Avenida de 16 de Septiembre is the heart of the city. The Juarez market is several blocks east; the Cathedral, the Guadalupe Mission, and the History Museum are directly to the right.

Driving Across. Several miles southeast of downtown, the Cordova Bridge of the Americas permits auto and pedestrian traffic both ways and is free. Downtown, take the Stanton Street bridge into Mexico and the Santa Fe Street Bridge back to the states. Your toll is approximately a dollar going over and about two coming back. (These prices fluctuate constantly.) Wherever you pull up, you'll find gentlemen directing, guiding, and otherwise doing their best to convince you how crucial their parking skills are. You don't have to buy this routine but they'll be with your car when you're gone. A dollar tip is customary.

On any trip south of the border, remember that American dollars are accepted as readily as Mexican pesos and that the recent devaluation has produced a new currency as well as modified the old one. The existing denominations are now utilized *minus* three zeros; for instance, 20,000 old pesos equals 20 new pesos. It is quite acceptable to haggle over prices in markets and with cabbies but not at restaurants or department stores. Quite often, the bill is presented with a dollar sign. Treat this as pesos until you are told otherwise. If you need to convert your money to pesos or vice versa, consider the following houses or stop at one of the ubiquitous *casas de cambio* that are sprinkled throughout downtown El Paso.

El Paso International Airport

EL PASO FOREIGN CURRENCY EXCHANGE
Open daily all year • 915-779-1098

Downtown

CHASE BANK • MAIN AND MESA STREETS
Weekdays • 915-546-6500

Greater El Paso

WELLS FARGO
Eight locations • Varying hours
915-532-9922 for locations and hours

TOURIST SERVICES

EL PASO TOURIST INFORMATION CENTERS
Civic Center Plaza • Daily 8–5 • 915-544-0062
El Paso International Airport • Daily 9–5 • 915-772-4271 ext. 275

Well staffed and full of brochures, flyers, and magazines, these centers can do more than answer questions. The Civic Center Plaza location is also the headquarters for the El Paso-Juarez Trolley Co. and the site for departures on the trolley tour.

EL PASO-JUAREZ TROLLEY CO.

One Civic Center Plaza • 915-544-0062 • Daily
Adults $11 • Children under 12 $8.50
Mission Tours on Thursday during the summer only

There is no better way to see Juarez than via the trolley. The convenience and value of this service make it the best way to familiarize yourself with the area (*see* **DRIVING TOUR**). The charge is a lot less than any of the costs or hassles associated with driving your own vehicle into Mexico.

TEXAS TRAVEL INFORMATION CENTER

Anthony Exit on Interstate 10 (Mile Marker 0) • 915-886-3468
Open daily 8 a.m. to 5 p.m. except New Year's and Christmas

If you haven't stopped at one of the Texas Department of Transportation Centers before, do so now. After quizzing a trained travel counselor about your itinerary, pick up the *Texas State Travel Guide*, a 272-page gold mine produced by the Texas Department of Transportation, regularly updated, and handed out free of charge.

TOUR BUS OPERATORS

Fiesta Tours • 915-544-4646
Golden Tours • 915-779-0555
Gringo Tours • 915-637-2298
Johnny's Tours • 915-549-7025
Outrider Tours • 915-592-9721
Rancho Grande Tours • 915-771-6664

Half- and full-day tours of El Paso/Juarez are conveniently scheduled by these coaches. Shopping, sightseeing, the Juarez Race Track, and bullfights are more easily enjoyed while someone else does the driving. Pickup and drop-off to major hotels. Group and children's rates available.

Other Helpful Numbers

American Express Office: Sun Travel. 3100 N. Mesa, Suite B.
915-532-8900. Monday through Friday from 7:30 a.m. to 5:00 p.m.
Airport: 915-772-4271.
Local Bus Service: Sun Metro. Union Depot at 700 San Francisco.
915-533-3333. El Paso's local transit system covers the entire city
and begins service daily at 4:41 a.m. with the last bus returning by
11:06 p.m. Fares range up to 75¢.
Bus Terminal: Greyhound Bus Lines. 200 W. San Antonio.
915-532-2365.
Train Station: Union Depot. 700 San Francisco St. 915-545-2247.
Automobile Rentals: Advantage, Avis, Budget, Dollar, Enterprise,
Hertz, National, Thrifty.

Emergencies/Medical Assistance: 911.
American Consulate (Juarez): (0115216) 11 31 64.
Mexican Consulate: 910 E. San Antonio Ave. 915-533-3644.
U.S. Customs: 9400 Viscount. 915-540-5800.
Time and Temperature: 915-532-9911.

DRIVING TOUR

Head to the **El Paso-Juarez Trolley Company** office at the Civic Center, or if you're staying at one of the following hotels, call in advance for a complimentary shuttle: the Airport Hilton, El Camino Real Paso del Norte, Embassy Suites, Holiday Inn Sunland Park, Howard Johnson, Quality Inn, and the Radisson Inn Suites. Children four and under ride free; for kids under 13 it's always $8.50; adults pay $11.

The trolley runs every day on an hourly circuit beginning at 10 a.m., with the final sweep picking up the stragglers beginning at 5 p.m from April–October and 4 p.m. from November–March. Allow at least three to four hours total for the nine stops on the tour (though you'll probably only visit one of the three restaurant stops).

Keep in mind that the tour starts in the more modern section of Juarez and ends up in the oldest area. Consequently, American shopping habits are more common at the initial five stops and Mexican ones—for instance, negotiating prices—at the last four. This type of bargaining is not welcome at restaurants (Stops #4 and #5) or at the newer markets (Stops #1 and #2). **The trolley's route is subject to change. Make sure you have the most up-to-date schedule and list of stops.**

From the Civic Center, the trolley proceeds east to the Free Bridge and heads across to **Silver Castle** (#1). This shop specializes in handcrafted, solid sterling silver jewelry in the Taxco style.

Plaza de las Americas (#2) is where the tour gets going. Located in the old Pronaf shopping center, it has been rebuilt as an indoor mall with a leather store, an oriental shop, and a cinema that shows American movies with Spanish subtitles. You'll be dropped off at **Decor**, which features furniture and furnishings including glass blowers practicing their trade. There are restaurants in the area, and it's a short walk to **Chihuahua Charlie's** (#4).

The **JJ Market** (#3) offers the only opportunity to haggle in the Pronaf area. This small shop specializes in curios, and the ladies behind the counter are tough negotiators. Ask for the owner—he cuts a much better deal.

Chihuahua Charlie's (#4) is one of the liveliest stops on the tour and one of the more expensive. Breakfast, lunch, and dinner as well as 16-ounce margaritas keep it hopping. During the summer, don't be surprised if a fiesta is being held early on Saturday afternoons featuring *mariachis* and *folklorico* dancing.

From Chihuahua Charlie's to **Los Arcos** restaurant (#5) is a short stroll along the avenida. This eatery specializes in seafood served in the style of Mazatlan, Culiacan, Mexicali, and Guadalajara.

Casa Oñate (#6) features *curiosidades*—everything from leather goods like boots and handbags and saddles to gold and silver jewelry.

Casa Maya (#7) stocks less leather goods and goes overboard on handmade Mexican blankets, wool rugs, dream catchers, mandellas, and the like.

City Market or **Centro Mercado** (#8) is one vendor after the next selling every item imaginable and haggling with customers new and old over price, quality, and breeding (*see* **SHOPPING**). There are over a hundred stalls vending fresh food, packaged Mexican staples, hand-crafted items, clothing, jewelry, knick-knacks, leather, and produce. There is also a restaurant.

BIRD'S-EYE VIEW

SCENIC DRIVE

Take the Downtown Exit from I-10 • Take Mesa north to Rim Rd. and take a right • Follow Rim Rd., which becomes Scenic Dr., two miles to the Murchison Park pull-off

After the view itself, the best part about the vista from Murchison Park is that the City of El Paso has placed a dozen explanatory tablets that describe the different sights—Fort Bliss, downtown, Juarez, the University of Texas El Paso, etc. Pass on the pay-per-view telescopes if it's one of the many hazy days. Sunset is best (and safest).

MUSEUMS

AMERICANA MUSEUM OF SOUTHWEST CULTURAL HISTORY

Convention & Performing Arts Center • 5 Civic Center 915-542-0394 • Tuesday–Friday 10–5 • Free • W+ • Gift shop

Featuring a permanent exhibit entitled *The Art and Legacy of a Vanished People,* the Americana Museum presents a comprehensive display of pre-Columbian pottery of the Southwest. The many examples of Sedentary Culture craftsmanship are augmented by numerous annual exhibits of local and regional artists. Creations by local artists and Indian artisans from the Apache, Cherokee, Navajo, and Ute tribes are available in the gift shop.

BORDER PATROL MUSEUM

8901 Montana at Hawkins • 915-778-1118 Monday–Thursday 10–2 • Free • Gift shop

This museum recently moved into a new building right behind the Border Patrol's El Paso Sector Headquarters. With no funding from the federal government, an extensive collection of acquired and donated memorabilia pertaining to the Border Patrol and its founding in 1924 has been assembled. Rotating exhibits highlight the various Border Patrol sectors and aspects of fulfilling the Border Patrol's mission, such as firearms and smuggling techniques.

CENTENNIAL MUSEUM OF THE UNIVERSITY OF TEXAS EL PASO

UTEP Campus at the corner of Wiggins Way and University

Tuesday–Saturday 10–5 • 915-747-5565 • Free • W

Displays include pottery, stone tools, and shell jewelry of prehistoric Mexico, mineral and rock specimens, dinosaur bones, fossils, and other relics from the Ice Age.

CHAMIZAL NATIONAL MEMORIAL

800 San Marcial • 915-534-7273 • www.nps.gov/cham/
Daily 8–5 • Closed Thanksgiving, Christmas, New Year's
Free • W+

The Chamizal Memorial is a monument to the peaceful settlement of a century-old dispute over the minor changes in the course and character of the Colorado and Rio Grande rivers. The name *chamizal* refers to the *chamiza* (salt bush) which prevails along the river plains where the changes in course took place. Those changes were remedied by the Chamizal Settlement, initiated in 1962 by Presidents Kennedy and Mateos, and were implemented by a concrete-lined channel that prevents the river from changing course. In addition to a historical museum, the 55-acre park grounds boast a 500-seat performing arts theater, a 1,000-volume reference library, and Los Paisanos Gallery, which exhibits different artists from Mexico and the United States. Quite often Chamizal is the site of Music Under the Stars, fiestas, and festivals, including the renowned Siglo de Oro (*see* **ANNUAL EVENTS**).

EL PASO MUSEUM OF ART

One Festival Plaza • 915-532-1707 • Tuesday–Saturday 9–6
Sunday 12–5 • Free (donations accepted) • W+

Located in the heart of downtown El Paso right across from the Convention Center and the Paso del Norte Hotel, the museum's permanent collection is best known for the gift of Samuel Kress. With nearly 60 pieces, it includes works from the Early Renaissance (1300–1500), High Renaissance (1467–1600), and the Baroque-Rococo (1600–1800). Ten to twelve temporary exhibitions are scheduled per year. Contact the EPMA for information on the exhibit schedule, art classes, lectures, concerts, and access to their reference library.

EL PASO MUSEUM OF HISTORY

Interstate 10 West at Ave. of the Americas North • 915-858-1928
Tuesday–Sunday 9–4:50 • Guided group tours by appointment
Free • Donations accepted • Gift shop • W

Much history has settled in El Paso's dust. For more than four centuries, explorers, conquerors, gunfighters, and settlers found a natural
all-weather passageway where the Rio Grande could be crossed and the
southernmost Rocky Mountains relented. The mission of the El Paso
Museum of History is to chronicle this heritage and interpret its many
historical artifacts. The scope of this museum is apparent in the cultures
it examines: Spanish, Mexican, and Anglo. In addition to providing
workshops, lectures, classes, and special exhibits, the Museum's collections include blacksmithing and leatherworking tools, fans and shawls,
cavalry items, bottles, Victorian era furniture, and historic clothing.

EL PASO SCIENCE MUSEUM—INSIGHTS

505 N. Santa Fe at the corner of Santa Fe and Missouri
915-534-3000 • Tuesday–Sunday 9–5
Adults $5, seniors and military $3, students $2

Each year, more than 100,000 guests visit this popular El Paso museum. Insights is designed to be interactive, i.e., visitors must activate the
displays by performing some kind of activity like touching, jumping, or
pushing. With over one hundred exhibits, it's as much fun for adults as
for kids. Topics include the senses and other phenomena like electricity, gravity, shadows, and—a favorite—bubbles. Traveling exhibits are
often featured.

FORT BLISS MUSEUM COMPLEX

An unusual mix of old and new, Fort Bliss was Black Jack Pershing's
headquarters while trying to capture Pancho Villa, as well as the site of
Werner von Braun's laboratory following World War II. With over
1,700 square miles in and around El Paso, America's air defense center is
a vital component of the El Paso economy. The present location—La
Noria Mesa—is number six. When first garrisoned in 1849 by Brevet
Major Jefferson Van Horne, only six companies were detailed. All operations were relocated to Fort Fillmore, New Mexico, and it wasn't until
1854 that Fort Bliss was reestablished. Now more than 300 students
from 22 nations study at the U.S. Army Air Defense Training Center.
The German Air Force Defense School is also based at Fort Bliss. Take
the Airway exit off of Interstate 10, proceed north, and veer left past El
Paso International Airport. You'll run right into the main gate. No pass
or fee is required to enter the base to visit any of the museums, however, proof of insurance and a driver's license are required. Entry at night
is restricted to base personnel.

FORT BLISS MUSEUM

Buildings 5051–5054 • Pleasonton and Pershing Roads
915-568-4518 • Daily 9 to 4:30 • Closed holidays • Free

This adobe replica of the first Fort Bliss uses a Sutler's Store for visitor orientation and as a gift shop. A six-minute slide show presents a brief overview of early El Paso. Seven period rooms feature reproductions of uniforms, equipment, and furnishings accurate to 1857. The collection in the north building contains artifacts from the history of Fort Bliss beginning with the Civil War, the occupation and torching of the fort by Confederate troops, and other El Paso area locations of the post including Concordia Ranch, Garrison Town, and Hart's Mill. Ask about the one-of-a-kind American flag that flies over the museum before you head inside for a look at Black Jack Pershing's riding crop.

THIRD ARMORED CAVALRY REGIMENTAL MUSEUM

Bldg. 2407 • Forrest and Chaffee Roads • 915-568-1922
Monday–Friday 9 to 4:30 • W

Like the Fort Bliss Museum, a visit starts with a brief introduction to the museum at the Orientation Gallery. The Third Cavalry has an unparalleled heritage in the U.S. Army. The second oldest regiment in active service, it was first "baptized in fire and blood" (Winfield Scott) as the Regiment of Mounted Riflemen during the Mexican-American War (1847). Formed at the Jefferson Barracks, Missouri, the Regiment later became the Third United States Cavalry. Now known as the Third Armored Cavalry, its history includes 39 campaigns in eight wars—as well as a list of over 50 generals who have emerged from its ranks.

The Main Gallery houses most of the collection as well as timelines that pinpoint the history of the regiment within the broader scope of American history. The collection of Third Cavalry Regimental Standards (battle flags) is the most comprehensive of any unit in the U.S. Army. Also on display is a history of Third Cavalry military weapons, equipment, and uniforms from its earliest days to modern high tech gizmos that amaze and annihilate.

UNITED STATES ARMY AIR DEFENSE ARTILLERY MUSEUM

Bldg. 5000 • Pleasonton Road • 915-568-5412
Daily 9 to 4:30 • Closed holidays • W

This one is easy to find; look for the huge missiles out front. The history of air defense is featured beginning with the development of U.S. Army antiaircraft guns to combat the Red Baron and his fellow aces during World War I (1917) and continuing up to the most famous weapon of post-Vietnam warfare, the Patriot Missile—aka, the Scud-buster. Efforts to contain and control World War II's best known land-to-land missile, the V-1 or Buzz Bomb, are examined. In addition to defense-oriented land-to-air projectiles, other technologies depicted by dioramas, photographs, models, and graphics include radar, search-lights, sound locators, and fire control equipment.

MAGOFFIN HOME STATE HISTORICAL PARK

1120 Magoffin Avenue • 915-533-5147
www.tpwd.state.tx.us/park/magoffin/magoffin.htm
Daily 9–4 • Admission • W+ but not all areas

In 1875, Joseph Magoffin built the present 19-room territorial-style house of sun-dried adobe on a site settled by his father decades earlier. It stands on more than an acre of landscaped gardens. The Magoffin family occupied the house for more than a century, even after the City of El Paso and the State of Texas jointly acquired the house and proper-ty in 1976. Furnishings, paintings, and other family treasures are dis-played as well as other items relating to historic El Paso.

WILDERNESS PARK MUSEUM

2000 Transmountain Road • 915-755-4332
Tuesday–Sunday 9–4:45 • Free • W

Numerous dioramas, accurate and vivid, describe man in the South-west during prehistoric, pre-Columbian, as well as more modern times. The permanent collection is full of eye-catching displays: arrowheads, ceremonial feathers, and turquoise jewelry. Each is presented with its own vista on historic cultures. If your tribe is too restless to remain indoors, take them outside to the Nature Trail which winds its way around the museum and past replicas of a kiva, a pithouse, and a pueblo.

HISTORIC PLACES

CONCORDIA CEMETERY

Located between US 54, Interstate 10, Yandell Drive,
and Stevens Street • 915-542-1591

Right next to the spaghetti bowl—where Interstate 10 and Highway 54 mesh—stand row after row of headstones, tombstones, and El Paso history. Since the nineteenth century, Concordia has served as the final resting place for all of El Paso—Gentile and Jew, famous and infamous. Perhaps the most notable occupant is John Wesley Hardin, murdered at the Acme Saloon (1895) by John Selman. The son of a Methodist min-ister, Hardin took to homicide at the tender age of 15, killed three sol-diers sent to arrest him, and never kicked the habit. More than 30 men met their maker after meeting Mr. Hardin. To catch up with John Wes-ley, find the western entrance to the Chinese section of the cemetery and head just west and north (toward New Mexico and the Franklin Mountains).

EL PASO MISSION TRAIL

I-10 East, Avenue of the Americas Exit south to Zaragosa

These two missions and a presidio are located in the oldest part of El Paso, an area locals call the Lower Valley. Though most of the original settlement of this area by the Tigua Indians and the now extinct Piros was on the south side of the Rio Grande in El Paso del Norte (Juarez), the course of the Rio Grande has changed over the centuries and so has the international status of the missions (*see* **CHAMIZAL NATIONAL MEMORIAL**).

YSLETA DEL SUR PUEBLO (TIGUA INDIAN RESERVATION)

108 S. Old Pueblo Rd. • 915-859-3916 • Summer: Daily 8 to 4:30 Winter: Wednesday–Sunday 8 to 5 • Admission • W

Tiguas (pronounced TEE-wahs) are the descendants of settlers who arrived in Texas three hundred years ago and are recognized as the oldest identifiable ethnic group in the state. Their heritage is the Pueblo grouping of native North Americans which includes the Hopi, the Taos, and the Zuni tribes. Soon after fleeing Santa Fe during the Pueblo Revolt (1680), the Tiguas built the Ysleta mission. Today, their 37-acre reservation offers demonstrations of native crafts, a visit to their sacred mission, or a stop at Speaking Rock, their popular gaming and entertainment complex (*see* **GAMING** *under* **SPORTS & ACTIVITIES.**)

MISSION YSLETA

Zaragosa and Alameda • 915-859-9848

Easiest-to-find, Ysleta is a natural first stop on a Mission Trail tour. Completed in a New Mexican interpretation of the Spanish colonial style (1851), this white-washed adobe structure honors San Antonio, patron saint of the Tiguas. (Control of the parish was transferred to the Society of Jesus in 1881 who renamed the mission Our Lady of Mount Carmel.) It replaced two earlier sanctuaries dating back to the late 1600s and the mid-1700s.

These sanctuaries all endured calamities of some sort, particularly flooding. Yet each time waters subsided (1740 and 1829), the community gathered together to rebuild their mission, bringing new energy and materials to revitalize the work of the forefathers. Mission Ysleta incorporates materials from the last three centuries including walls and bells from the 1744 sanctuary. Note the silver dome roof and bell tower; they took several years to rebuild after a disastrous 1907 fire.

As much a part of the mission's history as the structure itself, the Tigua tribe manifests a heritage that can be traced to the Pueblo grouping of Native Americans such as the Hopi, the Taos, and the Zuni. Accompanying Otermín from the Isleta pueblo near Albuquerque three centuries ago, they cling to the remaining 66 acres of their reservation. A 1751 grant of four leagues (roughly 20,000 acres) by Charles V of Spain was overlooked, ignored, or disregarded by the Texas Legislature, which sold all but several hundred acres as public lands (1871).

In addition to their dwindling domain, less than ten full-blooded members remain. Altogether slightly more than a thousand members have been identified; they are the oldest ethnic group recognized in Texas. Several causes have contributed to their decreasing numbers: marriage outside the tribe; their unusual urban setting; belated recognition of tribal status by Congress (1968); and, a perplexing federal regulation concerning hereditary membership (two-thirds of the 500-plus American and Alaskan tribes recognized by the federal government don't abide by similar hereditary criteria, known as blood-quantuum-levels).

SOCORRO MISSION
Socorro Road (FM 258) at Nevarez • 915-859-7718

This is the oldest continuously active parish in the United States (1681). When the Tiguas settled Ysleta, other tribes, such as the now-extinct Piros, settled to the east and built the Socorro Mission. Though the earliest structures (1691) were destroyed by floods, the hand-crafted *vigas* (ceiling beams) survived and have been incorporated into the design of the present mission (1843). Socorro is an outstanding example of Spanish Mission architecture, yet the *vigas* and the *latilla enrejados* (smaller branches), which form a distinctive herringbone pattern, reflect notable Indian influences. Nearby archaeological excavations have led to the discovery of the foundation of the original structure.

CHAPEL SAN ELIZARIO
San Elizario Plaza off of FM 258 • 915-851-2333

Rather than fostering the faith like Ysleta and Socorro, the purpose of San Elizario was to defend it—from the Apaches and the Comanches. Established in the 1780s as a *presidio* (fort) by the Spanish government, it was relocated 37 miles north to the growing community of San Elizario in 1789 and was garrisoned well into the nineteenth century. When this portion of Old Mexico became American territory via the Treaty of Guadalupe Hidalgo (1848), San Elizario's pre-eminent position was evident by the billeting of American troops locally and the selection of San Elizario as the first El Paso county seat (1850).

The present San Elizario Chapel, completed in 1887, anchors the southeast side of the San Elizario plaza in a graceful Spanish Mission style. Look west from its entrance, out across the plaza. This vista was selected by Steven Spielberg as the final scene for *Fandango* (1985), starring Kevin Costner. To your left, the plaza's south side, stands a long, one-story building: Los Portales. The name comes from the distinctive inset gallery, called a portal, that faces the plaza. Built for the García family in the mid-1850s, this Territorial structure was used as an El Paso County Courthouse and later as a schoolhouse whose first instructor was Octaviano Larrazola, who went on to serve New Mexico as governor and senator.

Past Los Portales and not immediately visible from the plaza is the **San Elizario Jail**. Barely a block from the plaza's southwest corner, this mud-bricked, one-story building was built during San Elizario's Mexican period (1821–1848) and after El Paso County's organization became the first jurado, courthouse and jail (1850). Some of the jail's notoriety came from a caper commonly attributed to Billy the Kid.

Unlike his well-known Lincoln County escape, San Elizario may have been the only jail the Kid broke *into*. He was purported to have impersonated a Texas Ranger, bluffed the guards, and freed an amigo, Melquiades Segura, from one of the jail's iron cages (1876). A less humorous escapade occurred the following year at the culmination of the El Paso Salt War, whose murderous climax in December 1877 occurred in and around San Elizario's now peaceful plaza.

Paseo del Convento runs along the rear wall of the chapel, i.e., the portion farthest from the plaza. On this block stands the old **Butterfield Overland Mail** building, which dates from the 1840s and was used to house John Butterfield's local way station prior to the Civil War.

EL PASO UNION DEPOT

700 San Francisco Avenue • 915-545-2247 (Amtrak)

This red-bricked, high-steepled masterpiece shines from its 1981 renovation. Union Depot was built at the turn of the century (1906) when El Paso was coming of age as the junction of the Southern Pacific, the Atchison, Topeka & Santa Fe, and the Mexican Central railroads. It serves as the downtown terminal for Sun Metro, El Paso's local transit system, and as the Amtrak station. Each holiday season, the depot hosts performances of El Paso's concert choir and chamber orchestra, El Paso Pro-Musica.

GUADALUPE MISSION

Avenida 16 de Septiembre at the Plaza • Juarez

Located in the heart of Juarez, this mission is the soul of the region. It was from this church and the plaza before it that Juarez and El Paso began. Completed in 1668 after almost 10 years of construction by Mansos Indians, this is the initial component of the Mission Trail and predates Ysleta, Socorro, and San Elizario.

OTHER POINTS OF INTEREST

EL PASO ZOO

4001 E. Paisano Dr. (across from the County Coliseum) 915-544-1928 • Daily except New Year's, Thanksgiving, and Christmas • Monday–Friday 9:30–4 • Weekends and holidays 9:30–5 • Adults $2, seniors $1, children $1

Over 400 species are featured at this 18-acre facility. The show stoppers are the sea lion shows at 11 a.m. and 4 p.m. and the elephant feeding between 9:30 and 10:00 a.m. and at 2 p.m.

FRANKLIN MOUNTAIN STATE PARK

Downtown El Paso to the New Mexico border • 915-877-1528
www.tpwd.state.tx.us/park/franklin/franklin.htm

The Franklin Mountain range divides El Paso into east and west. Over 24,000 acres of this rugged range are located within the state park (and the El Paso city limits). There are plenty of hiking trails, picnic shelters, and numerous access points, but Franklin Mountain is one of the most undervisited parks in the state given its urban setting.

LOS MURALES ("THE MURALS")

El Paso's many cultures are nowhere better and more vividly expressed than in its numerous murals. The colorful creators range from well-known mainstream artists like Tom Lea, who got a federal contract to produce *Pass of the North* at the Federal Courthouse (1938), to the unknown muralist whose *Lagrimas* ("Tears") graces the wall of a building in the historic Chihuahuita district. Stop by the El Paso Juarez Trolley Company office at the Civic Center and pick up a copy of the El Paso Junior League's four-color, 20-page brochure *Los Murales*. With maps, addresses, and descriptions of the murals, it's the essential guide.

MOUNT CRISTO REY (SIERRA DEL CRISTO REY)

Interstate 10 West, Sunland Park Exit to Doniphan

Where the states of Chihuahua, New Mexico, and Texas meet there stands a towering 27-foot statue of Christ beckoning his flock, which is always present for the Feast of Christ the King (the last Sunday in October). Unfortunately, unless you travel in a group, you can fall victim to the numerous thieves who infest the slopes of Sierra de Muleros. Quarried of Cordova cream limestone near Austin, it was sculpted by Urbici Soler in the late 1930s. The trail up the mountain is 5,650 feet long (about a two-hour hike) and includes the fourteen stations of the cross. The sculpture stands atop a nine-foot base, is perched 4,675 feet above sea level, and includes a 33-foot-high cross.

SPORTS AND ACTIVITIES

Amusement Parks

SPORTSPARK EL PASO

1780 N. Zaragosa off Interstate 10 E. • 915-857-7676

This private outdoor facility has lighted softball fields, lighted volleyball courts, T-ball and youth baseball diamonds, softball and hardball batting cages, a playground, and a two-story clubhouse with concessions and televisions tuned to ESPN.

PUTT-PUTT GOLF & GAMES

8836 Montana at Hawkins • 915-779-2226
Sunday–Thursday 9 a.m.–12 a.m. • Friday–Saturday 9 a.m.–1 a.m.

Three 18-hole lighted miniature golf courses for golfers of all levels. Also available are a video game arcade, bankshot basketball, and a snack bar.

WESTERN PLAYLAND

Ascarate Park • 6900 Delta Drive • 915-779-3914
Open summers, Wednesday through Sunday
Admission varies: one price for all or entrance fee and per ride

For bigger kids, Western Playland features rides, wet and dry, with intimidating names like El Bandido, Snake Mountain, and the Himalaya. Youngsters have their choice of rides, and the video arcade attracts quarter pushers of all ages.

WET-N-WILD WATER WORLD

Interstate 10 Exit 0 at Anthony • 915-886-2222
Open from mid-May to mid-September • Admission

Kind of like a combination Jurassic Park/Noah's ark theme: volcanic gardens inundated with tons of water. With free-fall slides, flumes, and tubes, it's just south of the Texas/New Mexico state line by I-10.

Baseball

EL PASO DIABLOS

Cohen Stadium • 9700 Gateway North • 915-755-2000
Ticket prices: $4/$5/$6 • Game time: 6:30 p.m.

For over 20 years, El Paso's home team has been the Diablos of the Texas League, a farm team in the Milwaukee Brewers organization. The Diablos host visiting squads from within the Western Division—Midland, San Antonio, and Wichita—as well as interdivision rivals from Jackson, Shreveport, Arkansas, and Tulsa. Promotions like free lottery tickets, giveaways, and post-game concerts run all season long. As the sun sets behind the Franklin Mountains and things begin to cool off, a night at the ballpark can be pleasant as well as inexpensive. Located on the east side of town in a first-rate facility.

Basketball

UTEP MINERS

UTEP Special Events Center • 915-747-5265 • W+ but not all areas

It wasn't long ago (1966) that Texas Western, now known as the University of Texas at El Paso, shocked America by winning the Final

Four and bringing home the NCAA crown. A member of the Western Athletic Conference, the Miners host the Sun Bowl Tournament each December. Previous invitees include Indiana, Michigan, Ohio State, Iowa, Iowa State, USC, Pepperdine, and Tennessee. Tickets for Miners games start as low as $5.

Betting

SUNLAND PARK RACETRACK & CASINO
Interstate 10 West, Sunland Park Exit west • 505-874-5200
Daily • Free parking and admission • W+

(see HORSE RACING)

JUAREZ TURF CLUB
One block south of the International Bridge • 915-775-0555
Open from 9 a.m. daily

Pick your poison—baseball, basketball, football—they cover them all including college and pros. Full service restaurant and bar.

Bullfighting

PLAZA MONUMENTAL
Pan American Highway • Juarez • April through September

In the interior of Mexico at the great arenas, or *plazas de toros*, bull-fights are held from October through March. Along the border, however, the opposite holds. In Juarez, *corridas* are held during the heat of the year beginning in the spring and lasting all summer long at one of Mexico's largest arenas. Pay the extra dollar or two to be seated on the *sombra* (shady) side and leave the *sol* seats for those who can take the heat. Don't get suckered into buying a sunny or a shady seat for the late corrida. If you feel your negotiating skills (in Spanish, no less) are not sufficient, contact **Victor Garcia** at 915-525-5341. His services include transportation to and from the arena as well as securing tickets.

Fishing

There's plenty of fishing around El Paso. Unless you're traveling toward the Big Bend and can budget some time for catfish near Tornillo, your best bet is north to New Mexico. Remember that Texas and New Mexico require fishing licenses. More information about licensing is available from the Texas Parks & Wildlife Department at 915-598-4741 and the New Mexico Department of Game and Fish at 505-524-6090.

El Paso Area:

HIDE-A-WAY LAKES

40 miles south from El Paso off Hwy 20 near Tornillo • 915-764-2555
Private. Catfish. $5 a hook and $5 a vehicle.

PLAIN VIEW LAKES

40 miles south from El Paso off Hwy 20 near Tornillo • 915-764-2750
Private. More catfish but $6 a hook and $6 a vehicle.

New Mexico:

ELEPHANT BUTTE RESERVOIR

70 miles north of Las Cruces off of I-10 (90 miles from El Paso)

Public. Now we're fishing. Elephant Butte is the largest reservoir on the Rio Grande and popular for all water sports. Elephant Butte Reservoir and the adjacent State Park enjoy a national reputation for striped bass with some over 50 pounds. Other catches include white bass, smallmouth and largemouth bass, catfish, and crappie.

CABALLO LAKE

60 miles north of Las Cruces off of I-10

Public. Less than 10 miles south of the southern tip of Elephant Butte Reservoir, Caballo Lake is not as popular or as crowded as its upstream neighbor. Head either to the lake or below the dam at its south end for largemouth bass, white bass, crappie, and walleye.

Football

UTEP MINERS

Sun Bowl Stadium at UTEP • 915-747-5234
Admission • W+ but not all areas

Western Athletic Conference football is showcased each fall featuring teams like Air Force, Brigham Young, and those mighty Wyoming Cowboys. In addition, the Norwest Sun Bowl highlights El Paso's Sun Carnival. Tickets for Miner games start as low as $10 for adults and $7 for kids.

Golf

With its abundant sunshine and plentiful water, El Paso does not want for golf courses. Private ones, such as the Coronado Country Club (915-584-3841) or the El Paso Country Club (915-584-0511), require guests to be escorted by a member. Fort Bliss offers military personnel and retirees the Underwood Golf Course (915-562-1273) at moderate rates of $8 during the week and $10 on weekends. The following list includes public courses and the semi-private Horizon Golf and Tennis Club.

ASCARATE MUNICIPAL GOLF COURSE
Ascarate Park • 915-772-7381

Weekdays: $8 or $5 for seniors
Weekends: $10 or $5 for seniors after 12:30 p.m.

CIELO VISTA MUNICIPAL GOLF COURSE
1510 Hawkins • 915-591-4927

Weekdays: $10 • Weekends: $12

HORIZON GOLF AND TENNIS CLUB
Horizon City • 915-852-3150

Weekdays and weekends: $25

PAINTED DUNES DESERT GOLF COURSE
12000 McCombs Road • 915-821-2122

Weekdays: $10 or $7 after 4:30 p.m. Juniors and seniors: $7 during the week. Weekends: $12 or $8 after 4:30 p.m.

Hockey

EL PASO BUZZARDS
El Paso County Coliseum • October–March season • 915-534-7825

Maybe it's the desert sun that makes the Buzzards so popular. It could also be their two recent league championships in Western Professional Hockey League play.

Horse Racing

SUNLAND PARK RACETRACK & CASINO
Interstate 10 West, Sunland Park Exit west • 505-874-5200
Daily • Free parking and admission • W+

A trip to Sunland Park is an El Paso tradition, particularly given the natural affinity of Texans for horse flesh. It's only grown more popular with its state-of-the-art slots and video gaming. Located just across the New Mexico state line, the view of the Franklin Mountains over the infield lake is a memorable one—particularly if savored with a winning ticket at the Franklin Lounge.

Riley's restaurant in the Turf Club offers fine dining (full bar), and Poor Albert's Food Court offers fun and fast foods. Catch stakes races from December through May, including the Riley Allison Thoroughbred Futurity, and the Sun Country and West Texas Futurities in the spring. Or, if you time it right, show up that first Saturday in May for the Kentucky Derby with a live transmission (and wagering) from Churchill Downs. Regardless of the season, there's always simulcast racing seven days a week.

Tennis

El Paso's dry, sunny days keep courts packed year-round except in the summer months during the heat of the day. The real treat is serving them up at night when the cool evening makes playing a pleasure. Both the eastside YMCA at 2044 Trawood (915-591-3321) and the westside YMCA at 7145 N. Mesa (915-584-9622) have courts and welcome guests, as does the more centrally located YWCA at 1600 N. Brown (915-522-7475).

The City of El Paso offers an enormous number of courts at more than a dozen parks all across town. Call Parks and Recreation at 915-541-4331 for locations, conditions, and hours. In addition, lighted courts are open to the public at the following El Paso high schools from 5:30 to 7:30 p.m. during the school year, and from 10 a.m. to 7:30 p.m. during the summer: Austin, Coronado, Del Valle, El Paso High, Irvin, and Montwood.

El Paso's traditional tennis bastion, the El Paso Tennis Club (2510 N. Vrain • 915-532-4373), hosts clinics and tournaments year-round including the Eric Alwan Celebrity Invitational/Chicken-Fried Steak Cook-Off. Tennis West (1 Tennis West Lane • 915-581-5471) is a private facility that welcomes visitors from other IHRSA-affiliated clubs.

COLLEGES AND UNIVERSITIES

UNIVERSITY OF TEXAS EL PASO
915-747-5000 • W+ but not all areas

To any visitor, the most visible feature of UTEP is its unusual Bhutanese architecture, one of a kind nationwide and a tribute to El Paso architect Henry Trost. What strikes the eye but eludes the mind are the battered walls which slope outward by seven inches from top to bottom. Bhutanese design elements in many of the 76 buildings on campus include deep-set lower windows, ornamental friezes of brick and tile below the roof line, and the low-hipped roofs. Other notable structures on campus include the 52,000-seat Sun Bowl Stadium and the 12,222-seat Don Haskins Center (*see* **SPORTS AND ACTIVITIES**).

To any follower of higher education, the most notable aspect of the University of Texas El Paso is its commitment to Hispanic students and graduates. Six out of every 10 students are Hispanic, an estimated 50 percent are first-generation university students, and more Hispanic UTEP graduates go on to pursue doctoral degrees than from any other institution nationwide.

A growing strength at UTEP is its unique bilingual and binational programs, offered to over 17,000 students enrolled at this second-oldest component of the University of Texas system. Founded by the Texas Legislature (1913) as the State School of Mines and Metallurgy, the present 366-acre site and architectural theme were selected three years later after fire destroyed the original eastside location. The mineral-laden areas around El Paso—New Mexico, southern Arizona, northern Mexico, and far west Texas—were ideally suited for mining research. The School of Mines became the College of Mines (1919), Texas Western College (1949), and ultimately the University of Texas El Paso (1967).

PERFORMING ARTS

EL PASO CONVENTION & PERFORMING ARTS CENTER

1 Civic Center Plaza • Santa Fe at San Antonio • 915-534-6000

Located in the heart of downtown El Paso and within walking distance of major hotels, Mexico, and City Hall (considered a part of the complex). Facilities include the 2,500-seat Abraham Chavez Theatre, a Grand Hall flanked by large meeting rooms, and the 60,000-square-foot Exhibit/Convention Hall, site of several trade shows annually.

EL PASO COUNTY COLISEUM

4100 E. Paisano Drive (Paisano at Boone) • 915-534-4229

The coliseum hosts many El Paso events including concerts, ice capades, tractor pulls, the Southwestern Livestock Show and Rodeo (February) and the NARC Championship Rodeo (November).

EL PASO PRO-MUSICA

915-532-7653

Founded to present quality choral and instrumental chamber compositions, Pro-Musica presents musical selections ranging from Renaissance to contemporary during its October to March concert season, including Christmas concerts at historic Union Depot (see **HISTORIC PLACES**) and the International Chamber Music Festival each January (see **ANNUAL EVENTS**).

EL PASO SYMPHONY ORCHESTRA

Abraham Chavez Theatre • 915-532-3776
Tickets from $5–$23 (performance) or $45–$145 (season)

Each season, the El Paso Symphony Orchestra presents a varied series from September through April featuring eight paired concerts in addition to KinderKonzerts, a pops concert series, and six Young People's concerts.

MCKELLIGON CANYON COUNTY PARK & AMPHITHEATER

McKelligon Canyon Road • 915-532-0981 (Park)
915-565-6900 (Theater)

Set high in the east side of the Franklin Mountains, find this 90-acre park by taking Interstate 10 to Highway 54 (also called the Patriot Freeway). Head north toward Alamogordo and exit Fred Wilson Avenue. Take a left under the freeway and you'll be going toward the Franklin Mountain range. When you run into McKelligon Canyon Road, follow it to the 1,500-seat Amphitheater.

SPECIAL EVENTS CENTER

UTEP Campus • 915-747-5234 (Tickets)
915-747-5330 (Basketball) • Admission varies • W+

Used for basketball games, concerts, and other programs, the UTEP Special Events Center seats 12,222.

SUN BOWL STADIUM

UTEP Campus • 915-747-5234 (Tickets)
915-747-5330 (Football) • Admission varies • W+

The site of the Norwest Sun Bowl, Sun Bowl Stadium is home turf for UTEP, a member of the Western Athletic Conference.

SHOPPING

One of a Kind

EL PASO CHILE COMPANY

909 Texas Avenue • El Paso • 79901 • 915-544-3434
www.elpasochile.com • 800-274-7468
Monday–Friday 10–5 • Saturday 10–2

One very hip hot store. Think of the Kerr family's chile company as a border-style Williams-Sonoma. For over a decade, *paseños*, as well as aficionados from across the country and around the world, have stopped by (or phoned up or logged on to www.elpasochile.com) for chile products like peppers, powders, salsas, wreaths, and, of course, ristras (hanging bunches of chiles). Not surprisingly, El Paso Chile Company does a booming mail order business (call for a catalog).

Pick up an autographed copy of Park and Norma's bestselling *The El Paso Chile Company's Texas Border Cookbook* or the sequel, *Burning Desires*. Park's more recent books—*Beans*, *Tortillas*, and *Chiles*—are available, as is his latest masterpiece, *The El Paso Chile Company Margarita Cookbook*.

Gift boxes start at less than $20 and are packed with your choice of marinades, powders, salsas, spices, tortilla chips, and BBQ sauce. You can even enjoy chiles in a variety of spicy fettucinis, linguinis, and pestos. A good stop either before or after a visit to the Galeria San Ysidro just a block up Texas Ave.

EL PASO SADDLEBLANKET

601 N. Oregon (Exit 19 of I-10) • 915-544-1000
Monday–Friday 9–5 • Saturday 10–5 • Closed Sunday

Cash, checks, pesos—*no le hace*—it's just like Old Mexico. And well it should be. El Paso Saddleblanket is the largest distributor, wholesale or retail, of Mexican *artesanias* including ceramic, textile, and *talabarteria*. Follow the billboards across West Texas and southern New Mexico to plenty of parking and huge showrooms of baskets, clothes, glassware and tinware, jewelry, pots, rugs, serapes, skulls, and horns.

Dozens of different handcrafted Mexican saddles, saddlebags, saddleblankets, and saddle purses are piled from floor to ceiling, and no one is long without assistance from attentive staffers. Handcrafted Navajo and Zuni items are displayed next to handwoven oriental rugs, Guatemalan goods, and Pendleton woolens. Tens of thousands of pieces are stacked on shelves, displayed in cases, and piled on the floors of the 36,000-square-foot, two-story building.

An interesting final note: Only 20 percent of El Paso Saddleblanket's business is retail trade. Wholesale accounts range from mom-and-pop operations to major retailers in America and overseas. Call for more information on retailing opportunities.

GALERIA SAN YSIDRO

801 Texas Ave. • 915-544-4444 • Monday–Friday 9–5
Saturday 9-3 • AE MC V

If you've admired the furnishings at the Gage Hotel (Marathon), the Inn of the Anasazi (Santa Fe), or the Cibolo Creek Ranch (Shafter), then you already know the Galeria San Ysidro. Decorative furnishings range from cowboy to country to all styles of Mexican—provincial, Indian, even a little Colonial. Exquisite wrought iron from neo-Classic to Pueblo Deco is available and can be designed and made to order. While you're down on Texas Ave., take a stroll over to the El Paso Chile Company a block away.

J.B. HILL BOOT COMPANY

335 Clark Drive • 915-599-1551 • www.jbhillboots.com
Monday–Friday 8–5 • AE MC V

J.B. Hill boots are priced at the upper end of the spectrum and are sold through select high-end retailers like Neiman-Marcus, exclusive specialty retailers such as Billy Martin's, and, if none are available in your locale, directly through the J.B. Hill showroom in El Paso. The product line encompasses styles for men and women, including an array of boots made from traditional calf and water buffalo, as well as from exotics such as alligator, lizard, ostrich, shark, stingray, and others.

JUAREZ CITY MARKET

Avenida 16 de Septiembre • Daily from sunrise to sunset

This is a true *mercado* in the heart of Mexico's fourth largest city. The number of handmade and hand-crafted items is endless: aisle after aisle of household furnishings, decorative items, kitchen utensils, raw produce, Mexican cheeses, packaged foodstuffs, and other essentials and non-essentials unique to Mexico like *metates*.

Stop before, during, or after your visit for a drink at *Neveria Camacho* on the market's east side as Tony "The Whistler" pokes fun at tourists and locals. After you run the gauntlet and make it inside, most of the proprietors are patient, friendly, and easy to deal with. See the lady at the cheese counter for *mole poblano* and rich, flavorful Mennonite and *asadera* cheeses. Choose from scores of *chiles: Ancho, arbol, mirasol, mulato, pasilla, piquin* and *poblano* are a few.

Other great food items include dried shrimp for soups, *nopalitos* and *tunas* (cactus palms and fruits), *piñon* nuts, pumpkin seeds, raw sugar, raw tamarind, and bottled vanilla. If a vendor doesn't have what you need, he or she will either find it for you or convince you to buy something in stock. Much of Mexico's commerce has been traditionally transacted this way.

To the north of the market is another Juarez institution, **CASA MENDOZA**, which has been in business since the early 1940s. This is your opportunity to snap up household and kitchen items at a fraction of what you'd pay in the States, including blue-rimmed glasses in every size and shape imaginable, all sorts of galvanized products, and cheap *talavera*.

Also nearby is the **RIO GRANDE PHARMACY** where legions of American shoppers buy moderately priced, high-quality pharmaceuticals. All products are produced by the same parent companies—such as Eli Lilly and Pfizer—but are sold at substantial savings. The Rio Grande Pharmacy is a reputable business dating back to the 1950s, and the staff speaks English. Catch a cab, walk across, or take the trolley to Stop #8 and enjoy the sights and sounds of the market.

ROCKETBUSTERS

115 S. Anthony St. • 915-541-1300 • By appointment only

The next time you bump into Tom Cruise, ask him how he likes his Rocketbusters. Mr. Cruise was among Tinsel Town's first Rocketbuster fans; a short list of those partial to Marty Snortum's works of art (also known as cowboy boots) includes Billy Crystal, Steven Spielberg, Oprah Winfrey, and Eric Clapton. Rather than head to Paris, Munich, Tokyo, or New York for your pair, give a call and mosey over to the Rocketbuster factory a few blocks east of the Union Depot (*see* **HISTORIC PLACES**) on Anthony Street. More than likely, you'll have to ring the door bell to be admitted. Prices start in the hundreds, and if you get a hankering for the limited edition James Dean, Roy Rogers, Gene Autry, or Dale Evans styles, plan on dropping several thousand. Either way, Marty stands behind his staff's work—in a pair of Rocketbusters.

Factory Outlets

Unlike the rest of the United States, the idea of a factory store out in El Paso is not a picturesque shopping center filled with designer seconds. It's either the factory itself or a retail facility nearby. Lower labor costs, the Rio Grande River, and local cotton farms are reasons why this city dominates many manufacturing industries, in particular, western wear.

Bootmaker Tony Lama got his start in downtown El Paso after a stint at Fort Bliss. The business he started is one of several major boot-makers operating locally. El Paso is the world's denim capital with two million pairs of jeans trucked out each week sporting labels like Levi, Wrangler, Lee, Calvin Klein, Guess?, and Jordache. Though you won't find a Levi factory outlet, following are some of the better known, high-volume retailers, as well as the factory outlets that make shopping El Paso a bargain.

AZAR NUT FACTORY STORE

1800 Northwestern Drive • 915-877-4079 • I-25 west to Transmountain Exit, head east, take a right on Northwestern Monday–Friday 10–6 • Saturday 10–2 • All major cards

Almond, Brazil nut, cashew, filbert, pecan, pistachio, black walnut, white walnut: they're all at Azar's headquarters. A sampling of other items includes candied nuts, yogurt peanuts, clusters, gift baskets, cocoa, coffees, and teas.

FARAH FACTORY STORE

8889 Gateway West • 915-593-4481 Monday–Friday 10–7 • Saturday 10–6 • Sunday 11–5 • Cr

Right at the factory, the Farah line is best known for men's and boy's labels like John Henry, Savane, and Farah. The savings on casual wear and dress wear, including slacks and sport coats, run from 30 to 60 percent off suggested retail.

LUCCHESE BOOTS

6601 Montana Avenue • 915-778-8585 Monday–Saturday 9–6 • AE MC V

Handmade lasts, hand-stitched uppers, and an all-leather boot have earned Lucchese its reputation. Save up to 40 percent on boots pulled from shipment for minor defects.

SAHARA SPORTSWEAR

Colony Cove I Center • 7040-V N. Mesa • 915-833-8169
Monday–Saturday 10–6 • MC V

Shirts, shorts, sweaters, warm-ups, bags, and hats by Sahara are on sale, as well as Sahara's line of products for colleges and professional baseball.

TONY LAMA BOOTS

7156 Gateway East at the factory • 915-772-4327
12151 Gateway East (I-10 at Zaragosa Exit) • 915-858-0124
4900 Interstate 10 West at the Mesa Exit • 915-581-8192
Monday–Friday 9–7 • Saturday 9–6 • Sunday 12–6
Major credit cards

El Paso's own Tony Lama went from soldier to cobbler to master bootmaker during the course of a career that spanned the better part of this century. Same selection at all three stores.

Malls

BASSETT CENTER MALL

I-10 at Geronimo • 915-772-7479
Monday–Saturday 10–9 • Sunday 12–6

Anchored by Mervyn's, the Popular store, Ross, Service Merchandise, and Target, Bassett Center boasts 80 specialty stores and restaurants as well as a six-screen movie theater.

CIELO VISTA MALL

I-10 at Hawkins • 915-779-7070 • Monday–Saturday 10–9
Sunday 12–6

Anchored by Dillard's, J.C. Penney, Montgomery Ward, and Sears. General Cinema operates a 10-screen movie theater at Cielo Vista.

PLACITA SANTA FE

5024–5034 Doniphan Drive • Take the Mesa Exit from Interstate 10, head south, and take a right just before the railroad tracks on Doniphan. Right behind Furr's.

More than a dozen different boutiques, galleries, shops, and tiendas crowd the site of the old Paradise Motel. The story of the Paradise includes a clandestine meeting between Black Jack Pershing and Pancho Villa. Doniphan Drive used to be the primary route north and west out of El Paso, and the Paradise, built at the turn of the century, holds the distinction of being the first motel in town.

Long known for its vices, the reputation of the Paradise began to wane as hookers, gun runners, and bootleggers took over. Now revitalized and restored for shoppers, the Paradise has handmade clothing and accessories, handcrafted spurs and jewelry, fine art, teddy bears, and antiques, all at the top of a long list of items available.

SUNLAND PARK MALL

Interstate 10 at the Sunland Park Exit • 915-833-5595
Monday–Saturday 10–9 • Sunday 12–6

Anchored by Dillard's, J.C. Penney, and Mervyn's, Sunland Park Mall is one of El Paso's newest and was developed by the same company that brought the world the Mall of the Americas. The mall has a six-screen cinema.

SIDE TRIPS

CARLSBAD CAVERNS NATIONAL PARK, NEW MEXICO

Take Montana Avenue east out of El Paso. It soon becomes Highway 62–180. Follow the signs 42 miles past Guadalupe Mountains National Park and into New Mexico to the White's City intersection. Carlsbad Caverns is to your left about seven miles. Total drive time is less than four hours from El Paso's east side.

See separate listing under **CARLSBAD CAVERNS NATIONAL PARK.**

GUADALUPE MOUNTAINS NATIONAL PARK, TEXAS

Take Montana Avenue east out of El Paso. It becomes Highway 62-180. Take 62-180 straight to the Visitor Center at Guadalupe Mountains National Park. Drive time is approximately three hours.

See separate listing under **GUADALUPE MOUNTAINS NATIONAL PARK.**

HUECO TANKS STATE HISTORICAL PARK

Highway 62-180, 24 miles east of El Paso • 6900 Hueco Tanks Rd.
El Paso • 79936 • 915-857-1135 • Open daily 8–6
(October–March) and 7–7 (April–September) • Admission: $4
www.tpwd.state.tx.us/park/hueco/hueco.htm

Just east of El Paso, beneath the limestone and granite Hueco Mountains lies more history than most museums can catalog, let alone exhibit. No site in West Texas can match the legacy of the Hueco Tanks, which is dominated by three low rock masses. Made of syenite porphyry, a type of granite, they intruded into a softer layer of rock about 34 million years ago and gradually became exposed as the overlying rock eroded. Depressions, called *huecos* by the Spanish, then formed, trapping late summer rains. (There are no springs.)

This fresh water source—in the middle of the northern reaches of the Chihuahuan Desert—has drawn man and beast to the Hueco Tanks for thousands of years. The legacy of the huecos is preserved in thousands of images of man, animal, and mythical figures, called pictographs, painted on the rocks and in images called petroglyphs that are carved or chipped into the stone. The images represent three periods in Native

American culture: the Desert Archaic, the Jornada Branch of the Mogollon Culture, and the more recent Apache, Comanche, and Kiowa.

An example of this heritage is a group of pictographs that recounts an 1839 siege of a Kiowa war party by Mexican troops garrisoned at San Elizario. More than likely, the Mexican troops were guided by Tigua scouts. Thousands more pictographs exist including graffiti courtesy of Forty-Niners and other travellers who made use of the Butterfield Overland Trail station, whose ruins can be found just north of the tanks in the park.

With 20 multi-use campsites, a sewage dump station, showers, and restrooms, Hueco Tanks is a popular overnight and/or multi-day excursion. In addition to the limitless number of hours that can be spent exploring for Indian art, another popular draw is the area's outstanding birding, detailed in the State of Texas's *Birds of Hueco Tanks State Historical Park* checklist (available at the headquarters).

The park's greatest claim—other than the celebrated petroglyphs and pictographs—is its rock climbing, certainly supreme in Texas and arguably without compare in the United States during winter. When summertime sends surface temperatures well above 100 degrees, however, those hot rocks are anything but inviting (as are the cold-blooded reptiles who thrive once winter ends).

During the six-month stretch from mid-October to mid-April, however, while other climbing meccas like Yosemite and the Shawangunks are draped in winter's white, Hueco Tanks is at its best: sunny days and cool nights. Snow is not uncommon; four to five inches are recorded each winter. Bring a good sleeping bag and don't make trails without a copy of *Hueco Tanks—A Climber's and Boulderer's Guide* by John Sherman, *et al.* (Chockstone Press: 1991). Pricey for some at $25, it's meticulously researched and, even more importantly, written by climbers for climbers. A substantial percentage of the routes were pioneered by the authors.

INDIAN CLIFFS RANCH
I-10 East to Fabens Exit (mile marker 49) then north four miles
P.O. Box 1056 • Fabens • 79838 • 915-544-3200 or 915-764-2283

Practically self-contained, the Indian Cliffs Ranch boasts everything from hayrides to movie sets to mesquite-smoked barbecue at the Cattleman's Steakhouse. Groups of two to two thousand make tracks for Indian Cliffs which has extensive catering and party facilities, as well as on-site activities like a children's zoo, longhorn and buffalo, and the Fort Apache playground. Most El Pasoans have enjoyed a steak dinner at Cattleman's, whose reputation has earned mention in several national publications in addition to sweeping local honors for best steak. Plenty of bus and RV parking.

LINCOLN, NEW MEXICO

Highway 54 northeast from El Paso through Alamagordo to Tularosa Right (east) on Highway 70 past Ruidoso to Hondo • Left (west) on Highway 380 to Lincoln • Drive time is approximately three hours by car • 505-653-4025 (Lincoln County Heritage Trust)

Almost untouched by development, the town of Lincoln's only street is lined with century-old stores and adobe homes whose quiet ways belie Lincoln's violent past. The Lincoln County War pitted the rival cattle operations of James Dolan and L. G. Murphy versus those of John Chisum, Alexander McSween, and John Tunstall. The catalyst was the murder of Tunstall. A devoted admirer, Billy the Kid (whose real name was William Bonney), set out to avenge his death, and the war began. The culmination was a five-day shootout.

Much of Lincoln is operated by the State of New Mexico and the Lincoln County Heritage Trust, including the Lincoln County Courthouse, the San Juan Mission, the Tunstall Store Museum, Dr. Wood's House, and the Wortley Hotel.

OLD MESILLA AT LAS CRUCES, NEW MEXICO

Take I-10 west past Las Cruces and Exit Avenida de Mesilla south Drive time is approximately one hour by car • 800-343-7827 (Las Cruces info) • 800-545-2040 (NM info)

The signing of the Gadsden Purchase took place in Mesilla, which was bigger than Las Cruces and El Paso and was the largest city between San Antonio and San Diego. Mesilla flourished during the mid-1800s as a supply center for Fort Fillmore and as a changing station for the Overland Mail. Mesilla's wild side was apparent with events like Billy the Kid's first murder trial, his conviction, and his escape.

Fortunately for present-day visitors, Mesilla's charm and integrity were preserved when the Santa Fe Railroad chose Las Cruces for its route. Mesilla's day as Doña Ana County's first city had ended. The easy drive from El Paso proceeds north and then west along Interstate 10 and south at the Avenida de Mesilla exit. Drive over and stop at **La Posta (505-524-3524)**, one of only two Overland Mail Route changing stations in existence. It's located right off the Plaza and is open Tuesday through Sunday for lunch and dinner (try the green chile enchiladas).

Art galleries, gift shops, and other restaurants line the plaza whose soul is **San Albino Church**, originally constructed in 1855 and rebuilt in 1906. The well-known **Gadsden Museum (505-526-6293)** chronicles Mesilla's colorful past.

RUIDOSO, NEW MEXICO

Highway 54 northeast from El Paso through Alamagordo to Tularosa
Right (east) on Highway 70 to Ruidoso and Ruidoso Downs
Drive time is approximately 2½ hours • 800-253-2255

Long before Texans made Houston the air-conditioning capital of the world, they lowered the temperature by heading for high country getaways like Ruidoso, Taos, and Durango. The alpine meadows, pine trees, and light afternoon showers in the Sacramento Mountains make Ruidoso shine as the home of the world's richest horse race, the multimillion dollar All-American Futurity held Labor Day weekend (505-378-4431). The All-American culminates a meet packed with well-known stakes races, all highly competitive and many with enormous purses.

Next door to Ruidoso Downs, the **Museum of the Horse** (505-378-4142) houses a collection of 10,000 artifacts, bridles, harnesses, sculptures, and spurs to tell the history of horse and men.

By the time winter rolls around (and the horse races have gone south to Sunland Park), Ruidoso turns into one of America's southmost ski towns. Many stay here while schussing on nearby Ski Apache, the highest point on the 460,000-acre Mescalero Apache Indian Reservation.

A wonderful way to get to know this area is at the **Inn of the Mountain Gods** (800-545-9011). With its own golf course, tennis courts, and other amenities, this high-altitude getaway is a perfect reason to visit Ruidoso regardless of season. For those who haven't visited in a while, the treacherous municipal airport has been converted into a Jim Colbert golf course called the Links at Sierra Blanca.

WAR EAGLES AIR MUSEUM

Santa Teresa Airport • Santa Teresa, NM • 505-589-2000
Admission $5, seniors $4, under 12 free • Closed Mondays

Take exit 19 off Interstate 10 (Mesa Street) and go west several miles into New Mexico. Avoid the right fork onto FM 260 which stays in Texas. Follow the signs to the Santa Teresa Airport, and to your left stands the War Eagles hangar. Dozens of fascinating planes, most of them flyable, are on display. The showstopper is a P-38 Lockheed Lightning, one of only eight remaining worldwide of this fast, high-flying WWII interceptor. Other notable craft include the two fighter-bomber warhorses of the Korean Conflict—the Soviet Mig-15 and the American F-86—and a Stealth Fighter (no photos allowed). The gift shop specializes in model aircraft and has a selection of books, caps, patches, pins, and t-shirts. An informal air show featuring an assortment of planes is scheduled the first Saturday morning of the month from May through September.

WHITE SANDS NATIONAL MONUMENT, NEW MEXICO

Highway 54, 88 miles north and Highway 70, 14 miles west
Daily except Christmas • Summer 8–7 • Winter 8–4:30
$4 per vehicle • W+ • Gift shop • Concessions • 505-479-6124

For those familiar with Great Sand Dunes National Monument in Colorado's San Luis Valley, get ready for an entirely different experience. Located in the heart of the world's largest gypsum dune field, White Sands is huge—almost four times as large as its Colorado counterpart. Consequently, the dunes are not so crowded and only a tenth as tall, e.g., 50 to 60 feet high versus almost 700 in Colorado. White Sands is located in the northernmost portion of the Chihuahuan Desert as compared to Great Sand Dunes, which sits in a corner of the fertile San Luis Valley.

Finally and most vividly, White Sands dazzles, its dunes a finely ground gypsum rather than the wind-blown topsoil that accumulated to form Great Sand Dunes. Stop at the Visitor Center for an explanation of this area's geologic past and the unique biosystem that has evolved around it. If a short hike is in order, walk the one-mile self-guided Big Dune nature trail. If behind the wheel with the a/c full blast sounds more appealing in this desert setting, take her for a spin on the sixteen-mile Heart of Sands loop drive. Parking areas along this paved route allow for short walks, and pullouts for wayside exhibits explain the nature of the dunes and their origin as well as some of the animal and plant life that have adapted to this harsh environment.

If you're timing this visit closely, be sure to call in advance to find out whether missile testing at the adjacent White Sands Missile Range conflicts with your schedule. Occasional delays of up to two hours can close the Dunes drive. Note, however, that the Dunes drive has longer hours than the Visitor Center: 7 a.m. to 10 p.m. in the summer; 7 a.m. to sunset in the winter.

ANNUAL EVENTS

January

INTERNATIONAL CHAMBER MUSIC FESTIVAL

First Baptist Church • 805 Montana
Admission varies • 915-532-7653

While the rest of America looks to summer festivals for first-class chamber music, El Paso has established a series of concerts each January that brings some of the music world's brightest stars to the Sun City.

February

SOUTHWESTERN INTERNATIONAL LIVESTOCK SHOW & RODEO

El Paso County Coliseum • Admission • 915-532-1401

This ten-day extravaganza features one of America's top 15 PRCA rodeos (based on total payout). Cowboys and cowgirls from 34 states, Mexico, Canada, and Australia vie for over $150,000, with additional prize money for the final day's Bull Busters. The rodeo makes the Southwestern Livestock Show possible for thousands of exhibitors. Other activities include a horse show, a county fair and market, an exotic snake show, a children's barnyard, a western gala, and a chili cook-off.

March

SIGLO DE ORO FESTIVAL

Chamizal National Memorial • Free • 915-534-6277

Different troupes from throughout the Spanish-speaking world come to El Paso to compete in this international classical drama competition. Spanish operas and literature are featured.

June/July/August

¡VIVA EL PASO!

McKelligon Canyon Amphitheater • 915-565-6900
Tickets: $7–$14 for adults • $5–$10 for children

After you take your seat high on the east side of the Franklin Mountains, a cast of 50 professional singers, actors, and dancers brings to life El Paso's multi-cultural heritage. This summerlong show of dance, song, and history is in one of the most popular outdoor dramas in the country. Dinner by Doc's Bar-B-Que is served from 6:30 until 8 p.m. Snacks and drinks are also available. Bring a sweater for the cool summer nights.

September

JUAN DE OÑATE FIRST THANKSGIVING FESTIVAL

McKelligon Canyon • Free

Each year on the last Sunday in April, El Pasoans gather to commemorate the First Thanksgiving, a celebration of the expedition of Don Juan de Oñate. In 1595, Oñate was granted the right to conquer New Mexico by the King of Spain. Three years later, he led over 100 men, their families, servants, and herds north from Chihuahua into the great desert. This colonizing effort, the first in America, occurred before many Mayflower passengers were born. Oñate's pioneering route went due north from Chihuahua to El Paso rather than following the Rio Conchos to its confluence with the Rio Grande and then northwest. The four-mile-long train took four blistering months to reach the Rio Grande and the future site of El Paso (April 20, 1598). After ten days of rest, the expedition celebrated with America's first play, America's first Thanksgiving, and a proclamation (*La Toma*) claiming the land for the King of Spain.

October

BORDER FOLK FESTIVAL
Chamizal National Memorial • 915-532-7273 • Free

A celebration of El Paso's multicultural heritage staged on the lush lands of Chamizal National Memorial, Border Folk Festival features music, dance, poetry, storytelling, and workshops. Many tasty foods and other concessions are available.

October

AMIGO AIRSHO
Biggs Army Airfield at Fort Bliss • 915-532-5387
Admission: Adults $10 • Children $8 • W but not all areas

Be sure to bring your camera or video equipment because the list of demonstrators is as good as any nationwide. Expect the Navy's Blue Angels and the Army's Golden Knights to be joined by professional aviators performing heart-stopping stunts. Walk the show grounds and view military and civilian aircraft, vintage autos, and classic Harleys. Many non-aviation activities are scheduled around the busy two-day show, including a kick-off concert and bowling, golf, racquetball, softball, and volleyball tournaments. Contact the Amigo Airsho for dates, prices, and information on reasonably priced hotel and air packages.

EL PASO JUAREZ INTERNATIONAL CLASSIC
Downtown El Paso/Juarez • 915-544-9400

This 15-kilometer (9.3-mile) run winds its way back and forth across the border twice en route to proclaiming a champion.

KERMEZAAR
El Paso Convention Center • 915-593-8337 or 915-534-0609

The largest arts and crafts show in the Southwest features hand-crafted goods including textiles, paintings, and ceramics.

November

WORLD FINALS RODEO
El Paso County Coliseum • 915-545-1188

Nine days of rodeo and a tenth day that's all bull riding bring 600 cowboys and cowgirls in from across the country and around the world. All are members of the 12,000-strong North American Rodeo Commission and are competing for a $25,000 added purse.

November & December

SUN CARNIVAL SPORTS FESTIVAL & PARADE
Citywide • 800-915-BOWL • Admission varies • W

For starters, Savane sponsors the All-American Golf Classic featuring outstanding collegiate golfers from the U.S. and Japan. In late November, over 300,000 spectators line Montana Street from Campbell to Copia for the Thanksgiving Day parade. Two classics wrap up the citywide celebration: the Sierra Providence Sun Classic Basketball Tournament and the nationally televised Norwest Sun Bowl.

RESTAURANTS

($ = Under $7.50, $$ = Under $15, $$$ = $15+ plus tax & tip)

The self-proclaimed Mexican food capital of the world seems destined to hold onto its crown as the popularity of this cuisine expands along with El Paso and Juarez themselves. Other traditional assumptions about dining in El Paso and Juarez no longer apply. Several well-known establishments not listed below are on-going concerns, but have let standards fall to the extent that they can be considered health risks.

American

SAN FRANCISCO GRILL
Downtown at San Francisco, El Paso, and Mills • 915-545-1386
Daily • Lunch and dinner • $–$$ • Cr • W+ but not all areas

Owned by the proprietors of the **Mesa Street Bar & Grill** in Kern Place, the SFG is as clubby as El Paso gets. High marks for the hearty sandwiches and the excellent pastas. If you're considering the San Francisco Club, go for the soup and sandwich combo (the club is monstrous). Best dessert? Go for the *crème brûlée* (the key lime runs a close second). The full bar stocks Anchor Steam.

JAXON'S RESTAURANT AND BREWING COMPANY

1135 Airway • 915-778-9696 • 4799 N. Mesa • 915-544-1188
Daily • Lunch and dinner • $–$$ • Cr • W+ but not all areas

An El Paso power lunch starts with tortilla soup or an order of *que-sadillas*. Don't pass up the blue corn tostadas, the fajitas, or the unbeatable burger. If you have room left share a mud pie or, better yet, order a single slice for the table. It's that big. At dinner, hand-cut steaks are their forte. Bar.

Barbecue

EL PASO CITY LIMITS

8838 Viscount • 915-598-7722 • Monday–Saturday
Lunch and dinner • Closed Sunday • $–$$ • AE D MC V • W

City Limits is known for its dollar rib night and specializes in mesquite-smoked barbecue, steaks, and catfish. City Limits (located near the airport) has a sports bar. Their sister restaurant on the west side is the **Rib Hut** at 2612 N. Mesa at UTEP (915-532-RIBS). Order the baby back ribs and ask for extra sauce for ribs and fingers. Bar.

STATE LINE

1222 Sunland Park Drive • 915-581-3371
Daily except Saturday lunch • Lunch and dinner • $–$$$ • Cr • W+

A popular stop for families with its large patio courtyard, booths and tables indoors, and lively decor straight from *Back to the Future.* It only gets more crowded right after a day at the track. Favorites include El Paso's biggest (and arguably best) beef ribs, the well-marinated brisket, an all-you-can-eat country-style platter, and the burgers. Don't order the popular cobbler with ice cream till you see how much of an appetite you have left.

TEXAS BAR-B-Q CO.

1316 Texas Ave. • 915-546-9051 • Monday–Friday • Breakfast and lunch • $ • Major credit cards for catering orders only • W

For most barbecue fans, the picture of John Wayne says it all. These folks have their priorities, and mesquite-smoked brisket is tops on their list. The breakfast menu boasts nearly a dozen different burritos as well as two servings that'll carry you till Santa Fe: the Mexican plate and the Country Plate. Consider trying your favorite portion served as a burrito rather than ordering a sandwich. Texas Bar-B-Q Co. caters, custom smokes, and serves to-go brisket, chicken, hash, hot links, or pork any way you want—by the pound, as a plate, or in a sandwich.

Bistro

CAFE CENTRAL

1 Texas Court across from the Camino Real • 915-545-2233
Monday–Saturday • Lunch and dinner • $$–$$$ • Cr • W

This is the best restaurant in the book. Changes in season and inspiration prevent any set menu from being printed but pray that *frutas del mar* is being served when you are seated: green lip mussels, calamari, scallops, and shrimp reduced with garlic, white wine, butter, and fresh herbs. The only thing closer to perfection is Art Lewis on the saxophone Friday nights. Anything served with the *chinois* sauce (made up of soy sauce, cilantro, ginger, and garlic) is superb. The entire menu lists favorites like the superb Caesar salad and the *tacos tres colores* (made up of lobster, chicken, and beef). Bar.

Chinese

UNCLE BAO'S

5668 N. Mesa • 915-585-1818
9515 Gateway West • 915-592-1101
Daily • Lunch and dinner • $–$$$ • Cr • W+

Several years ago, the folks at *Texas Monthly* ranked Uncle Bao's as good if not better than anyplace in San Francisco's Chinatown. Since then, Uncle Bao's has opened up a second location on the westside and only increased in popularity. If you pass on the Citrus Beef, know that Uncle Bao offers tremendous portions and consistent, Americanized Chinese cuisine. Weekend buffet from 11:30 a.m. to 4:00 p.m. Bar.

Continental

MARTINO

417 Avenida Juarez • 011 52 16 12 33 70
Daily • Lunch and dinner • $–$$ • Checks

Martino's is the sole surviving bistro on Juarez's once-great strip. With several hundred choices, it's simplest to ask for Oscar as your waiter and enjoy his selections as well as his mean Stoli martini, shaken right at the table. Pass on the salad and the soup course (dramatic but weak) and save room for your entrée—the quail or the *carne asada a la tampequieaña*. A basket of shoestring fries is mandatory. Yes, they are cooked in beef fat. Bar.

Italian

ARDOVINO'S

206 Cincinnati Ave. • 915-532-9483
865 N. Resler (at Red Road) • 915-760-6000
Monday–Thursday 11–9 • Friday–Saturday 10–10 • $–$$ • AE MC V

You can tell someone is from El Paso if they have a favorite pizza at Ardovino's. Since 1961, the Chicago-style pie at the Kern Place restaurant has been the city's best. Proof of that came recently when Ardovino's was heralded as one of the top 100 independent pizzerias nationwide. Now there's a second location across from Franklin High School.

BELLA NAPOLI

6331 N. Mesa • 915-584-3321 • Tuesday–Saturday Dinner
Sunday lunch and dinner • Closed Monday • $–$$
AE MC V • W but not all areas

El Paso comes to Bella Napoli for veal entrées like *ossobucco, picata,* and the specials. Try the eggplant parmigan—*magnifico.* Live opera on Thursday nights. Beer and wine.

CAPPETTO'S

2716 Montana Ave. off Piedras • 915-566-9357 • $–$$ • Cr • W

Great meals get off to good beginnings at Cappetto's because of its excellent Italian salad. Loaded with olives, pepperoni, salami, and scallions, it's the perfect complement to the piping hot bread. An outstanding heavy red sauce enhances the many pasta dishes. Bar.

Border Regional

Mexican Food

There are all kinds of restaurants in El Paso, but only one great cuisine. This is it. The neighborhood, the building, the decor, they don't matter. The *salsa* tells you more about the operation than any guidebook can. Is it prepared on-site, is it fresh, does it have character? Salsa also tells the style of cuisine. Have a seat at Griggs and sample the traditional red salsa; it's typical of the New Mexican recipes that the Griggs family has passed down for over a century. Their servings favor milder palates and feature less firey peppers. Just like their salsa.

Restaurants listed in Juarez often go to extremes to ensure a pleasant dining experience by using filtered water. As with all cases in Mexico, stick to Mexican food and save the flambé for the country club. Seafood is a judgment call. There are usually enough enticing alternatives that the choice doesn't come up. El Paso-based chains like Avila's and Leo's are included, recommended, and offer good food and good value.

AVILA'S

East side—10600 Montana • 915-598-3333
West side—6232 N. Mesa • 915-584-3621
Daily • Lunch and dinner • $ • Cr • W

The *salsa*—a green one—is hot, rich, and thick. Always follow the chips and salsa with an order of *chile con queso.* It goes well with all of Avila's time-tested entrées: rolled meat tacos and any enchilada plate. Be sure to save room for an order of El Paso's best *sopapillas.*

CASA JURADO

4772 Doniphan • 915-833-1151 • Bar • Closed Monday
226 Cincinnati • 915-532-6429 • Beer & wine • Closed Sunday
Lunch and dinner • $–$$ • Cr

The spicy bite of the tortilla soup is tempered by cool avocado slices. The distinctive orange *salsa* is full of chiles, tomato, and oregano. Entrée recommendations include *chili verde con carne* and the *flautas,* beef or chicken.

DELICIOUS MEXICAN EATERY

3314 Fort Blvd. • 915-566-1396
1335 Montwood • 915-857-1396
6415 N. Mesa • 915-845-7474
Daily • Breakfast, lunch, and dinner • $ • Checks • W

Continual efforts throughout West Texas and New Mexico have yet to uncover a better *gordita* than at Delicious. Literally "little fat one," these deep-fried corn patties are hollowed out, stuffed with every imaginable filling, and quickly gobbled up. The *chile rellenos* make you wonder what you've been eating all these years. In order to serve up the freshest possible relleno, the Borrego family buys chiles in season from New Mexico, California, and Mexico. If you've never had a *relleno burrito,* this is your chance.

FORTI'S MEXICAN ELDER

321 Chelsea • 915-772-0066 • Daily
Lunch and dinner • $–$$ • Cr

The best of the big boys. No one in El Paso has run a restaurant as well as Consuelo Forti has for the past twenty years, and one of the reasons is that no one has run her kitchen except chef Robert Loya. Try the chicken *salpicón.* Served cold, this shredded chicken salad is prepared with a lime and cilantro vinaigrette. For a bite of everything, skip breakfast and order the Combination Plate #3—an enchilada, a taco, a tamale, a chile relleno, chile verde or rojo, guacamole, beans and rice. Beautiful presentation, better food. Don't pass up the *flan* (dessert custard) or the Mexican lemonade (regular or strawberry margaritas).

GRIGGS NEW MEXICAN FOOD

5800 Doniphan • 915-584-0451
9007 Montana • 915-598-3451
701 S. Mesa Hills • 915-584-0451
Daily • Lunch and dinner • $–$$ • D MC V • W

Known for its New Mexican style cooking—milder and less force-ful—the flavorful, red salsa has little bite and makes a wonderful intro-duction to Mexican food for first timers apprehensive about steam com-ing out their ears. For a safe entrée, order a plate of green enchiladas.

GUSSIE'S TAMALES AND MEXICAN BAKERY

2200 N. Piedras • 915-566-8209
Daily 8 a.m. until 8 p.m. • $ • Checks

Don't be deceived: this is not your typical *panaderia* (bakery). In addi-tion to *biscochos*, corn cookies, *pan de huevo*, *polvorones*, and *timbales*, east-side El Pasoans know Gussie for her heavenly *tamales*. They're full of her wonderful spirit, and Gussie tolerates no shortcuts like *maseca*, or animal fat. If you need the cure, enjoy the excellent *menudo*. Take-away only.

H&H CAR WASH

701 E. Yandell at Ochoa • 915-533-1144
Daily except Sunday • Breakfast and lunch • $
Car wash: Monday–Friday 9–5 • Saturday 9–3

Mandatory rations on any visit to the Pass. A true cross-section of locals can be found at H&H. Witness the parade of Mercedes, Lexus, Isuzu Troopers, and Buicks. The H&H concept—a combination 1950s car wash, gas station, and diner—embodies the American dream. Mak-ing it come true are Antonia in the kitchen and Artemisa at the counter. The two of them together are your ticket to the *carne picada*, the best breakfast in this book—chopped sirloin tips, onions, tomato, and chiles, stir-fried and served with a side of salsa prepared fresh at H&H. The milder green salsa is a jalepeño blend, and the higher octane red is made with *chile de arbol*. For the *carne picadillo*, the sirloin is replaced with ground beef. By the time you finish eating, your car is washed, starched, and ironed for $10. Trucks are $12–15.

JULIO'S CAFE CORONA

Avenida 16 de Septiembre • (0115216) 13 33 97 or 13 08 33
Daily • Lunch and dinner • $–$$ • MC V

Pass on the El Paso location and head straight to Juarez for a bowl of *Tlalpeño* soup, a hearty chicken broth made with much too much chick-en, cilantro, lime, and a hint of *chipotle* (dried, smoked red jalepeño). You should try the *salpicón*—cold, shredded beef salad in a chipotle, lime, cilantro vinaigrette and tossed with red onions, tomato, cheese

and avocado. Or try the *machaca* with egg—shredded, dried beef prepared with scrambled egg and a red chile sauce. Dessert is easy: *cajeta
crepes*—three rolled crepes, smothered in *cajeta* (a Mexican caramel
sauce), and topped with toasted pecans.

KIKI'S

2719 N. Piedras • 915-565-6713
Daily 10:30–10 • $–$$ • MC V • W call ahead

Rated as one of the top 50 Hispanic restaurants in the country, Kiki's
is famous for its crab plates like enchiladas, machaca, and tacos. Other
good choices include the beef and chicken machaca as well as the green
chicken enchiladas. Beer and wine.

L&J CAFE

3622 Missouri by the Concordia Cemetery • 915-566-8418
Exit Copia off I-10, go north to Missouri, and take a right
Restaurant: Mon.–Fri. 11–8 • Saturday 11–6 • Closed Sunday
Bar: Mon. Tue. Thu. 10 a.m.–12 p.m. • Wed. Fri. Sat. 10 a.m.–2 a.m
Sun 12–12 • $ • Cr

With great food, good prices, and a long bar, the L&J boasts a crew
of regulars who make the cast of *Cheers* look like new kids on the block.
Founded in the 1920s by Tony Flores (grandfather of Leo, the present
owner), it first opened for business with a hitching post out front,
endured Prohibition, and survived countless raids by the Texas Rangers.
The wonderful red sauce on the stacked enchiladas blends red chile,
chile de arbol, and *pasilla* to perfection. They taste even better at the bar.
Diehards order them *montado*—topped with an egg sunny-side-up. Try
the *caldillo* or the *chile verde* the second time around. Beer and wine.

LA HACIENDA CAFE

1720 W. Paisano • 915-533-1919
Daily • Lunch and dinner • $–$$$ • Cr • W

Recent changes at La Hacienda include an expanded patio area fea-
turing mesquite-grilled entrees. Old favorites and authentic Mexican
food are prepared indoors at La Hacienda. If the food wasn't so consis-
tently good, the restaurant would be a museum.

El Camino Real crossed the Rio Bravo near La Hacienda, which was
built in 1849 or 1850. Known as Hart's Mill, or *el Molino*, it served one
of El Paso's earliest settlements and was adjacent to Fort Bliss later in
the nineteenth century. Unfortunately, finding La Hacienda can be a
substantial undertaking. Call for directions (or stay at the nearby Sunset
Heights Bed & Breakfast). Full bar at Rosa's Cantina, home of the one-,
two-, and three-bell margarita.

LEO'S

7872 N. Loop • 915-593-9025
5315 Hondo Pass Ave. • 915-757-9025
5103 Montana Ave. • 915-566-4972
2285 Trawood Dr • 915-591-2511
8001 N. Mesa • 915-833-1189
Daily • Lunch and dinner • Each location
closes on a different day • $ • AE MC V

If the food at El Paso's best-known Mexican restaurants reminds you of Avila's, it's because they're family. The salsa is similar, too, but with more cilantro. Excellent burritos and *chile con carne.*

RUBIO'S RESTAURANT

5734 Alameda near Paisano • 915-771-8545
Tuesday–Friday 11–6 • Weekends 7–4 • Closed Monday
$ • MC V • W

Don't be surprised if the whole Rubio family is at work cooking, waiting tables, or working the cash register. Start off with El Paso/Juarez's best *chile con queso.* Made with white cheese, flame-roasted chiles, chicken broth, tomato, and onion, all the Velveeta in the world won't prepare you for this one. Though the *flautas* are legendary, their specialty is beef *fajitas,* and their secret is a different cut of meat. Add a side of *frijoles rancheros,* and all you'll need is a slice of coconut cream pie to end the perfect meal. Beer and wine.

Steaks

CATTLEMAN'S STEAKHOUSE

At Indian Cliff Ranch (*see* SIDE TRIPS *above*) • 915-544-3200
Monday–Friday 4:30–10 • Saturday 4–10 • Sunday 12–9
$–$$$ • AE DC MC V • W+

Listed as serving the Best Steak in America by *People* magazine and a perennial choice for the best steak in El Paso, Cattleman's is El Paso's best-known steakhouse. The monstrous portions and two-pound T-Bone can satisfy the biggest appetites, and there is more to do before, during, and after dinner at the Indian Cliff Ranch than at most amusement parks. Fort Apache, a grist mill, a children's zoo, hayrides, an Indian maze, and movie sets are all within walking distance.

CLUBS AND BARS

CHIHUAHUA CHARLIE'S

P.T. de la Republica • (0115216) 3 17 80 or 3 99 40
Daily • Lunch and dinner • AE MC V

Their slogan is "We don't speak English but we promise not to laugh at your Spanish." Live music, massive 16-ounce margaritas, and the lively binational crowd make Chihuahua Charlie's a noisy favorite. Easily reached by crossing the Cordova Bridge of the Americas, Chihuahua Charlie's is Stop #5 on the El Paso/Juarez Trolley Tour (*see* **DRIVING TOUR**). Bar.

COMIC STRIP

6633 N. Mesa • 915-581-8877 (Hotline)
Tuesday–Saturday after 6:30 p.m.

If you're tired of spending six or seven dollars on first-run movies, drop three bucks some weeknight and head to the Comic Strip. You'll get more than your money's worth, and that's not including Tuesday night's two-for-one specials. Friday and Saturday nights cost more but that's when top national touring comedians make it to town. One show nightly at 8:00 p.m. Tuesday through Thursday; Friday and Saturday shows start at 8:30 and 10:45. Open seating. Alcoholic and non-alcoholic beverages. Must be 17 or older if not accompanied by an adult. Bar.

KENTUCKY CLUB

629 Avenida Juarez • Juarez • (0115216) 2 06 47

The legend. Enjoy this last vestige of a bygone era in Juarez's history at the Kentucky Club's enormous hand-carved bar, staffed by barmen in black tie whose tenure at the Kentucky Club routinely exceeds the age of their patrons. Worth a trip in themselves are the Ramos gin fizz and the margarita, shaken over ice and served neat.

ACCOMMODATIONS

($ = Under $40, $$ = $40–$75, $$$ = $75–$100, $$$$ = Over $100)
Room Tax 14%

With over six thousand hotel rooms available in the El Paso/Juarez area, every budget and style can be matched. This list is broken down by area and should not be viewed as all-inclusive.

East Side

AMERISUITES HOTEL

8250 Gateway East • 915-591-9600 or 800-255-1755 • $$

This two-story hotel located on the south side of Interstate 10 has 126 units, each with kitchen, bedroom, and bath, all with cable TV, pay-per-view movies, and room phones (charge for local calls). Amenities include pool and spa, free airport shuttle, and complimentary breakfast.

LA QUINTA LOMALAND

11033 Gateway West • 915-591-2244 or 800-531-5900 • $$

This two-story motor inn has 138 units including non-smoking rooms with cable TV (Showtime), pay-per-view movies, and free local calls. Denny's and Guenther's Edelweiss are right next door. Amenities include outdoor heated pool, complimentary continental breakfast and free coffee in the lobby, and free parking. Small pets OK. Discount rates for AAA and Sam's Wholesale Club available.

Airport/Mid-City

EL PASO AIRPORT HILTON

2027 Airway Blvd. • 915-778-4241 or 800-742-7248 • $$$–$$$$

With spade at the ready, Conrad Hilton led the ground-breaking ceremonies at the four-story Hilton right as you leave El Paso International (200 yards away). With 121 units and 151 suites, there is also an Executive Level ($$$$). All rooms feature cable TV (Showtime), pay-per-view movies, and room phones (charge for local calls). Amenities include Magnim's restaurant, lounge, and piano bar, heated outdoor pool, jacuzzi, health club with sauna, courtesy airport shuttle around the clock, and free parking. Small pets OK.

EL PASO MARRIOTT

1600 Airway Blvd. • 915-779-3300 or 800-228-9290 • $$$$

This six-story Marriott has 296 units including two-bedroom suites and non-smoking rooms with cable TV (HBO) and pay-per-view movies, and room phones (charge for local calls). Amenities include two restaurants—Chatfield's and La Cascada—and McGinty's lounge, indoor/outdoor pool, health club with sauna, gift shop, courtesy shuttle to airport, free parking, and an American Airlines ticket office. Pets on the first floor only.

EMBASSY SUITES

6100 Gateway East • 915-779-6222 or 800-EMBASSY • $$$$

This eight-story hotel located right by I-10 has 185 suites with satellite TV, pay-per-view movies, a microwave or stove and oven, coffee maker, and refrigerator. Amenities include Chloee's restaurant and lounge; an indoor pool; a health club with jacuzzi, sauna, and steam room; a gift shop; a courtesy shuttle to airport, complimentary cooked-to-order breakfasts; a manager's reception each afternoon featuring open bar and complimentary hors d'oeuvres; and free parking. Pets allowed for $50 non-refundable fee (ouch!).

LA QUINTA AIRPORT
6140 Gateway East • 915-778-9321 or 800-531-5900 • $$

This two-story motor inn has 121 units including suites and non-smoking rooms with cable TV (Showtime) and room phones (no charge for local calls). Amenities include two adjacent 24-hour restaurants, Denny's and the Kettle, heated outdoor pool, courtesy shuttle to airport, complimentary coffee and complimentary continental breakfast. Small pets OK. Discount rates for AAA, Allstate, and Sam's Wholesale Club members.

RADISSON SUITE INN
1770 Airway Blvd. • 915-772-3333 or 800-333-3333 • $$$

Each of the 150 rooms at this three-story hotel is a suite. Located right by the El Paso International Airport, smoking and non-smoking suites are available. All rooms include cable TV, a VCR, access to a complimentary video library, and no charge for local calls. Amenities include a complimentary cooked-to-order breakfast or continental breakfast, complimentary cocktails during the week, the Cafe at the Radisson restaurant and lounge, heated outdoor pool, health club with sauna, exercise room, game room, gift shop, same-day valet laundry, laundry room, courtesy shuttle to and from the airport, and free parking. No pets allowed. AAA, government, and limited AARP discounts available.

Downtown/Medical Center

CLIFF INN
1600 Cliff Drive • 915-533-6700 or 800-333-2543 • $$$

Antiques fill the lobby of this gracious establishment located within walking distance of Sierra Medical Center and other hospital facilities. The elegant single-story hotel emphasizes convenience while enabling guests to look after medical needs. Guests are offered complimentary transportation to and from doctor's appointments, as well as airport shuttles. The Cliff Inn has 78 guest rooms, kitchenettes, and suites including non-smoking rooms with cable TV (HBO) and room phones (charge for local calls). Amenities include the Three Continents Restaurant and Lounge, pool with jacuzzi, lap pool and tennis nearby, complimentary breakfast, complimentary hors d'oeuvres, and free parking. No pets.

CAMINO REAL PASO DEL NORTE
101 S. El Paso St. • 915-534-3000 • $$$$

What the Waldorf is to New York and the Adolphus is to Dallas, the Paso del Norte is to El Paso. Located right across from the Convention Center, this is not only El Paso's largest hotel, with 375 rooms and 32 suites, but it's a landmark in its own right. Designed by Henry Trost, the Paso del Norte opened with a lavish gala on Thanksgiving Day 1912 and is still the first name in El Paso accommodations.

Built of brick, steel, and terra cotta, the interior was done in fireproof gypsum from nearby White Sands, and the lobby, mezzanine, and dining rooms were finished with cherrystone, golden scagliola, and black serpentine marble and solid mahogany.

Non-smoking and handicap rooms are available, and all rooms have cable TV, pay-per-view movies, and room phones (charge for local calls). On property are the Dome Grill, Cafe Rio for more casual dining, and Uptown's club. Complementing any dining experience is a round of drinks at the historic Tiffany Dome Bar (perhaps the best bar in Texas). The dome is encased in its own temperature-controlled room and insured for over $1 million. Amenities include an outdoor heated pool and health club, gift shop, courtesy shuttle to El Paso International Airport, secured parking (fee), and a Delta ticket counter on the premises.

West Side

HOLIDAY INN SUNLAND PARK
900 Sunland Park Drive • 915-833-2900 or 800-446-4656 • $$

This two-story property located right off Interstate 10 at the Sunland Park exit has 166 units including non-smoking rooms, cable TV (HBO), pay-per-view movies, and room phones with free local calls. Amenities include the Sierra Grill restaurant and coffee shop, the Tack Room lounge, an outdoor pool, free airport shuttle, golf and tennis affiliations, and free parking. Small pets OK. AAA and AARP rates available.

Bed & Breakfasts

SUNSET HEIGHTS BED & BREAKFAST INN
717 W. Yandell • 915-544-1743 • Cr. • $$–$$$$

You'd think from what Dr. Roni Martinez offers that you were ensconced in a resort hotel. Try a renovated 1905 brick Victorian National Historic home full of Victorian furnishings, solid brass fixtures, and surrounded by wrought iron fencing. As far as convenience goes, this one can't be beat. El Paso's hardest-to-find Mexican restaurant, **La Hacienda**, is just down the street, and after a night in Juarez you can walk across the Santa Fe Bridge, get in your car, and arrive in two minutes without taking a single turn (a helpful plus after a night on the strip).

There are five rooms (including a suite with king size bed), each with private baths including immense claw-foot tubs. A home-cooked Mexican breakfast is served in the dining room. Dinners are available by reservation with a six-person minimum. Take the Porfirio Diaz exit from Interstate 10, and a right on Yandell to Randolph. Check in by appointment. Check out by noon. Outdoor unheated pool. No smoking. No pets.

YOUTH HOSTEL

GARDNER HOTEL—EL PASO INTERNATIONAL YOUTH HOSTEL

Member AYH • 311 E. Franklin • 915-532-3661 • $
One night's rent + tax required for any reservation
Cash, check, money order, or MC V accepted for deposit
No charge for cancellation up to 72 hours in advance
www.gardnerhotel.com

You'll be right in the middle of downtown El Paso when you stay at the Gardner. It's convenient to Union Depot with eastbound and west-bound service three times weekly and to the Greyhound bus terminal with daily arrivals and departures. If you're flying into El Paso, either take a cab downtown (about $15) or hop on the #33 bus to San Jacinto Park. The Gardner is a block north to Franklin Avenue and less than two blocks east.

Although the Gardner is the oldest continually operated hotel in town (1922), it's not a dump. The recent lobby renovation reeks of oiled wood, polished marble, tanned leather, and gilded antiques. The Gardner has 50 rooms, eight of which are dedicated to the hostel ($17.50 per person per night plus linens), along with a kitchen, dining area, common area, and laundry.

The scoop on the hostel is that it's better than average. Points are added for the common area, the laundry, overall convenience, and round-the-clock access to the property as well as to the bunk rooms. Points are deducted for the smaller than average bathrooms, the cramped kitchen, and the nagging list of AYH rules and regulations.

Right next door is one of the city's better-known burger stands, the **Big Bun**. Nothing on the menu tops two bucks. From El Paso to the Big Bend, forget about hitching a ride. You'll only get sunburnt and disappointed. Either take Amtrak from nearby Union Depot (three times a week) or catch a Greyhound bus from the downtown terminal located across from the Civic Center (daily). Cars can be rented in Alpine upon arrival. Commissary.

FORT DAVIS

JEFF DAVIS COUNTY SEAT • 1,200 • (915)

For over four centuries, visitors to the Davis Mountains have marveled at this mountain island in the Chihuahuan Desert. Black bear and cool mountain breezes are found in stands of pine and oak that surround the tallest town in Texas. Winter snows are welcome; it's still ranching country here. But tourism is clearly becoming the top industry in town as the popularity of the old fort, Davis Mountains State Park, the University of Texas McDonald Observatory, and nearby Big Bend National Park increases year after year.

Spanish explorer Antonio de Bermejo journeyed through Limpia Canyon less than a hundred years after Columbus discovered America (1583). His countrymen, however, preferred to settle closer to *el Camino Real* which led from Mexico City to El Paso and then north to Santa Fe. (Something about Apaches and Comanches.) Too far removed to be of much interest to Mexico or the Republic of Texas, it was only when Fort Davis was garrisoned that Anglo-Americans began to settle the Apache Mountains (as they were then called).

Those who recall Jeff Davis remember him as President of the Confederacy. During the Pierce Administration, he was Secretary of War and ordered the fort to be established (1854). It was also as a result of his efforts (the Civil War) that the fort was abandoned. His name now graces the fort, the town, and the county. During the War Between the States, neither blue nor grey triumphed here; it was the Apache who burnt the yellow and limber pine fortress to the ground.

Regarrisoned two years after Appomattox, Fort Davis became the headquarters for the Army's Department of the Pecos. The arrival of the railroad and the subjugation of the Native Americans led to the fort's closure. The town of Fort Davis survived as county seat for an immense ranching region and now as one of the most enjoyable tourist destinations in Texas.

TOURIST SERVICES

FORT DAVIS CHAMBER OF COMMERCE
P.O. Box 378 • Fort Davis • 79734 • www.fortdavis.com
915-426-3015 or 800-524-3015 • Monday 1–5
Tuesday–Friday 9–5

Located in front of the Overland Trail campground, the Fort Davis Chamber has plenty to offer visitors planning to come or already in town. Call or e-mail at the website for info packets, event schedules, and restaurant and accommodation updates. Also available are several publications on Fort Davis and flyers on local and area attractions.

GUIDEBOOKS AND PUBLICATIONS

JEFF DAVIS COUNTY MOUNTAIN DISPATCH
P.O. Box 1097 • Fort Davis • 79734 • 915-426-3077
Annual subscription: $21

If you want to make the most of your visit or enjoyed it enough to keep in touch, get a subscription to the *Dispatch*. A weekly, it runs somewhere between 10 and 20 pages and covers local events, area activities, and the seasonal changes that occur at the fort, the observatory, and other attractions.

BIRD'S-EYE VIEW

SKYLINE DRIVE

Davis Mountains State Park
Four miles northwest of Fort Davis via State Highway 118

Pay four dollars at the park's entrance (or show a valid Texas Conservation Passport), meander down Park Road 3 until you see the Skyline Drive arrow pointing left, and put it in low gear. By the time you drive to the hill's crest, you'll come to a fork in the road. Bear right. When you kill your engine, the quiet will be deafening and the vistas amazing. The view from atop the Skyline Drive is unbeatable. Some rave about the Window at the Basin in Big Bend National Park, others extol the River Road along the Rio Grande, but if you want to experience what comes to mind when people say the word "Texas," look no further.

Depending on the season and the rains, the thousands of square miles that surround you can range from straw-colored to shades of green or even snow white. Snowfall is no rarity along these southernmost Rockies. Clearly visible to the north stands the University of Texas McDonald Observatory.

The prominent knob on the mountain off to the left of the observatory is Old Baldy. It sits atop Mount Livermore, the tallest peak in the Davis Mountains at 8,378 feet. Proceeding clockwise or to your right from the observatory are the Glass Mountains over by Marathon, pyramid-shaped Mount Ord on the far side of Alpine, closer and steeper Mitre Peak, Haystack and the Puertacitas, Chinati Peak down by Mexico, and Blue Mountain along the road to Valentine.

MUSEUMS

NEILL DOLL MUSEUM

On Court St. seven blocks west of the courthouse
915-426-3969 • Hours vary • Admission

Built as a summer house for Galveston resident Henry Trueheart, over 350 dolls from the nineteenth and twentieth century are displayed, with the oldest dating back to the 1830s. The collection also includes antique doll buggies, quilts, toys, and bottles. For an unusual treat, consider staying overnight. Bed and breakfast accommodations are available. No children.

OVERLAND TRAIL MUSEUM

Follow sign two blocks from Main Street by Stone Village
Open March–September • Call for hours
Adults $2 • 915-426-3904 (Historical Society)

Owned and operated by the Fort Davis Historical Society, this museum is located on the longest existing stretch of the Overland Trail still in use as an improved dirt road. Most portions of the Trail are either paved or have been passed over by progress. Set in the former residence of local barber, tinkerer, and Justice of the Peace Nick Mersfelder, the numerous exhibits detail Jeff Davis County's early days. The original post office from nearby Valentine is set up as are local artifacts including spurs, saddles, furnishings, and firearms. Photos, many from the 1800s, depict life at the fort, on pioneer ranches, and in town.

HISTORIC PLACES

FORT DAVIS NATIONAL HISTORIC SITE

P.O. Box 1456 • Fort Davis • 79734 • 915-426-3224
www.nps.gov/foda/ • Admission: $2 per person
Daily except Christmas • 8–6 (summer) • 8–5 (winter)
W+ but not all areas

Fort Davis was established in 1854 by the Eighth U.S. Infantry to protect travelers and mail coaches on the San Antonio-El Paso Road. It was named for the then current Secretary of War, Jefferson Davis. Fort Davis was abandoned for most of the Civil War and left to the Apaches who destroyed many of the original buildings. In 1867, it was reestablished by units of the Ninth U.S. Cavalry, one of the newly formed regiments consisting of soldiers of African-American descent. Known as buffalo soldiers, these troops served at Fort Davis from 1867 to 1885. The death of the Mescalero chief Victorio (1880) signaled the end of the Indian Wars in Texas and, too, the mission of the post.

In 1891, Fort Davis, having "outlived it usefulness," was abandoned by the military and reverted back to private ownership. The officers' quarters became some of the best rent houses in town, and by the turn of the century the Post Hospital was a favorite spot for picnics and dances. In the late 1920s, the property was leased by cowboy movie star Jack Hoxie as a movie set. In the 1950s, the Fort Davis Historical Society leased the property. The society was instrumental in having Fort Davis authorized as a National Historic Site (1961).

Today a visitor center, museum, and auditorium are located in restored barracks. A slide program is presented in the auditorium every half hour, and the sounds of a Dress Retreat Parade can be heard on the grounds at scheduled times. During the summer, park rangers and volunteers dressed as soldiers, officer's wives, and servants guide visits to some of the restored and refurnished buildings. In winter, these buildings are open for self-guided tours. Several miles of hiking trails can be found on the grounds, and a shaded picnic area is a perfect place to have lunch. Electric carts are available to handicapped or restricted visitors.

JEFF DAVIS COUNTY LIBRARY

Just south of the County Courthouse
Tuesday–Friday afternoons • 915-426-3802

"Get Booked" is the fitting slogan of the county's public library (located in the former Jeff Davis County jail).

PIONEER CEMETERY

Highway 118 south from Fort Davis ½ mile to cemetery sign
Open daily • No admission

A big blue highway department sign points across from the 118 Cafe to a rickety old gate. Open it and walk down the paved path several hundred feet to the grassy field that contains the graves of Fort Davis pioneers, soldiers of the Confederacy, and many whose tombstones have disintegrated and whose names have been forgotten. Quite common are wooden crosses, mute memorials in this abandoned meadow. For a town of less than a thousand, it's hard to imagine but modern Fort Davis makes use of two other cemeteries these days.

OTHER POINTS OF INTEREST

CHIHUAHUAN DESERT RESEARCH INSTITUTE VISITOR CENTER

Three miles south of Fort Davis on Highway 118 • 915-364-2499
April–August Monday–Friday 9–5 • Weekends 9–6
Free ($2 donation per car requested) • W

In the foothills of the Davis Mountains just south of Fort Davis, CDRI explores the enormous biotic province that extends from near Mexico City in central Mexico north through the Trans-Pecos and into the Rio Grande Valley of central and southern New Mexico and adjacent southeastern Arizona.

The Chihuahuan Desert is one of the four major deserts in the United States (the other three being the Great Basin, the Mojave, and the Sonora). Visitors learn about this vast and varied desert area at the Chihuahuan Desert Arboretum, a 40-acre area which has been divided into approximately 57 plant families, most of which were grown from seed. The 4,000-square-foot Cactus Propagation Greenhouse contains nearly 200 species of cactus and succulents that comprise the Institute's collection, among the world's largest.

The Visitor Center also features the self-guided Modesta Canyon Trail System to a series of hidden springs at the mouth of a beautiful wooded canyon and another route to Clayton Peak, the highest point on the property. The loop through the Canyon takes about an hour to walk, and the top of Clayton Peak by itself is about a half-hour jaunt.

DAVIS MOUNTAINS STATE PARK

Superintendent • Box 786 • Fort Davis • 79734 • 915-426-3337
Four miles northwest of Fort Davis via Highways 17 and 118
$3 per person per day • W+ but not all areas
www.tpwd.state.tx.us/park/davis/davis.htm

One of the most popular state parks, Davis Mountains State Park straddles the confluence of Keesey and Limpia Creeks and offers visitors a wide choice of activities, amenities and, above all, scenic splendor (see **BIRD'S-EYE VIEW**).

Rising from 4,900 to 5,675 feet above sea level, the park provides numerous facilities to enjoy the cool summers and mild winters of the Davis Mountains, including campsites, trailer sites with electric or full hookups, and 39 hotel rooms at the Indian Lodge (see **ACCOMMODATIONS**).

The park's interpretive center is open from 4 to 6 p.m. during the summer and from 3 to 5 p.m. the rest of the year. Hikers can take advantage of trails within the park as well as trek to nearby Fort Davis National Historic Site (3.5 miles one way). Texas Conservation Passport holders can enjoy trails in the recently acquired 1,400-acre Limpia Canyon Primitive Area. Passport holders can also participate in the park's unique bird banding program, which is offered from August to November and from March to May from 8 to 11 a.m. This is a rare opportunity in one of the state's top flyways. Reservations are suggested (915-426-3337).

MCDONALD OBSERVATORY

Highway 118, 17 miles north of Fort Davis • 915-426-3640
UT McDonald Observatory • P.O. Box 1337 • Fort Davis • 79734
www.as.utexas.edu/mcdonald/vc/default.html
Visitor Center open daily 9–5 except Thanksgiving, Christmas,
New Year's Day • Longer summer hours

William Johnson McDonald, a prosperous Paris, Texas, banker, willed over $1,000,000 in 1925 to the University of Texas for the creation of an observatory. Upon his death, this windfall caught everyone flat-footed including UT's Board of Regents and McDonald's heirs. As you can tell from the immense 82- and 107-inch reflector telescopes, housed in burnt orange and white domes, McDonald's wishes were carried out (though not without an out-of-court settlement to quiet his heirs). The facility search committee selected 6,800-foot Mount Locke high in the Davis Mountains, far from the lights of larger cities and the clouds of coastal Texas.

Recognized around the world for its research excellence, the University of Texas has once again focused attention upon the McDonald Observatory with the construction of a massive new scope atop adjacent Mount Fowlkes, the William P. Hobby-Robert Eberly Telescope. Unlike more traditional optical telescopes, the HET Telescope is a *spectroscopic survey telescope* or SST. Spectroscopic astronomy measures the amount and composition of wavelengths (or colors) of light from astronomical objects. This light is captured at the focus of the 91 computer-controlled hexagonal segments that compose the primary mirror. Think of these segments as forming a Texas-sized honeycomb (more than 10 meters wide). In a separate room beneath the SST, a fiber optic cable transmits the incoming light to a mass of spectroscopic instrumentation. This is where the research begins.

SSTs analyze data from more distant and fainter astronomical objects. They cost less, too: The $13.5-million SST is approximately 15 percent the amount spent on the recently constructed Keck telescope in Hawaii. This "Arecibo-type" telescope (named for a similarly configured Puerto Rican radio telescope) delves into many astronomical phenomena that present telescopes and observing schemes are incapable of studying. Opportunities include the measurement of astronomical distances and velocities, aspects of stellar evolution, dark matter, and variable stars such as R. Coronae Borealis, RV Tauri, and Algols.

The W.L. Moody, Jr. Visitors' Information Center, located at the base of Mount Locke, offers astronomy exhibits, films, a gift shop, and a bookstore. The center is open year-round from 9 a.m. to 5 p.m. During the day, weather permitting, solar viewing is performed at the Public Observatory at 11 a.m. and 3:30 p.m. using a 16-inch telescope with a Hydrogen-Alpha filter, permitting visitors a safe view of features on our nearest star.

Every Tuesday, Friday, and Saturday at sunset, the Public Observatory at the Visitors' Center is opened to the public. Enjoy a tour of the constellations and view the moon, planets, stars, and galaxies through large telescopes. No reservations are necessary, and the fees are $3 for adults and $2 for children 6–12. Family rates are available ($8 for families). The Center opens its doors usually half an hour before the Star Party start time. Bring your binoculars, and be sure to dress warmly—the mountain air gets cool after sunset. Because of the seasonal variance in time of sunset, the beginning times change monthly.

One night a month, typically on the Wednesday nearest the full moon, the 107-inch Harlan J. Smith Telescope is opened for the public to look through. Participation requires reservations six months in advance. The admission fee, schedule of dates, and complimentary tickets can be obtained by contacting the W.L. Moody, Jr. Visitors' Information Center.

SPORTS AND ACTIVITIES

Cycling

The Davis Mountains offer year-round cycling for all levels and at all distances. Most of the favored routes are on well-maintained state highways that are relatively free of traffic. A few basics: Watch for livestock. There is plenty of open-range (unfenced) grazing in Jeff Davis County. Make sure you have ample water, spare tubes, and tools for basic repairs. A cycling trip can be derailed for want of parts and/or service. The nearest full-service repair shop is down south at Desert Sports in Terlingua (888-989-6900) or in Midland at Peyton Bikes (915-699-1718).

For the less ambitious, the shortest and easiest routes are in town or close by. An excellent (and brief) route heads south from town on Highway 17 toward Marfa but bears west on 166 to the Point of Rocks (five miles one-way). Standard intermediate-length trips are to Marfa via Highway 17 (just over 20 miles) and the more demanding ride to Alpine via Highway 118 (around 25 miles). Though the one-way distance to Balmorhea on Highway 17 is 50 miles, there is a 2,000-foot elevation drop which makes much of this ride a breeze. The steepest portion is the section preceding Wild Rose Pass, which is not as tough as some hills in Austin.

Of course, the ultimate test is the 75-mile Scenic Loop. The highest road in the state, it offers long flats, scores of peaks and valleys, and gorgeous scenery. Texas doesn't offer any better cycling. If you ride clockwise from Fort Davis (Highway 17 south to Highway 166 to Highway 118 back to town), the toughest part comes last. Most choose to head counter-clockwise and face the music right off, past the Prude Ranch uphill to the Observatory and into, through, and out of Madera Canyon. The long ride downhill past Sawtooth Mountain leads into a few rolling hills and plenty of unfenced pastures before the lengthy, relatively level stretches around Blue Mountain and back into town. Many prefer to bite off pieces of this ride and enjoy a 20- or 30-mile hill workout or a series of sprints on the straightaways.

Guest Ranch

PRUDE RANCH
Six miles north of Fort Davis on Highway 118 • 800-458-6232

Since the 1920s, Texans have been heading to the mile-high Prude Ranch to escape broiling summers in the lowlands. The only difference is that today's guests are from all across America and around the world, and now there's something going on almost year-round.

The motto of the ranch is "we'll keep a horse saddled for you," and for starters, the Prude Ranch stables offer **horseback riding, trail rides**, and, for larger groups, **chuckwagon suppers**. On your own, there is hiking in and around several thousand acres of ranch property. If you're interested in **cycling**, the ranch is located right on the most scenic (and demanding) paved ride in Texas—the 75-mile Scenic Loop. Other facilities include a **basketball court**, a **rodeo arena**, a heated indoor **swimming pool**, and a **tennis court**.

Keep in mind that all of these activities are before you consider watching or participating in any of the scheduled events at the Prude Ranch, such as **rodeos**, including a recent Texas high school rodeo championship, **cycling** events, and the annual **Star Party**, which draws close to a thousand astronomers.

Horseback Riding

Mounts are available at several stables including the Prude Ranch (915-426-3201) and Paradise Mountain Ranch (915-426-3737). Most charge around $20 per hour with longer rides available.

Touring

See **SIDE TRIPS.**

SHOPPING

FISHER HILL GALLERY
Main Street (Highway 17) • 915-426-3246
Monday–Saturday 10–6

The house coffee at the Hotel Limpia is mixed here, and over a dozen different blends are available ground or whole bean at Fisher Hill. Several are brewed daily and served by the cup. Try the cool coffee de cream, served on ice with cream and sugar. Most of the antiques and hand-crafted items come from area ranches and homes.

HIGH COUNTRY NURSERY
Right across from Fort Davis National Historic Site
915-426-3155 • Monday–Saturday 9–6 • Sunday 1–6

Browse past aisles of varietals native to the Trans-Pecos, like evergreen sumac, tecoma stans, purple sage, Chisos red oak, and madrone. Antiques, collectibles, and an ongoing flea market are inside, as is a selection of colorful Mexican imports.

HOTEL LIMPIA GIFTS
Hotel Limpia • 915-426-3241
Daily 10–9:30 except Monday until 5 p.m.

The area adjacent to the Hotel Limpia Dining Room is devoted to gifts, collectibles, and books. Home accessories include western candlesticks, picture frames, reproduction tin signs, wind chimes, bells and baskets. Everything imaginable having to do with birds is on display—feeders, houses, blankets, and books. The shelves are stacked with westerns, cookbooks, and southwestern titles.

JAVELINAS & HOLLYHOCKS
Main Street across from the Hotel Limpia
915-426-2236 • Daily 9–6

There's something for everyone (and every age) in the charming collection of items, including books, local artwork, and educational toys for kids. A surprising number are nature-oriented or naturally made.

LINEAUS ATHLETIC COMPANY
P.O. Box 2021 • Fort Davis • 79734 • 800-626-6456

For over a decade, Lineaus Lorette has been designing, hand-crafting, and marketing medicine balls and other leather training products to organizations like the New York Giants, the Denver Broncos, and the USC Trojans. Stressing speed and quickness as well as strength, medicine balls have been valued by generations of coaches for providing the ideal workout—aerobic as well as anaerobic. His standard medicine ball weighs 12 pounds, has a 14-inch diameter, and sells for $200.

SIDE TRIPS

SCENIC LOOP
State Highways 17, 118, and 166

This is as good as Texas gets on paved public roads. Nearly 75 miles of rolling hills, winding canyons, and jagged peaks combine with open grassland for a memorable 1½ hour drive. And that's not counting stops. Head counterclockwise, i.e., from Fort Davis to Davis Mountains State Park on to the Prude Ranch. This route offers the best vistas: Mount Locke and the UT Observatory from the south and Sawtooth from the east.

Good picnic sites along the way include Davis Mountains State Park just outside of Fort Davis, along Highway 118 below the Observatory, at Madera Canyon beyond the Observatory, and the Point of Rocks (at the end of the Loop). Much of the Loop is unfenced, and cattle graze, sleep, and herd on or near the road. Always avoid low-water crossings during summer storms. And fork off to Kent, Valentine, or Marfa only if you are willing to enjoy added hours of scenery.

ANNUAL EVENTS

April–May

CHIHUAHUAN DESERT RESEARCH INSTITUTE ANNUAL PLANT SALES

CDRI Visitor Center • 3 miles south of Ft Davis • 915-364-2499
Last weekend in April • Memorial Day

Drought-tolerant and heat-resistant ornamental plants native to the Chihuahuan Desert are the highlight of these fundraisers. Develop your garden with varieties unavailable at most nurseries. The growth in popularity of this sale has led to the separate cactus and succulent sale on Memorial Day.

May

ALL BRANDS RALLY

Prude Ranch • 800-524-3015 • Registration fee

Designed for the motorcycle enthusiast, this weekend event begins with a Friday afternoon parade and goes on to include field events and a poker run with cash prizes. Camping costs are not included with the registration fee.

July

FOURTH OF JULY

In town and at the fort • 800-524-3015 • Fourth of July weekend
Free: Courthouse Festival • Admission: Dance

The busiest weekend in Jeff Davis County. At the fort, a formal flag-raising and retreat ceremony highlight a day full of uniforms, demonstrations, and pageantry. In town, the parade starts at St. Joseph's Catholic Church and heads down Main Street to the town square. Freight wagons, color guards, an infantry cadre from the fort, floats, and hundreds of mounted riders from area ranches participate. Everyone heads to the courthouse lawn for a good part of the late morning and early afternoon to eat and poke around the booths. Soon folks head out to the Prude Ranch for the team roping while others head home for supper and to get ready for a West Texas street dance. Show up early; by sundown, it's elbow to elbow out there.

HUMMINGBIRD ROUNDUP

Jeff Davis County • 800-524-3015 (Chamber of Commerce)
Last weekend in July • Registration fee

The Davis Mountains offer excellent birding, and participants tour various habitats in and around Fort Davis to identify and learn more about hummingbirds.

August

BLOYS CAMP MEETING

Skillman Grove • 17 miles west of Fort Davis on Hwy 166
Early August • Free (donations accepted)

Many West Texans and people partial to West Texas who gather at Skillman Grove are second-, third-, and fourth-generation attendees at this non-denominational camp meeting. Founded by Rev. Dr. William Benjamin Bloys, the first meeting (1890) lasted three days. Forty-seven attended. Campers slept on bedrolls and cooked in Dutch ovens, and the Reverend used an Arbuckle coffee crate for a pulpit. By 1909, 115 hacks and buggies, 450 horses and mules, and nine automobiles brought 575 campers to Skillman Grove.

These days, several thousand attendees participate in the week-long meeting. Many spend a night (or the week) in one of the 350 permanent cabins, while others bring RVs or stay in Fort Davis. Bible study comes after a full cowboy breakfast (donations only) with services offered in the morning, afternoon, and evening.

September

FRIENDS OF FORT DAVIS FESTIVAL

Fort Davis National Historic Site • 915-426-3224
Saturday of Labor Day weekend • Free

For more than a decade, this annual day-long event has featured a wide variety of activities and is one of only two days each year when there is no admission fee to the fort. Some activities highlight the fort's history, like the cavalry-infantry patrol demonstrations, the military drills, and the field camps. Some are just plain fun like the door prizes, the children's games, and wagon rides.

Other activities you won't find anywhere else include an 1884 baseball game pitting the Fort Davis nine versus Fort Concho's team from San Angelo. Played in authentic uniforms and using rules of that era, these two posts enjoy a heated rivalry with games played at both forts during the year.

A high point for many is the extensive Colt firearms exhibit at the auditorium. Also on hand are craftsmen demonstrating skills from the fort's heyday—broom squires, dollmakers, saddlemakers, blacksmiths, and photographers. Laundresses even set up Suds Row. Though the festival is a major fundraiser for the Fort, there is no admission charge. Funds are raised at the noon barbecue which features music by the

Corngrinders and at the silent auction with items ranging from antiques to collectibles and books.

CYCLEFEST

Prude Ranch • 800-458-6232 or 915-699-1718 (Peyton's Bikes)
Weekend varies • Fee

Not to be confused with Memorial Day's Hammerfest, Cyclefest is a two-day, family-oriented bicycling event at distances ranging from ten to 100 miles. All cycling is on portions of the beautiful 75-mile Scenic Loop. The long ride (you choose the distance) is scheduled for Saturday, and a shorter jaunt is planned Sunday morning to allow participants to head home early. The Prude Ranch, headquarters for Cyclefest, has activities for family members as well as bunks, meals, and entertainment for all comers.

December

FRONTIER CHRISTMAS

Downtown Fort Davis • 800-524-3015 (Chamber of Commerce)
First weekend • Free

With Santa parading into town, decorations, and a candlelit tour of historic homes, this event is an old-fashioned, family-oriented holiday celebration in the heart of Fort Davis.

RESTAURANTS

($ = Under $7.50, $$ = Under $15, $$$ = $15+ plus tax & tip)

BLUE MOUNTAIN DINER

Intersection of highways 118 and 17 • 915-426-2479
Breakfast, lunch, and dinner Monday–Saturday • Sunday brunch

You won't find any fried foods at a restaurant run by Layle Dees. Try instead fresh-baked breads, plenty of soups and sandwiches, homemade pizzas and lasagnas, as well as hearty breakfast fare.

BLACK BEAR RESTAURANT AT THE INDIAN LODGE

Davis Mountains State Park • 915-426-3254
Four miles northwest of Fort Davis via State Highway 118
Breakfast, lunch, and dinner daily • $

It's a West Texas tradition to corral the family, take a five-minute or maybe a fifty-mile ride through some of the state's prettiest country, and enjoy the inexpensive Sunday buffet complete with salad bar, choice of entrées, and homemade desserts. Pay the entrance fee to enjoy the Skyline Scenic Drive (*see* **BIRD'S-EYE VIEW**). If you're considering the 75-mile Scenic Loop around breakfast time, stop in for the early morning specialties like the breakfast tacos with choice of potato, *chorizo* (Mexican sausage), bacon, country sausage, or ham with egg.

HOTEL LIMPIA DINING ROOM

Main Street at the Town Square • 915-426-3241
Lunch and dinner Tuesday–Sunday • $–$$ • AE D MC V • W

The menu at the Limpia can satisfy all tastes and appetites. There's a vegetable plate, charbroiled steak, southwestern spaghetti, spinach lasagna, and several fish and chicken selections. All entrées are served family style with a selection of vegetables, soup or salad, biscuits, and mashed potatoes. Children are made welcome with plates like chicken-fried chicken or spaghetti, and all kid's meals include a beverage. If you care for a mixed drink with dinner, head upstairs to the Bandana Room and buy a temporary membership. Fee is waived for hotel guests. Reservations highly recommended.

RAUL'S BARBECUE

Intersection of Highway 118 and 17
Most days • Lunch and dinner (tends to close early) • $

Any visit to the Davis Mountains is incomplete without paying homage to the finest barbecue in West Texas. Located in a nondescript house on the east side of town just before Highway 17 forks to Balmorhea, Raul's is operated at the discretion of the namesake owner. If it's not open the first time you stop by, do yourself a favor—try again. Show up before quitting time—7:00 p.m. Brisket lovers can order by the pound or enjoy a *tejano* (on a bun). Ribs by the plate or to go.

THE DRUGSTORE RESTAURANT

At the Old Texas Inn • 915-426-3118
Breakfast and lunch daily • $ • AE MC V

The highlight of the Drugstore is the old fashioned soda fountain featuring hand-mixed floats, malts, sodas, sundaes, ice cream, and phosphates. The chicken fajita burrito and the chicken-fried steak are the menu's bestsellers. Choices also include half a dozen burgers, sandwich baskets, BLTs, and salads.

CLUBS AND BARS

THE BANDANA ROOM

Upstairs at the Hotel Limpia • 915-426-3241 • Nightly
Tuesday–Saturday

This full bar enjoys the distinction of being the only establishment in Jeff Davis County to serve alcohol. Enjoy the rustic setting upstairs over the Hotel Limpia Dining Room for drinks or dinner. State law requires non-members not staying at the hotel to buy a $3 temporary membership.

ACCOMMODATIONS

($ = Under $40, $$ = $40–$75, $$$ = $75–$100, $$$$ = Over $100)
Room Tax 10%

BUTTERFIELD INN
Main Street • 915-426-3252 • $$

Each of the four brightly painted cottages comes with bath and ample living area at this centrally located inn. All have cable TV (HBO), a jacuzzi tub, and a wood fireplace to take the chill off in the cooler months. A pay phone is available at the main building, site of the gift shop. No pets.

FORT DAVIS MOTOR INN
Highway 17 North • 915-426-2112 or 800-803-2847 • $$

With 36 units, this adobe-style motel offers smoking and non-smoking rooms as well as a handicap unit. Phones with free local calls, cable TV, and pine furnishings come with all rooms. AAA and AARP discounts available. Three RV spaces with full hookups are on site, but no showers or restrooms are available.

HOTEL LIMPIA
On the Square • 915-426-3237 or 800-662-5517 • $$–$$$

The two-story main building was built in 1912 of pink limestone quarried near Sleeping Lion Mountain and has 14 rooms including suites. Across Main Street stands the two-story Limpia West annex, an eight-room rustic rock structure constructed in 1925. The most recent addition is the Hotel Limpia Suites (behind the main building). All rooms feature cable TV (HBO).

As long as someone is at the front desk, a pot of fresh coffee, the Limpia Blend, is brewed in the lobby. Two spacious parlors and porches with rocking chairs await guests, as does the Hotel Limpia dining room, the Bandana Club upstairs (full bar), and a well-stocked gift shop with plenty of good books. Pets are welcome (charge). Like the Gage in Marathon, call early for springtime reservations. The Hotel Limpia has a busier summer season. Some weekends are booked years ahead, e.g., Fourth of July and the Star Parties.

INDIAN LODGE
Davis Mountains State Park • 915-426-3254 • $$–$$$
www.tpwd.state.tx.us/park/indian/indian.htm
Four miles northwest of Fort Davis via State Highway 118

Operated as a bed and breakfast by the Texas Parks & Wildlife Department, the original portions of the white adobe pueblo-style lodge were built by members of the Civilian Conservation Corps (1933). Note the pine *viga* and cane *latilla* ceilings, the 18-inch-thick walls, and some of the hand-carved furniture. The old and new wings have 39 rooms combined, each with cable TV, tile baths, and central heat and air. The air conditioning is the biggest surprise. Most nights, even in the summer, require a light blanket. Lodge guests can also enjoy the heated outdoor pool and recreation room.

An American-plan breakfast is served to overnight guests from 6:30 to 9:30 a.m. in the Black Bear Restaurant. Choose from bacon, sausage, eggs to order, pancakes, hashbrowns, cereal, juice, milk, and coffee. *Evenings at the Lodge,* featuring ethnic food and entertainment, are scheduled throughout the year and include Mardi Gras, St. Patrick's Day, Oktoberfest, and Halloween. Note that the lodge closes for the middle two weeks of January. Reservations are accepted up to one year in advance. Cribs, roll-aways, and room service not available. Pets not allowed in rooms.

PRUDE RANCH
Highway 118, six miles north of Ft Davis • 800-458-6232 • $$–$$$

This famous guest ranch (*see* **SPORTS AND ACTIVITIES**) offers 35 rooms with doubles or kings and private baths, 13 cabins with double and bunk beds, and seven bunk rooms that accommodate from 10 to 20 people (depending on age and familiarity). The Prude family goes out of its way to ensure you see it all and do as much as you possibly can. Part of that includes pulling the plug on all televisions and phones (though pay phones are available on the property). Wholesome portions of good ranch cooking are served in the dining hall. Other amenities include a heated indoor pool and a gift shop. Leashed pets only. AAA discount available.

Bed & Breakfasts

BOYNTON HOUSE GUEST LODGE AND BED & BREAKFAST
Atop Dolores Mountain • 915-426-3123 or 800-358-5929
$$–$$$ • W+

Perched atop Dolores Mountain, this white-bricked, red-tiled Mexican colonial (1985) is built around a solarium brimming with rose bushes, geraniums, and peach and banana trees. It offers views of Fort Davis, the Davis Mountain high country, and the open range heading toward Marfa and Alpine. Boynton House has four bedrooms and an apartment, each with private bath. No smoking. No pets. AARP discount available.

THE VERANDA COUNTRY INN
915-426-2233 or 888-383-2847 • $$–$$$$

This spacious historic inn was built in 1883 and is surrounded by walled gardens and courtyards. Located a block west of the Jeff Davis County Court House, the Veranda has eight guest rooms and a separate carriage house furnished with antiques and collectibles. Groups welcome. A full breakfast is included with each night's stay. No smoking. No pets.

WAYSIDE INN BED AND BREAKFAST
915-426-3535 or 800-582-7510 • $–$$$$

This country house (1941) has five bedrooms ($–$$) downstairs, each with private bath, and two larger bedrooms upstairs which share a bathroom and can be rented as a suite ($$$$). Antique and contemporary quilts and furnishings, along with Anna Beth and Jay Ward's full country breakfast, can be found inside. Count on pancakes, biscuits from scratch, baked eggs, Canadian or turkey bacon, and cereals. Anna Beth likes to use her china, silver, and cloth napkins but will accommodate those who prefer paper products. The private side entrance is for guests returning from star parties, the Marfa Lights, or a day on the river.

FORT STOCKTON

PECOS COUNTY SEAT • 8,524 • (915)

An important leg of the Comanche War Trail from the South Plains to northern Mexico each September included Comanche Springs (present-day Fort Stockton) and watering holes east of Marathon and around Persimmon Gap at Big Bend National Park, i.e, roughly the route of US 385 from Fort Stockton to Big Bend National Park. Plentiful water drew native Americans from many tribes, Spanish explorers like Domínguez de Mendoza (1684), and, ultimately, Uncle Sam (1858), who sought to protect the Government Road from San Antonio to El Paso with troops from Fort Lancaster (*see* **OZONA**).

Like most West Texas garrisons, the fort itself didn't last until the twentieth century, but the town survived and prospered. Fort Stockton is now the center of one of America's largest natural gas fields, as well as a convenient gateway to the Big Bend.

Though the Comanches are long gone, the importance of water to Fort Stockton remains clear. One of the town's biggest events is the annual Water Carnival, and millions of tourists know Fort Stockton as the biggest watering hole on Interstate 10 between Van Horn and Ozona—a 200-mile stretch.

TOURIST SERVICES

VISITOR INFORMATION CABOOSE

Interstate 10 and Highway 285 (Exit 257) • 915-336-8052
September–May: 11–6 Monday–Saturday • 12–6 Sunday
June–August: 10–8 Monday–Saturday • 12–8 Sunday

Right off I-10 by the golden arches, this is an easy way for travelers to pick up brochures and to check on upcoming events while beginning a stay in Fort Stockton or before going on. Parking is available for historic tours of Fort Stockton and winery tours at Ste. Genevieve via Roadrunner Bus Tours.

FORT STOCKTON CHAMBER OF COMMERCE VISITOR CENTER

1000 Railroad Ave. • 800-336-2166 • www.fortstockton.com
Monday–Friday 9–5 • Saturday 9–12

Located in the newly restored 1911 Santa Fe Depot, the chamber provides information on attractions in and around Fort Stockton as well as the rest of the Big Bend and Texas.

ROADRUNNER BUS TOURS

Pickup at Caboose, Chamber of Commerce, and other
points in town • 915-336-8052 or 915-336-2264
Historical Tours Monday–Friday 1:30 and 4:00 • Weekends 2 p.m. only
Admission: Adults $6.50, children $3.50
Winery Tours Saturday and Wednesday mornings only at 9:40
Admission: Adults $8, children $6.50

MUSEUMS

ANNIE RIGGS MEMORIAL MUSEUM

301 S. Main St. • 915-336-2167
September–May: 10–12 and 1–5 Monday–Saturday • 1:30–5 Sunday
June–August: 10–8 Monday–Saturday and 1:30–8 Sunday
Admission: Adults $1, children 50¢ • W

Built in 1900 by a group of local investors, the hotel is an excellent example of Territorial Architecture. The 14-room facility was built of adobe with wrap-around verandas and gingerbread trim. All rooms are well appointed: one features furnishings from the turn of the century, a second exhibits archaeologic finds from the area, a third covers the life of pioneer women, and others include Western memorabilia, geology, and rotating exhibits.

Annie Riggs came to Fort Stockton as an eight-year-old shortly after the Civil War. Several husbands and ten children later, she used the proceeds from the murder of her second husband (by her son-in-law) to buy out the original backers for $5,000. She owned and operated the hotel until her death in 1931.

HISTORIC PLACES

HISTORIC FORT STOCKTON
Monday–Saturday 10–1 and 2–5 • 915-336-2400
300 East Third Street • Admission: Adults $2 • Children $1

Owned by the City of Fort Stockton and managed by the Fort Stockton Historical Society, old Fort Stockton consists of original structures dating back to 1868 and reconstructed military buildings restored to their 1870s appearance. The fort was initially garrisoned in 1858 but abandoned at the beginning of the Civil War. Confederate forces only briefly occupied the garrison, and Union forces reoccupied the post from 1867 to 1886.

The Historic Fort Stockton Museum itself is located in Barracks #1. Start and view the informative video before you tour the rest of the premises. Afterward, head to the four original buildings (out of 35) still standing: the Guard House and three of the eight Officers' Quarters. The Guard House is worth a closer look; it contains jailer's quarters, three solitary confinement cells, and a larger holding cell.

OTHER POINTS OF INTEREST

PAISANO PETE
Intersection of Main Street and Dickinson Blvd

Paisano Pete, the world's largest roadrunner, stands 11 feet tall and 22 feet long and is available for viewing and photos round-the-clock all year long (including holidays).

STE. GENEVIEVE WINERY
I-10, Exit 285 McKenzie Road (25 miles east of Fort Stockton)

The largest winery in Texas is also America's fifth biggest. Ste. Genevieve marries University of Texas lands with the *savoir faire* of French winemakers. Over a thousand acres are under cultivation, producing more than a million bottles of wine.

SPORTS AND ACTIVITIES

Golf

PECOS COUNTY 18 HOLE MUNICIPAL GOLF COURSE
Highway 285 one mile northwest of Fort Stockton • 915-336-2050
Open Tuesday through Sunday

The home course of PGA tour member Blaine McAllister offers a 50 percent senior citizen discount off normal rates. Weekday green fees are $12.50, and weekend fees are $18.

ANNUAL EVENTS

July

WATER CARNIVAL
Comanche Springs Pool at Rooney Park • 915-336-2264 (Chamber)
Third weekend of the month • Admission • W

Each year, a different theme is incorporated into more than a dozen different performances ranging from musicals and dancing to synchronized swimming. All can be viewed at the Comanche Springs Pool on Thursday, Friday, and Saturday nights, with different admissions each night.

RESTAURANTS

($ = Under $7.50, $$ = Under $15, $$$ = $15+ plus tax & tip)

MI CASITA
405 E. Dickinson • 915-336-5368
Monday–Friday lunch and dinner • $ • W

Several salads are on the menu, including grilled chicken, taco, and a chef's. For a good Mexican fix, order one of the combination plates: the Mi Casita, the Montezuma, the Azteca, or the Cancun. A popular new item on the menu is the Bill Heine Blue Plate Special, featuring an ample serving of headcheese and a side of mouth-watering *frijoles*. All specials include iced tea or coffee and dessert.

SARAH'S CAFE
106 S. Nelson • 915-336-7700
Monday–Saturday • Lunch and dinner • $–$$ • MC V • W

Author James Michener and four-time Indy champ A. J. Foyt are among those privileged to have enjoyed a good Mexican plate from

Doña Sarah's kitchen. Sarah Nuñez, a Shafter native, opened for business in 1929. Her children and grandchildren run Sarah's now. Lots of folks stick with Sarah's Special: a *chile relleno*, a *chalupa*, a *taco*, an *enchilada*, some *guacamole*, rice and beans. Be sure to savor the legendary green sauce. It goes best with chicken dishes, like the chicken enchiladas. Beer and wine.

ACCOMMODATIONS

($ = Under $40, $$ = $40–$75, $$$ = $75–$100, $$$$ = Over $100)
Room Tax 13%

BEST WESTERN SWISS CLOCK INN
3200 W. Dickinson • 915-336-8521 or 800-528-1234 • **$$**

This two-story lodge located on the west side of town has 112 smoking and non-smoking units including suites and family rooms. Rooms include cable TV (HBO), pay-per-view movies, and phones with no charge for local calls. Complimentary coffee is served in the lobby. Annemarie's Alpine Lodge Restaurant is on the property and serves an inexpensive lunch buffet. Other amenities include an outdoor unheated pool, courtesy car for local transfers, and free parking. Small pets OK. AAA, AARP, and corporate rates available.

HOLIDAY INN EXPRESS
1308 N. U.S. 285 • 915-336-5955 • 800-HOLIDAY • **$$–$$$**

Each night's stay includes a continental breakfast, free local calls, and the local paper. All rooms include refrigerators, hairdryers, and cable TV with Disney and HBO.

LA QUINTA
2601 W. I-10 • 915-336-9781 or 800-642-4239 • **$$**

This two-story inn sits right on I-10 at Exit 257 and has 97 smoking and non-smoking units including suites. Rooms include cable TV (HBO) and phones (free local calls). Some have small refrigerators. Amenities include complimentary coffee in the lobby, an outdoor unheated pool, and free parking. Pets are welcome. AAA and AARP rates available.

GUADALUPE MOUNTAINS NATIONAL PARK

CULBERSON AND HUDSPETH COUNTIES
MOUNTAIN TIME • (915)

Unlike many national parks, Guadalupe Mountains has almost no appreciable development either in its vicinity or within the park itself. Come prepared. Enormous salt flats and rugged mountain ranges surround this already desolate area. The nearest gas station is 35 miles north across the New Mexico state line near Carlsbad Caverns National Park, and it's a much longer drive if you stay in Texas: 75 miles south to Van Horn and 110 miles west to El Paso. Commercial air service and rental cars are available in Carlsbad, New Mexico (55 miles), El Paso (110 miles), and Midland-Odessa (170 miles). The nearest air strip is 34 miles north at White's City (800-228-3767). Improved but not paved, it's seven-tenths of a mile long.

Most of the park's limited development borders Highway 62-180 along the park's eastern edge. The Pine Springs Visitor Center, the near-by Pine Springs Campground, and the Visitor Center at McKittrick Canyon are all accessible via paved or improved dirt roads from this highway. Highway 62-180 is the route that the TNM&O Bus Line (806-765-6641) travels (ask for the Pine Springs stop). Some of the more remote areas, Dog Canyon, for instance, are more than 100 miles by car even though as the crow flies they are less than 15. Because of this lack of development, most of the highest country in Texas remains as pristine as it was when Spanish explorers first encountered the Mescalero Apache in the sixteenth century. This policy has been mandated by the designation of over half the park, 46,850 acres, as wilderness area.

This has been the way of these mountains since before the Spanish and even up to its most recent residents, pioneering ranchers, who set up camps or headquarters in the lowlands and ventured into the high country only to herd strays or to hunt deer, elk, and bear. The sparse vegetation never supported much cattle; consequently, ranching operations were few, hands covered enormous ranges, and the infrastructure more common to greener pastures never developed.

Almost all of the present park is former ranch land that was donated expressly for a National Park or acquired with cooperation of ranch owners. The oldest structures standing are ranch headquarters such as the Williams Ranch which can be accessed only by four-wheel-drive roads or the Frijole Ranch (and nearby Manzanita Spring) right off Highway 62-180. For a more detailed historical explanation, see the following **HISTORIC PLACES.**

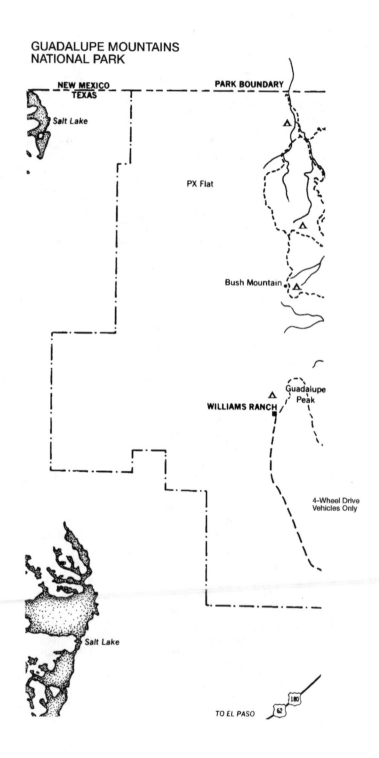

GUADALUPE MOUNTAINS
NATIONAL PARK

NEW MEXICO
TEXAS

PARK BOUNDARY

Salt Lake

PX Flat

Bush Mountain

Guadalupe
Peak

WILLIAMS RANCH

4-Wheel Drive
Vehicles Only

Salt Lake

TO EL PASO

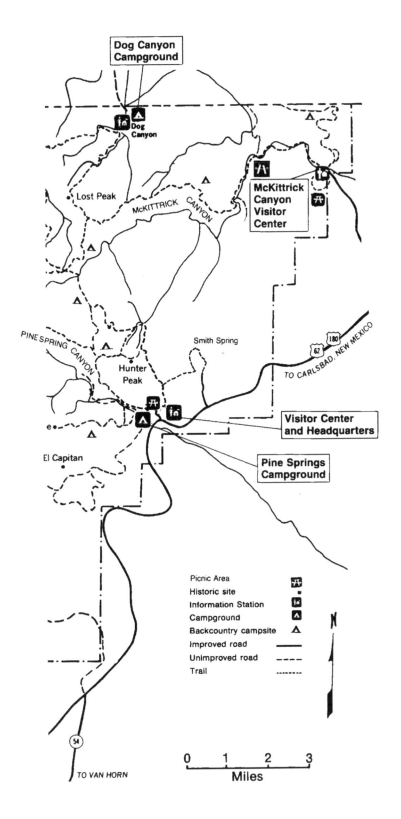

Dog Canyon
Campground

Dog
Canyon

Lost Peak

McKITTRICK   CANYON

McKittrick
Canyon
Visitor
Center

PINE SPRING CANYON

Smith Spring

62 180

TO CARLSBAD, NEW MEXICO

Hunter
Peak

Visitor Center
and Headquarters

e

Pine Springs
Campground

El Capitan

Picnic Area
Historic site
Information Station
Campground
Backcountry campsite
Improved road
Unimproved road
Trail

N

0   1   2   3

Miles

54

TO VAN HORN

TOURIST SERVICES

SUPERINTENDENT, GUADALUPE MOUNTAINS NATIONAL PARK

HC 60 • Box 400 • Salt Flat, TX • 79847-9400 • 915-828-3251
www.nps.gov/gumo/ • Visitor Center open 8:00–4:30,
slightly longer in summer, closed Christmas Day

There is no park entrance fee although campground use fees are charged. Use this address and phone number when contacting the Park Service for information. Don't go to Salt Flat, Texas, however, if visiting Guadalupe National Park is on the agenda (you'll only find a cafe and a post office). The visitor centers and ranger stations are located on the eastern and northern portions of the national park.

PINE SPRINGS VISITOR CENTER/HEADQUARTERS

Highway 62-180 • 915-828-3251
Daily 8–4:30 (winter) • 8–6 (summer)

Located adjacent to the Pine Springs Campground, this Visitor Center provides the full gamut of information, activities, and resources. Brochures and trail maps on the park, books covering regional history and natural sciences, exhibits, and a slide program are all available. Rangers not only provide the latest details on trails, campgrounds, and special conditions but also offer guided hikes and nightly programs at the Pine Springs Campground Amphitheater (seasonally).

MCKITTRICK CANYON VISITOR CENTER

Four miles west of Highway 62-180 from a turnoff
7 miles northeast of Pine Springs • Access closed nightly

Gateway to McKittrick Canyon, learn more about this Texas treasure and one-of-a-kind relic forest before you begin your day hike. No overnight camping is permitted in McKittrick Canyon.

DOG CANYON RANGER STATION

Located at the Dog Canyon Campground, this remote facility can be reached by foot via the Pine Springs or McKittrick Canyon Trails or by car via State Highway 137, a paved road, which extends west 59 miles from Highway 285 approximately 12 miles north of Carlsbad. Even phone lines go the long route. Although the Ranger Station is in Texas, it has a New Mexico number (505-981-2418). The distance from the Pine Springs Visitor Center is 12 miles by foot and 105 miles by vehicle.

GUIDEBOOKS AND PUBLICATIONS

THE GUADALUPES
By Dan Murphy • Carlsbad Caverns/Guadalupe Mountains Association

A brief introduction to the Guadalupe Mountains as well as the National Park that includes a portion of them. The geology, wildlife, and history of the area are included. Available at the Headquarters Visitor Center, Carlsbad Caverns National Park, as well as from the Carlsbad Caverns/Guadalupe Mountains Association at 505-785-2318.

BIRD'S-EYE VIEW

ATOP GUADALUPE PEAK
8,749 feet above sea level

A hell of a hike. The top of Texas is less than five miles from the Pine Springs Visitor Center, and that means views of the Chihuahuan Desert and the mountains of three states: Chihuahua, New Mexico, and Texas. Wear sturdy shoes, bring plenty of sunscreen, and take even more water. Directions, information, and trail maps are all available at the Visitor Center. Allow several hours each way.

With breaks, a summit siesta, and fatigue, this haul can easily stretch beyond half a day. On a clear day, vistas of more than 100 miles including the Davis Mountains and Mexico are not uncommon as are views of the Sierra Diablos directly south and the Delaware Mountains to the southeast. Of course, right in front of you is the *El Capitan* escarpment which stands as sentinel for the highlands and is another half-hour hike.

For those of you unwilling, uninterested, or unable to scale massive heights in a single bound, drive south on Highway 62-180 from the Pine Springs Visitor Center toward Guadalupe Pass and pull over at the scenic viewpoint. El Capitan, the jagged limestone monolith before you, has stood as a beacon to travelers for centuries as it hovers more than a mile above the surrounding flats. Even the accidental tourist can savor this sensation as he drives on Interstate 10 east of Van Horn and spies El Capitan more than 50 miles to the north.

HISTORIC PLACES

Much of the history of this region concerns cultures that hardly left footprints, let alone more substantial remnants. Dating from about 12,000 years ago, pottery shards, projectile points, and other artifacts reveal man's earliest known sojourns through these hills. More identifiable is the presence of the Mescalero Apache. Stone circles several feet in diameter are found in both Guadalupe and Carlsbad Caverns national-al parks. They were used as roasting pits to prepare agave or mescal. This plant, an integral part of the diet of this band of Apaches, led to the white man's name for this people, the Mescalero.

The U.S. Army came to the Guadalupes looking for a watering hole as early as 1849, but it wasn't until the late 1850s when John Butterfield's Overland Mail Route was established that there was regular traffic. As part of his contract with the government, Butterfield was awarded 320 acres for each of his changing stations (see **THE PINERY**). The Pinery was in use less than a year as the harsh climate and the harsher Mescalero Apaches forced the route south to more plentiful water and less hostile country.

Faint ruts in the desert and historic structures are all that still stand of the Overland Trail and the early ranches. As you look closely at these buildings (or their remains) and consider life out on this range, keep in mind that the hundreds of thousands of acres that surround Guadalupe National Park's Texas boundary are privately-owned ranches.

THE PINERY

Immediately east of Pine Springs Visitor Center

The Butterfield Overland Mail route ran between St. Louis and San Francisco. Over 2,700 miles long, the three- to four-week delivery actually had two stages: a westbound driver who departed St. Louis and an eastbound one who left San Francisco. Not surprisingly, the Lone Star State occupied the longest segment. The changing station at the Pinery was the halfway mark. The first eastbound stage met its westbound counterpart at the Pinery on September 25, 1858. Though the Butterfield Mail continued until March 1861, the Pinery was abandoned as a changing station. Guadalupe Pass was the highest point on the entire run, and a lower route via Fort Davis offered better protection and more water.

FRIJOLE RANCH

Follow the Frijole Ranch turnoff (less than two miles north of the Visitor Center), three-quarters of a mile to the ranch house.

Hardy ranchers like the Rader brothers homesteaded the Guadalupes even when the Apache roamed. The Rader brothers' Frijole Ranch headquarters (1876) is now open to the public and is used by the National Park Service as a cultural history museum. (Check at the Pine Springs Visitor Center for times and access.) Much less accessible is the **Williams Ranch** which can be reached only by four-wheel-drive vehicles over seven miles of rough road. Complete directions and a gate key are available from park personnel at the Visitor Center.

OTHER POINTS OF INTEREST

MCKITTRICK CANYON

Take the McKittrick Canyon turnoff seven miles north of the Visitor Center on Highway 62-180 and drive four miles to the parking lot. Open from 8 a.m. to • 6 p.m. (summer) or 4:30 p.m. (winter)

Steep canyon walls and a perennially spring-fed stream keep this relic forest alive thousands of years after a drier climate parched the Chihuahuan Desert. Four miles of self-guided trail along the floor of the canyon offer casual hikers sights commonly seen in many states not including Texas: little leaf walnut, velvet ash, big tooth maple, and the state's only reproducing stock of rainbow trout. The canyon is busiest during the fall when it wears autumn colors. Picnicking is permitted at the parking lot, in the canyon near the Pratt Cabin (2+ miles from the parking lot), and at the Grotto picnic area (3+ miles from the parking lot).

SPORTS AND ACTIVITIES

Camping

At the lower campgrounds, Pine Springs and Dog Canyon, it's first-come, first-served. These two areas are accessible by road and are also fee campgrounds ($8 per night per site). Pine Springs lies right off Highway 62-180 adjacent to the Visitor Center. Dog Canyon is on the north side of the park just a mile south of the New Mexico border and approachable by car only from New Mexico on State Highway 137. Proceed north from Carlsbad approximately 12 miles and then head west to access State Highway 137. By foot, Dog Canyon is a mere 12 miles from Pine Springs via the Tejas Trail through some of the park's most scenic terrain. Both campgrounds can accommodate RVs as well as tents, and each has running water, handicapped-accessible restrooms, and picnic tables.

Due to the natural dryness as well as the limited fuel, *open fires are prohibited.* The reasons for this were quite evident during the spring of 1993 when a fire started by an errant match covered more than 6,500 acres. This was not an isolated incident. A lightning strike on Frijole Peak caused a 6,000-acre burn in 1990. The moral of the story is to bring a camp stove if you like your coffee hot. Registration is a must; permits are required for overnight camping and are available at the Pine Springs Visitor Center or at the Dog Canyon Ranger Station.

Hiking

The novice hiker as well as those unfamiliar with the demands of this region are counseled to look elsewhere for introductory remarks on both topics. As wonderful as this park can be, plenty can go wrong: The cactus is sharp, the cliffs are steep, the snakes are poisonous, and the water is scarce. Winds of over 100 mph are not uncommon around Guadalupe Pass, snow accumulation of several feet is typical in protected areas of the high country, and temperatures can reach a high of 100 degrees during the summer and below zero in winter months.

First of all, either stop by a visitor center or phone the Carlsbad Caverns/Guadalupe Mountains Association at 505-785-2318 for a copy of *Trails of the Guadalupes* by Don Kurtz and William D. Goran and the Guadalupe Mountains National Park topo map (*Trails Illustrated* topo map #203). Both are indispensable. The booklet details trails, temperatures, mileage, rainfall, and other important information. The topo map is tearproof, waterproof, $7.95, and much more practical than purchasing any or all of the 7.5-minute USGS series that apply to Guadalupe Mountains National Park: *Guadalupe Peak, Guadalupe Pass, PX Flat,* and *Patterson Hills.* Whatever your trek, be sure to pack plenty of water.

The curse of the Texas hiker strikes again as there are no high country watering holes of any sort. For day hikes, it is generally recommended to carry a half gallon per person. Overnight hiking typically requires a gallon per person per day on the trail. At two pounds per quart or eight pounds per gallon, you be the judge. During the hotter summer months, H_2O consumption will increase substantially.

Some good day hikes include to Smith Spring—2.3 miles (3.8 km) from the Frijole Ranch House (round trip), and to the top of Texas and back—the 8.4-mile (13.6-km) Guadalupe Peak hike from the Pine Springs Campground (round trip). All longer trails are rewarding hikes. Take the time to discuss your interests and abilities with a park ranger before deciding on longer trails or overnight hikes like the Tejas Trail (11.9 miles/19.2 km).

RESTAURANTS AND ACCOMMODATIONS

See **CARLSBAD CAVERNS NATIONAL PARK or VAN HORN.**

LAJITAS

BREWSTER COUNTY • 48 • (915)

Once the hot Chihuahuan summer cools off and snow birds and tourists arrive, Lajitas comes to life. In centuries past, the onset of autumn brought the Comanches to Lajitas and its San Carlos crossing, known as the best ford across the Rio Grande from Del Rio to El Paso.

Historians credit H. W. McGuirk with the founding of the town (1899). McGuirk was a rancher with mining and mercantile interests who eventually sold his holdings and relocated to New Mexico before Lajitas came of age. During the turbulent times of the Mexican Revolution and World War I, Lajitas served the immense Big Bend region as a cavalry post. Border raids by Mexican bandits at Glenn Spring (present-day Big Bend National Park), in nearby Presidio County, and at Columbus, New Mexico, heightened the importance of the garrison. The legacy of this era is the modern recreation of the Lajitas Cavalry Post as a resort.

HISTORIC PLACES

LAJITAS TRADING POST
1 Clay Henry Rd. • 915-424-3234 • Daily • 8 a.m. to 8 p.m.

The trading post was built during World War I and, in its early years, resupplied the U.S. Cavalry as well as Mexican forces from across the river. Still a general store, it serves tourists as well as locals from both sides of the river with a wide range of merchandise: groceries, picnic supplies, beer, ice, bait, gas, diesel, a fax machine, and a notary public. Billy the Kid can also be found at the trading post continuing the daunting legacy of Clay Henry and Clay Henry Jr., his illustrious beer-drinking forefathers.

Around the corner, stop in at **Arrowhead Sotol Products** (915-424-3224). Owner Larry Harris gathers and cures the stalk of the sotol plant, whose length can exceed six feet. He then handcrafts furniture, walking sticks, and even golf clubs using the durable shaft. Collectibles include wind chimes, earrings, and silver jewelry.

SANTA MARIA Y SAN JOSE MISSION
At the west end of Lajitas on the Rio Grande

Town father H. W. McGuirk built this 20- by 40-foot Catholic church shortly after he settled in Lajitas. A focal point of the early community, it fell into disrepair and wasn't renovated until 1990. (An interior renovation was completed in 1999.) Note the stained glass windows, crafted by Jim Box (1990). Santa Maria y San Jose now hosts weddings and other celebrations, as well as weekly Catholic and Episcopal services.

Keep an eye out just east of Lajitas for the town's tiny cemetery. Dating back to the era of founding father McGuirk, the graveyard is worth a visit to view rarely seen, oven-shaped *hornitos* ("little ovens") made of native stone and built over gravesites. The Lajitas Cemetery stands on the north side of FM 170 just down the hill from Lajitas on the Rio Grande.

SPORTS AND ACTIVITIES

See also **BIG BEND NATIONAL PARK.**

Golf

LAJITAS GOLF COURSE
Open every day of the year • 915-424-3211

Right along the Rio Grande, this nine-hole course rarely gets crowded (ask golf pro Paul Lee). Green fees are $20 all day on weekends and holidays and $17 all day during the week. Carts available.

Horseback Riding

LAJITAS STABLES
Just east of Lajitas • 915-424-3238
Daily from sunrise to sunset with a siesta in the summer

Unlike Montana or Colorado stables, once winter sets in these wranglers don't close shop. Lajitas Stables offers several packages ranging from a one-hour ride ($22) to multi-day trips or ride/raft packages at $130–$150 per person per day. Plenty of gentle, dependable mounts are available for greenhorns.

Rafting

See separate listing **BIG BEND NATIONAL PARK.**

SIDE TRIPS

SAN CARLOS, CHIHUAHUA, MEXICO

San Carlos is a traditional Mexican village of 2,500 south of Lajitas. A little bit of farming, ranching, mining, and a *candelilla* waxworks keep it going. Depart the Lajitas Trading Post at ten in the morning. San Carlos native **Kiko Garcia** (915-424-3221) uses a Suburban to traverse the 18 miles of rugged dirt roads in about an hour and a half.

Highlights include San Carlos Canyon and its lush springs, lunch at Señora Garcia's house, and an afternoon visit to a second canyon or the ruins of the old Spanish *presidio*, one of five built in the late 1700s to protect Spanish citizens from marauding Apaches and Comanches. Arrive back in Lajitas between 5:30 and 6:00 p.m. For those interested in spending the night, consider **Gloria's Bed & Breakfast** (915-424-

3446), which also offers shuttle service to San Carlos in addition to accommodations ($$).

ANNUAL EVENTS

February

CHIHUAHUAN DESERT CHALLENGE MOUNTAIN BIKE RACE AND FESTIVAL

Lajitas on the Rio Grande and surrounding area • 915-424-3471

This four-day event has been selected as one of the top 25 off-road races in the world by *Velo News*. The Chihuahuan Desert Challenge is the first race of the year on the NORBA calendar and features fun rides to San Carlos and the ghost town of Buena Suerte as well as a circuit race, time trials, and a cross-country event for cash prizes and NORBA points. Over 800 entrants participated in the 1999 event, which is sponsored by Terlingua's Desert Sports (888-989-6900 or www.desert-sportstx.com) and hosted by Lajitas on the Rio Grande.

November

FRANK X. TOLBERT—WICK FOWLER MEMORIAL CHILI COOK-OFF

CASI CHILI COOK-OFF

First weekend of November

See separate listing under **TERLINGUA.**

RESTAURANTS

($ = Under $7.50, $$ = Under $15, $$$ = $15+ plus tax & tip)

BADLANDS RESTAURANT

Lajitas on the Rio Grande • 915-424-3471
Daily • Breakfast, lunch, and dinner • Saloon opens at 5 p.m.
$–$$ • AE MC V • W

The family-friendly menu features plenty of appetizers, salads, sandwiches, and side orders. In addition to BLTs, burgers, and barbecue, this eatery just north of the Rio Grande offers numerous Mexican food entrées—*burritos, enchiladas, fajitas, tacos,* and an excellent *picadillo* (sauteed beef tips). During the holidays, special Thanksgiving and Christmas buffets are served ($$). Bar.

DOS AMIGOS AND THE COMANCHE MOON CAFE

Paso Lajitas • Mexico • Daily
Breakfast, lunch, and dinner until 8 p.m. • $

Immediately west of Lajitas, a big dry wash cuts two deep dips in FM 170. In the middle of the second one, fork left on a sandy car path and meander about 100 yards toward the river. Parking is plainly visible and safe. A boatman ferries you across at a dollar per person round trip. High water can push market rates up (pay when you return). A short stroll and you're in front of Dos Amigos. Maybe Bill, Lisa, Zane, and Cody Ivey, who own and operate the Terlingua Ghost Town, will be there.

A little bit farther now and you'll find yourself at the Comanche Moon, a favorte haunt of Giddings Brown, the general manager of Lajitas on the Rio Grande. Both serve home-cooked Mexican specialties like *enchiladas, tacos, flautas,* and *tostadas* (also called *chalupas* in these parts). Last time I checked, Mexican beers were a buck. The Comanche Moon closes a little earlier (around seven). After you arrive back on the American side, a dollar covers the guy who patrols the parking lot in your absence.

CLUBS AND BARS

BADLANDS SALOON

Lajitas on the Rio Grande • 915-424-3452
Nightly until 12 a.m. except 1 p.m. on Saturdays

There's usually something brewing on weekends during the high season. Bands cater to all tastes and play country & western, *tejano,* and rock & roll. Bar.

ACCOMMODATIONS

($ = Under $40 $$ = $40–$75 $$$ = $75–$100 $$$$ = Over $100)

LAJITAS ON THE RIO GRANDE

915-424-3471 • 800-525-4827 • www.lajitas.com • $$–$$$

A wide range of lodging is available in Lajitas. All units at the Badlands Hotel, the Cavalry Post Motel, La Cuesta Motel, and the Officer's Quarters are air-conditioned. Accommodations include hotel rooms, one- and two-bedroom condos, bunkhouses, and houses with daily, weekly, and monthly rates. Rooms include cable TV and phones (charge for local calls). Rates are typically reduced from June 15 to September 15.

The Lajitas RV Park has 78 sites as well as a camping ground complete with restrooms, showers, and picnic tables. Amenities include the Badlands Restaurant and Saloon, the Lajitas Mercantile, the Frontier Drug Company featuring an old-fashioned fountain and gift items, a pool, laundry room, the Lajitas Golf Course, tennis courts, bike rentals, and plenty of free parking. The resort has its own 4,777-foot paved airstrip just east of the property. Bring your own rope for tie-downs. Pets welcome.

LANGTRY

VAL VERDE COUNTY • 30 • (915)

Though the railroad may have built Langtry, Roy Bean gave it lasting renown. Situated near the rail line that connected the Gulf and West coasts, Langtry first achieved fame for its proximity to Dead Man's Gulch, site of the completion of the Southern Pacific's transcontinental Sunset Route in 1883 (*see* **PECOS RIVER BRIDGE OVERLOOK**). With the construction came much mayhem. This rowdy piece of the Lower Pecos River Valley required a Justice of the Peace; Bean began his work the week before he was appointed.

As a jurist Roy Bean had no compare, be it ordering the defendant to buy the house a round (at Bean's saloon) or fining a dead man the sum of his worldly possessions. With age came even greater autonomy: Bean defied Governor Culberson and circumvented the state's anti-prizefight law in 1896 by hosting a heavyweight title bout within sight of some Texas Rangers but beyond their domain on a sand bank in the middle of the Rio Grande. In that fight, Peter Maher, fresh from a victory over Gentleman Jim Donnell, lost to Bob Fitzsimmons, but it was Bean who won everlasting fame.

TOURIST SERVICES AND MUSEUM

JUDGE ROY BEAN VISITOR CENTER

Loop 25 one mile south of Highway 90 • 915-291-3340
Open from 8 a.m. to 5 p.m. except December 24, 25, 26,
and New Year's Day • Free • W

With the exception of the State Capitol, the Judge Roy Bean Visitor Center is the only state-operated travel information center that is not at an entry city like El Paso or Brownsville. Before you visit the Jersey Lilly, pick up a copy of the *Texas State Travel Guide,* plan your vacation with the assistance of a Department of Transportation travel counselor, and tour the cactus garden. Most of the 100+ varieties are Chihuahuan Desert natives.

Roy Bean's courtroom and billiard hall stands out back. It was called the Jersey Lilly (Bean was smitten with the English starlet Lillie Langtry and continually invited her out west). When Miss Langtry finally assented to his invitation, His Honor had been dead and buried for several months. Judging from Bean's condition and Langtry's remote desolation, no one in Miss Lillie's party was heard to mutter "better late than never."

SIDE TRIPS

PECOS RIVER BRIDGE OVERLOOK

18 miles east of Langtry
Scenic viewpoint from the south side of the east bank • W+

An earlier bridge, constructed in Roy Bean's day (1891), was the highest in the world and stood over this once empty canyon long before Lake Amistad filled up the bottom 80 feet (1969). The present one towers 273 feet above the Pecos.

Just up river and a couple of miles west of the Pecos on private property is Dead Man's Gulch. Much like the celebration at Promontory Point in 1869, speeches and a silver spike commemorated the completion of the Sunset Route across the southern United States here by Irish and Chinese crews in 1883.

Even more noteworthy was the route's centennial celebration. Former state senator Don Kennard invited Lt. Governor Bill Hobby to join the party planning to overnight under the stars in early January 1983, and the rush was on. A short list of attendees included Majority Leader Jim Wright, historian T. R. Fehrenbach, several Railroad Commissioners, Texas Supreme Court Justice Jim Wallace, and then-State Treasurer Ann Richards.

SEMINOLE CANYON STATE HISTORICAL PARK

Park Superintendent • Box 820 • Comstock • 78837
915-292-4464 • www.tpwd.state.tx.us/park/seminole/seminole.htm
19 miles east of Langtry • 45 miles west of Del Rio
Open daily except during public hunts (check for dates)
Entrance fee • W+ but not all areas

Located just south of the confluence of the Pecos River and the Rio Grande, Seminole Canyon is the site of Fate Bell Shelter which contains some of North America's oldest and most impressive Native American pictographs (rock paintings). Over 200 Pecos River-style sites exist but none like this one. Considered by experts to be among the most important rock art in the New World, Fate Bell is accessible only via guided tours at 10 a.m. and 3 p.m. Wednesday through Sunday (weather permitting). Moderately strenuous hiking is involved.

Seminole Canyon State Park contains many other activities: campsites with water and with water nearby, eight miles of hiking trails, a six-mile mountain biking loop, picnic tables and grills, and plenty of opportunities for wildlife observation and photography. Several ecosystems are present at the park—the Chihuahuan Desert, the Tamaulipan Thorn Scrub, and the western edge of the Texas Hill Country—and provide for an unusual diversity of flora and fauna.

MARATHON

BREWSTER COUNTY • 600 • (915)

Named for its likeness to the plains where the Athenians defeated the Persians (490 B.C.), Marathon was founded by Captain Albion Shepherd (1881), a member of the Southern Pacific Railroad's original surveying party. More important than the railroad was nearby Camp Peña Colorado (see **OTHER POINTS OF INTEREST**). Peña Colorado was the last of the frontier forts, and its abandonment in 1893 signaled the end of the Indian Wars in Texas. By then, the Marathon area had become prime cattle country with thousands of acres of pasture claimed by enterprising ranchers (see **GAGE HOTEL**).

To this day, resupplying and ranching are the town's twin industries. The railroad still passes through; Amtrak stops in Alpine, a 30-minute drive west. Most visitors to Big Bend National Park (55 miles south via US 385) pass through Brewster County's second largest community, located just over four thousand feet above sea level. The assortment of lodging, dining, and shopping have made this tiny town as much a draw as the park itself, and its allure beckons newcomers and old hands back to the Big Bend.

TOURIST SERVICES

MARATHON CHAMBER OF COMMERCE
P.O. Box 163 • Marathon • 79842

If you'd like general information, drop a note to the Chamber at the post office box or stop by the Gage Hotel, a designated State Information Site for Big Bend National Park (see **ACCOMMODATIONS**).

OTHER POINTS OF INTEREST

THE POST AKA CAMP PEÑA COLORADO
Four miles south of Marathon via Avenue D

Established in 1879 as one of the last posts of the Army's frontier defense system, by the time Camp Peña ceased operations (1893), the West was won in Texas. Camp Peña was one of many frontier forts garrisoned by buffalo soldiers, former slaves whose regiments played such a crucial part in ending the Indian Wars. A term first coined by Native Americans, buffalo soldier was used to describe the fighting spirit and the tight, curly hair of the troops. Nowadays, the Post is a rendezvous for dances, weddings, and the ever popular Fourth of July celebration (*see* **ANNUAL EVENTS**). Stop by the front desk at the Gage Hotel for the word on upcoming events.

SHOPPING

BELL STUDIO/GALLERY
Ritchey Building

In addition to his own artwork, Charlie Bell (of the world renowned Bell brothers, which includes Bob and David) offers instruction in papermaking, drawing, painting, and ceramics.

CHISOS GALLERY
Highway 90 one block east of the Gage Hotel • 915-386-4200

Specializing in Mexican collectibles as well as Southwestern art, the Chisos offers hand-crafted Tarahumara goods, religious articles, and Mexican antiques.

EVANS GALLERY
21 South First St. • 915-386-4366

Located on the south side of the tracks in the old Chambers Hotel, this gallery features quality art photography.

FRONT STREET BOOKS
Highway 90 just east of the Gage Hotel • 915-386-4249
www.fsbooks.com • Monday–Saturday 9–6 • Sunday 9–2

The sister store to the original operation in Alpine, this edition of Front Street orients its inventory to travelers and guests at the Gage Hotel with plenty of guides, West Texana, and magazines.

GAGE GEAR

Highway 90 right next to the Gage Hotel • 915-386-9042

Once upon a time, this gift shop filled up much of the lobby of the Gage Hotel next door. Then too many items and not enough space forced it out the door and into its own quarters where worried guests find everything they left back home like cameras, film, batteries, flashlights, socks, backpacks, and assorted knick knacks.

JOHNNY B'S

Highway 90 between Gage Gear and Café Cenizo
915-386-4111 • Monday–Sunday 8–6 Sunday 10–6
Closed Wednesdays • Cash and checks

Pull up a seat in one of the booths or at the counter of this old-fashioned soda fountain where traditional favorites like burgers, shakes, banana splits, and lime rickeys are prepared to order.

SOTOL GALLERY

Highway 90 one block east of the Gage Hotel • 915-386-9011

The Sotol is devoted strictly to black-and-white photography of the Big Bend and Chihuahuan Desert region. Prices for the traditional silver prints and hand-coated platinum and palladium prints start at $200.

SPRING CREEK GALLERY

Highway 90 three blocks east of the Gage Hotel • 915-386-4350

If it's Western décor or furnishings that you're looking for, then this gallery offers one-stop shopping for the entire house. Spring Creek Gallery offers unique Western home décor furnishings and accessories, clothing, artwork, jewelry, dinnerware by Frankoma, glassware by Bamco, Western Heritage lamps, terra cotta decorations and coaster sets, and handmade metal artwork. It also has hide-covered leather furniture, as well as crackle furniture, along with Mexican furniture and accessories for the living room, kitchen, bath, and bedroom. Special order Western fabrics and cowhide furniture are also available.

V6 COLLECTION

Highway 90 one block east of the Gage Hotel • 915-386-4559

Go West! A complete collection of authentic Western collectibles, clothing, and accents graces the new and improved quarters of the old Marathon State Bank. Double D Ranchwear, jewelry by Paul Wiggins and other Texas artisans, buckle sets, tooled leather briefcases, suitcases, and wallets, Western furniture, and hand-blown glassware are some of the many items that the V6 will ship anywhere in the U.S.

WEEKS & LITSCHAUER

Highway 90 just east of the Gage Hotel • 915-386-4452

The husband and wife team of Garland Weeks and Mimi Litschauer operate one gallery featuring two studios. Her paintings include plein air landscapes and oils. His traditional, representational, figurative sculptures are cast in limited edition bronzes (commissions accepted).

ANNUAL EVENTS

July

FOURTH OF JULY DANCE

The Post • Four miles south of Marathon via Avenue
Fourth of July weekend • Admission Required for Dance Only

Most of Marathon and a good bit of Brewster, Jeff Davis, and Presidio counties show up for this memorable shindig out at the Post. There's no charge to go jaw or gawk, but the dance costs.

RESTAURANTS

($ = Under $7.50, $$ = Under $15, $$$ = $15+ plus tax & tip)

CAFÉ CENIZO

At the Gage Hotel • 915-386-4205
Breakfast and dinner daily • $–$$ • MC V • W

Folks from across West Texas think nothing of driving an hour or two for dinner and/or drinks at this beautifully appointed restaurant and bar. Chock full of gorgeous Western collectibles and memorabilia, the highlight of Café Cenizo is the one-of-a-kind White Buffalo Bar. The inviting patio is perfect for dining on starlit summer nights. Domestic and imported beers and Texas wines are featured. Reservations recommended. Bar.

ACCOMMODATIONS

($ = Under $40, $$ = $40–$75, $$$ = $75–$100, $$$$ = Over $100)

CAPTAIN SHEPHERD'S INN

Located a block north of the Gage Hotel
915-386-4205 or 800-884-4243 • $$$–$$$$

Run as a bed and breakfast by the Gage Hotel (*see* **GAGE HOTEL**), this inn has been Marathon's pre-eminent address since it was erected in 1899 by the town's founding father, Albion Shepherd. The main house, a two-story adobe finished in Greek Revival and furnished in Victorian, has five bedrooms ($$$), all with private baths. The carriage house, let as a two-bedroom suite ($$$$), offers a large common area featuring a fireplace, sitting and dining areas, and a full kitchen.

The staff of the Gage Hotel handles all details of your stay including reservations and payment. A direct line from the foyer of Captain Shepherd's Inn to the front desk at the Gage is available to make dinner reservations, ask travel questions, and handle emergencies. All facilities of the Gage including the pool are at the disposal of inn guests. A generous continental breakfast is served including baked goods, fruit, cereal, juices, and coffee.

GAGE HOTEL
Highway 90 • 915-386-4205 or 800-884-4243
www.gagehotel.com • $$–$$$

Countless articles in publications like *The New York Times* and *Condé Nast Traveler* have described the allure of this West Texas landmark. The site of innumerable weddings, reunions, and Big Bend outings, the Gage continues in its historic role as headquarters for trips out West. Built in the 1920s, it originally served as headquarters for the 500,000-acre ranch of Alfred Gage, a Vermont native who came to Brewster County to punch cattle in the 1880s and ultimately bequeathed one of the state's greatest ranches four decades later.

The addition of **Los Portales** to the west of the original hotel complements the design of Gage's original architect, Henry Trost. The outdoor pool and covered patio offer welcome relief from the West Texas sun. The renovated **Wilson House** across the street is ideal for a family of four and boasts a massive floor-to-ceiling rock fireplace.

All of the 37 rooms (and Wilson House) are appointed with Mexican, Indian, and Anglo artifacts (but no televisions). The knowledgeable front desk can book rafting on the Rio Grande, horseback and bicycle rides locally, hunting on area ranches, or stargazing at McDonald Observatory. The Gage offers packages featuring noted photographers, musicians, and chuckwagon cooks as well.

MARATHON MOTEL & RV PARK
West Highway 90 • 915-386-4241 • $

Located at the west end of town, there are four inexpensive cabins, each a duplex. For larger parties, a house with a room downstairs and a kitchenette and rooms upstairs is available. Full RV hookups (including cable TV) are available. If you're coming through during hunting season—October, November, December—or during the spring, call Mary or John Hoover in advance to see if any rooms are left.

MARFA

PRESIDIO COUNTY SEAT • 2,424 • (915)

Collar a copy of the film *Giant* starring Rock Hudson, Liz Taylor, and James Dean, and you'll get a good look at Marfa. The vistas are as grand today as four decades ago when this town was knee-deep in movie stars and everyone was an extra. The name Marfa comes from a Dostoevsky novel that a railroad official's wife was reading when tracks were first laid west. Cattle has been king since Milton Faver founded the Cibolo Creek Ranch south of town before the Civil War. Unlike Alpine with its university and Fort Davis with its fort, observatory, and state park, Marfa keeps to cattle and each November holds one of the top bull sales in America, the Highland Hereford Breeders Association sale.

TOURIST SERVICES

MARFA CHAMBER OF COMMERCE

131 E. San Antonio • P.O. Box 635 • Marfa • 79843
915-729-4942 • Monday–Friday 10–12 and 1–5

Tourist information, t-shirts, mugs, caps, and books and merchandise on the Marfa Lights are available.

GUIDEBOOKS AND PUBLICATIONS

BIG BEND SENTINEL

Box P • Marfa • 79843 • 915-729-4342
Annual subscription: $27

The best of the Big Bend's weekly newspapers, the *Sentinel*, is full of news about the Big Bend area and covers Marfa, Alpine, Fort Davis, and all the national and state parks.

MARFA LIGHTS

By Judith M. Brueske, Ph.D. • $6.95

Full of eyewitness accounts, this is the most comprehensive work on the Lights available. Pick up a copy at the Marfa Chamber or Ocotillo Enterprises in Alpine (*see* **ALPINE**).

BIRD'S-EYE VIEW

PRESIDIO COUNTY COURTHOUSE

Weekdays during office hours if custodian is available

The view from the fifth-story perch is more than adequate compensation for the 86 steps you'll climb en route. High among Marfa's many steeples, wrestle with the unwieldy set of binoculars and set your sights on the Big Bend's foremost tabernacle, Cathedral Mountain, clearly visible to the southeast.

MUSEUMS

CHINATI FOUNDATION

Highway 67, half a mile south of Marfa at Fort D.A. Russell
1 Cavalry Row • 915-729-4362 • Thursday–Saturday 1–5 or by
appointment • Free during regular hours • W

A not-for-profit arts organization, the Chinati Foundation is so out of place in Marfa that it actually fits in. The first aspect to the *Fundacion Chinati* worth noting is that the buildings that house the art also form an integral part of the collection.

The Chinati Foundation is committed to alternative museum forms, and in Marfa they selected a superb setting. The permanent installations of works by John Chamberlain, Claes Oldenburg, Roni Horn, Carl Andre, and Donald Judd are not ensconced in magnificent structures with designer nametags like Johnson, Pei, or Wright, but in a collection of renovated and reinterpreted buildings—including abandoned ones in town that the Foundation and Judd salvaged, and the remnants of Fort D.A. Russell, south of Marfa.

Secondly, consider that many of the works, particularly Judd's, were created to be integrated into their architectural surroundings, and in some instances—most notably at the Fort—the renovation of the often-dilapidated buildings was subsumed into the art. This becomes apparent not on a crowded October day during the foundation's open house (*see* **ANNUAL EVENTS**) but when you and a few others have the collection to yourselves during the off-season, i.e., the other 51 weeks of the year.

Finally, consider the art itself. It is not as intimidating as it first seems. Ask your guide for assistance and explanation. They are quite familiar with the art and often the artist.

Your guided tour begins at Fort D.A. Russell, where the most recent addition to the permanent collection is an installation by Kabakov. Entitled *Shkola No. Shest* ("school number six"), it's appropriate that the Russian tongue is used not only because of Kabakov's designs but because Marfa was named for a character from Dostoevsky's *The Brothers Karamazov*.

Your group and guide will then proceed into town to several other properties. Be sure to take the time to include a stop at the old Wool & Mohair house, which has been renamed the Chamberlain Building. More than 23 works by artist John Chamberlain are displayed; all feature his interpretations of salvaged automobile shells, pieced together and refitted.

OTHER POINTS OF INTEREST

MARFA LIGHTS
At Historical Marker on Highway 67/90, nine miles east of Marfa

When the sun goes down, the cars pull up. People who need an excuse to go parking late at night in the middle of nowhere have been pretending to look for the Marfa Lights for better than a century. Whereas the rest of the country winks at the mention of submarine races, the locals, tourists, and even accredited scientists have marveled at this unexplained phenomenon.

The first sighting was by Bill Ellison in 1883. Since then, the different interpretations of these nightly apparitions has expanded geometrically, particularly during Prohibition: St. Elmo's Fire, phosphorescent minerals, lanterns of massacred troops, and swamp gas. About the only good rule of thumb is that the more a car's windows are fogged up, the less chance of a confirmed sighting.

PRESIDIO COUNTY COURTHOUSE AND JAIL
Town Square

Presidio County ranks up there with Ellis and Wise counties for Texas's most picturesque courthouse. Certainly the setting is more dramatic. Built in Second Empire style for $60,000 in 1886, consider that renovation costs a century later totaled $350,000. Until 1993, the adjacent jail was the longest continually operated jail in the state.

SPORTS AND ACTIVITIES

Golf

MARFA MUNICIPAL GOLF COURSE
At the end of Golf Course Road • 915-729-4043
Tuesday through Sunday • Greens fee

Welcome to the highest golf course in Texas. At an altitude of 4,882 above sea level, your tee shots will travel appreciably farther due to the thinner air. You may not notice, however, because of the panoramic views. Many a bogey has been overlooked (and gone unrecorded) while taking in views of Cathedral Mountain south of Alpine, Blue Mountain west of Fort Davis, and Chinati Mountain south toward Mexico. Better holes include the par three sixth hole with a water hazard in front of the green and the par five number seven (495 yards) with a dogleg right. Hardest hole on the course is the par four ninth hole, also a dogleg right, at 425 yards.

SIDE TRIPS

SHAFTER, TEXAS
40 miles south of Marfa on US 17

There's more to Texas than just oil and gas. Try silver and gold. What's left of Shafter stands beside Cibolo Creek, beneath *las Tres Hermanas* (three peaks named for sisters Anita, Aurora, and Ida Brooks). From 1883 until 1942, the Shafter Mine produced more than $23,000,000 in silver ore as well as gold, lead, and zinc. With over 100 miles of tunnels, the mine supported a mill, a smelter, and men's and women's clubs for the more than 200 miners, machinists, and their families.

Shafter now boasts less than 50 residents and has a general store, a well-marked pay phone, and an historic cemetery. Drive past the Catholic church through town and across Cibolo Creek. The cemetery is dead ahead as is a chronology of the town courtesy of the Speed family. Movie fans note that portions of the silver screen version of Michael Crichton's *Andromeda Strain* were filmed locally.

ANNUAL EVENTS

April

MARFA OLD TIMERS ROPING
Presidio County Fairgrounds off of Golf Course Rd. • 915-729-4942

Not a fancy, made-for-TV event but an annual tradition among friends, the Old Timers Roping is sponsored by the Marfa Roping Club. This is a roping competition for a variety of age groups but featuring teams with at least one member over forty and a second member over sixty. The minimum combined ages must exceed 100 with some teams in the 115-plus bracket.

September

MARFA LIGHTS FESTIVAL
Presidio County Courthouse • 915-729-4942
(Chamber of Commerce) • Labor Day weekend
Free: Courthouse Lawn Festival • Admission: dance & concerts

People may argue about the existence of the Marfa Lights, but no one disputes the popularity of this shindig. Activities begin the Friday evening before Labor Day with a street dance by the Presidio County Courthouse (admission). On Saturday and Sunday, a Lawn Festival (no charge) is held at the courthouse from 10 a.m. until 5 p.m. with vendors selling arts and crafts as well as food.

Other than the nightly viewing of the Marfa Lights, the highpoints are concerts on Saturday night (admission) and Sunday evening (admission). Both concerts are usually held at the baseball field on the east side of town. Book in advance for this one. Seeing one of the Marfa Lights is probably easier than finding a room in Marfa, Alpine, or Fort Davis over Labor Day weekend.

October

CHINATI FOUNDATION OPEN HOUSE
Fort D.A. Russell • 915-729-4362

Local, national, and international friends of the *Fundacion Chinati* gather for art, film, and music as well as dining, drinking, and dancing. Everyone is invited to join in (*see* **MUSEUMS**).

RESTAURANTS

($ = Under $7.50, $$ = Under $15, $$$ = $15+ plus tax & tip)

BLUE MOUNTAIN DINER
104 East El Paso • 915-729-3949 • Breakfast, lunch, and dinner Monday–Saturday • Breakfast and brunch on Sunday

The sister operation of a popular Fort Davis eatery, the Blue Mountain serves a variety of salads, sandwiches, and specials as well as an excellent breakfast which will tide you over on any roadtrip round the Big Bend. Located a block south of the post office across the railroad tracks.

CARMEN'S CAFE
317 E. San Antonio (E. Highway 90) • 915-729-3429 Monday–Saturday • Breakfast, lunch, and dinner • $

Enjoy a *gordita* at Carmen's. This West Texas specialty is a deep-fried cornbread patty sliced open and stuffed with meat, lettuce, tomato, and cheese and topped with *guacamole* and sour cream. Don't forget to add *salsa*. Other good choices: the *chile colorado*, the *asado* plate, and the chicken *enchiladas*.

MIKE'S PLACE
111 S. Highland Ave (next to City Hall) • 915-729-8146 Monday–Friday 7–7 • Saturday 7–2 • $

Mike's specialty is some of the best chili in West Texas and an equally famous burger. For a Mexican fix, order the *chile verde* or the *menudo*. Open since 1952.

TUMBLEWEED GRILL
500 E. San Antonio Ave (E. Highway 90) • 915-729-4065 Tuesday–Saturday lunch and dinner • Sunday lunch • $–$$

Specializing in Angus steaks, smoked meats, and barbecue, the Tumbleweed is your first stop there on the right when you come into Marfa from Alpine and cross Alamito Creek. Daily lunch specials.

ACCOMMODATIONS

($ = Under $40, $$ = $40–$75, $$$ = $75–$100, $$$$ = Over $100)
Room Tax (in Marfa) 13%

CIBOLO CREEK RANCH
34 miles south of Marfa off Hwy 67
Tours by appointment only • 915-229-3737 • $$$$

If you think you've seen it all, head on down Shafter way. The Cibolo Creek Ranch is without compare nationwide, let alone in Texas. Old Fort Cibolo, constructed in 1857 by Milton Faver, has been renovated with the assistance of the Texas Historical Commission and, in the process, has received three National Historic Site designations and five Texas State Historical markers.

By choosing spring-fed Cibolo Creek for his headquarters, Faver took advantage of the ideal climate at his mile-high domain: moderate temperatures, low humidity, and plenty of shade trees. Guests can go hiking and view wildlife; the birding is outstanding. It only gets better indoors. Each of the rooms is furnished with western and Mexican antiques and features saltillo tile floors and traditional ceilings—cottonwood *vigas* and oak *latillas* and *rajas*. Most have fireplaces. You can't tell by looking, but central air and heat have been masterfully incorporated into the renovation.

Kudos to the ranch kitchen, which specializes in cross-cultural cuisine featuring Asian, American, and Mexican specialties. Each day's menu is influenced by the morning's harvest from the ranch's organic orchards and gardens. The nightly tariff includes all meals and non-alcoholic beverages. Complete banquet and catering facilities are available. Wine aficionados will appreciate Cibolo's cellar, which includes selections from California, the Pacific Northwest, France, Spain, Germany, and Italy. Add-ons include mountain tours, cooking classes, sporting clays, horseback riding, and alcoholic beverages.

The Cibolo staff can make arrangements for all off-ranch activities including day and overnight float trips on the Rio Grande, touring the nearby state and national parks, as well as visits to the University of Texas McDonald Observatory. The reservations office can also arrange for charter air transfers utilizing the ranch's 5,300-foot, fully-lit airstrip.

HOTEL EL PAISANO
207 N. Highland • 915-729-3145 • $$–$$$$

After entering the cool, dimly lit, tile-floored lobby, notice the black and white stills from the George Stevens production of Edna Ferber's novel *Giant* (1956). El Paisano was the headquarters for the crew. Throughout the lobby, placards and photos remind visitors of the heady days when Elizabeth Taylor, Rock Hudson, and James Dean strolled the streets of Marfa.

El Paisano was built in 1930 and entered into the National Register of Historic Places in 1978. Designed by Henry Trost, master architect for "arid America," El Paisano is a two-story property located on Highland Avenue, Marfa's central boulevard, directly across from the Presidio County Courthouse. The nine units are all suites of various sizes and come with fully equipped kitchenettes, TV (HBO), and coffee makers. Available in the building are a hotel restaurant, an indoor pool and sauna, a game room, gift shop, and beauty salon. No pets allowed. Government rates are available.

HOLIDAY CAPRI INN
MOTEL THUNDERBIRD
Highway 90 West • 915-729-4326 or 729-4327 • $

Both properties are located across Highway 90 from each other and are run out of the same office at the Trading Post of the Southwest. Both phone lines ring here, and it also serves as the front desk for all 52 rooms including singles, doubles, and triples (sleep six). Rooms include cable TV with basic channels only and phones (50¢ charge for local calls). Amenities include a pool shared by both properties, the Trading Post of the Southwest gift shop, an adjacent barber shop, and free baby beds.

MENTONE

LOVING COUNTY SEAT • 107 • (915)

You've heard about it, you've read about it, here's your chance to stop by and visit America's wealthiest county. Each year the runners-up jockey for silver and bronze, has-beens like Orange County, California, Westchester County, New York, and Fairfax County, Virginia. Mineral-rich Loving County always leads the pack. The last Texas county organized (1931), Loving County has the smallest population of any county or parish nationwide and was named for trail driver Oscar Loving, whom Robert Duvall portrayed as Gus in *Lonesome Dove*.

The only church is the former schoolhouse. There was no replacement—kids are bussed out of county for their lessons. There are no doctors, no hospitals, and, only two community organizations in Loving County: the 4-H Club and the County Historical Society.

Stop by the county's lone diner, the A&G Cafe, for breakfast, lunch, or dinner during the week or until 3 p.m. on Saturday. These folks know the meaning of a dollar—the Wednesday lunch special is steak. In the most recent federal election, better than 80 percent of the county's 107 citizens participated—which may go to prove that if more of us took the time to vote we might all be as well off as Loving County.

PECOS

REEVES COUNTY SEAT • 12,069 • (915)

More than any other watering hole in West Texas, Pecos has a lore about it that goes far beyond the state's borders. Besides claiming Pecos Bill and Calamity Jane, locals brag on the world's first rodeo—held in Pecos on July 4, 1883. All the hoopla goes with the word Indians used to describe the crooked river running down from New Mexico—*pecos*. White men used that same word to describe other riparian activity, however; to "pecos" a fellow meant to murder him and throw his body in the same crooked river with a rock overcoat.

Known officially as the Town of Pecos City, Pecos also achieved lasting fame as the source of the Pecos Cantaloupe. Once crops exceeded local demand, farmers began marketing the cantaloupes to the Texas & Pacific Railroad, whose arrival in 1881 put the town on the map. Situated at the intersection of Interstate 20 and US Highway 285, present-day Pecos is an important crossroads for West Texas and serves as a distribution center for far-flung farming, ranching, and oil and gas interests.

TOURIST SERVICES

PECOS CHAMBER OF COMMERCE
111 S. Cedar • P.O. Box 27 • Pecos • 79772 • 915-445-2406

Located right next to the West of the Pecos Museum off of US 285, the Pecos Chamber also serves as the visitor bureau. From the Chamber, it's a short stroll to the West of the Pecos Museum, Clay Allison's grave, and a replica of the Jersey Lilly Saloon.

MUSEUMS

WEST OF THE PECOS MUSEUM
Highway 285 and 1st St. • 915-445-5076
Monday–Saturday 9–5 • Sunday 2–5
Closed Thanksgiving Day and December 18–25 • Admission

Housed in over thirty rooms of the #11 Saloon (1896) and the adjacent Orient Hotel (1904), this two-story structure is one of the most complete historical museums between San Antonio and El Paso. Established in 1962, the extensive collection of Texana and Western American artifacts is housed in and around an Old West Saloon where a double killing occurred in 1896. Out back stands a replica of the Jersey Lilly and the grave of Clay Allison, the "Gentleman Gunfighter."

ANNUAL EVENTS

July

WEST OF THE PECOS RODEO
Reeves County Rodeo Arena • 800-588-7326
Weekend closest to the 4th of July

The world's oldest rodeo has evolved into a fully sanctioned PRCA event and is the highlight of Western Week. Activities are held all week including the Rodeo Parade downtown, the Old Timer's Reunion at the West of the Pecos Museum, the Golden Girl Pageant, Fiesta Night in Old Pecos, a Western Art Show and Sale at the Civic Center, and dances nightly.

August

PECOS CANTALOUPE FESTIVAL
Reeves County Civic Center • First weekend • Free

The pride of Pecos is its world-renowned cantaloupe. Pecos celebrates each year's crop with this weekend of cantaloupe eating, seed spitting, and a cantaloupe look-a-like contest. The Cantaloupe Fly-in Breakfast is held at the airport. Also on the agenda are a golf tournament, a softball tourney, and, for the serious athletes, a putt-putt golf competition.

October

REEVES COUNTY FALL FAIR
Reeves County Civic Center
Early October Thursday–Saturday • Admission fee for concert

The county fair is the biggest time in Pecos and includes a sanctioned World Championship Barbecue Beef Cook-Off at the Sheriff's Posse Arena, the livestock show at the Civic Center, and scores of vendors. Each year, a top *tejano* band performs at the rodeo arena. Past entertainers include Mazz, Emilio Navaira, the Texas Tornadoes, and La Mafia.

ACCOMMODATIONS

($ = Under $40, $$ = $40–$75, $$$ = $75–$100, $$$$ = Over $100)
Room Tax 13%

BEST WESTERN SUNDAY HOUSE
I-20 at Exit 40 • 900 W. Palmer
915-447-2215 or 800-528-1234 • $$

This single-level motor inn is located on the south end of town and has 104 smoking and non-smoking rooms. Rooms include TV (HBO) and phones (charge for local calls). Amenities include the Alpine Lodge Restaurant, complimentary coffee in the lobby, outdoor pool, same-day valet laundry, and free parking. Pets OK. AAA, AARP, commercial, and military rates are available.

PRESIDIO & OJINAGA

PRESIDIO COUNTY • 3,072 • (915)

STATE OF CHIHUAHUA • 40,000+ • (011 52 145)

Known nationwide for its scalding temperatures (rare is the summer day without temperatures over 100 degrees), Presidio and Ojinaga are situated on the historic Chihuahua Trail, one of the Southwest's great commercial routes. Both cities share a distinct past and a promising future. *La Junta de los Rios* is the centuries-old name for this area, site of the confluence of the Rio Grande and Mexico's Rio Conchos. For thousands of years, Native Americans were drawn to the fertile floodplain; early Spanish accounts (1581) mention some of the later settlements. Over the next century and a half, military men and missionaries attempted to subdue this area and settle *la Junta,* but *Presidio del Norte* (present-day Ojinaga) was too distant a town and too low a priority for long-lasting success.

Commerce, not conquest or converts, led to settlement and is the focus of Presidio and Ojinaga's future. The Chihuahua Trail bypassed El Paso and Santa Fe and led from Chihuahua City across the Big Bend via Presidio del Norte to San Antonio and the Gulf port of Indianola.

First traversed by the Connelly Expedition (1839), it brought traders and pioneers like Milton Faver (*see* **CIBOLO CREEK RANCH** under **MARFA**), John Spencer, John Burgess, and Ben Leaton (*see* **FORT LEATON STATE HISTORICAL PARK**). The old ruts of the Chihuahua Trail are the future of both cities. The passage of the North American Free Trade Agreement (NAFTA) was critical to this region, and, much like the confluence of *los Rios Grande y Conchos,* the intersection of US 67 and the South Orient Railroad here promises great fortunes to future pioneers.

TOURIST SERVICES

PRESIDIO INFORMATION CENTER AND GIFT SHOP
US 67 Business (next to the Post Office) • 915-229-4478
Daily from 9 a.m. to 6 p.m.

There's always someone here during business hours to take your call and help with directions and other questions. The gift shop stocks gifts crafted by Tarahumara Indians including dolls, clay figurines, wooden bowls, and the ubiquitous Tarahumara drums. Other items include Zapotec folk art, maps, books, and Presidio brand gourmet barbecue sauce.

HISTORIC PLACES

FORT LEATON STATE HISTORICAL PARK
Three miles east of Presidio along FM 170 • 915-229-3613
Park Superintendent • P.O. Box 1180 • Presidio • 79845
www.tpwd.state.tx.us/park/fortleat/fortleat.htm
Daily 8–4:30 • Admission • W

Fort Leaton, the historic outpost of Ben Leaton, serves as the western gateway to the Big Bend Ranch State Park. Three veterans of the Mexican-American War—Ben Leaton, John Spencer, and John Burgess—quit Chihuahua City after the war to seek their fortunes on the recently established Chihuahua Trail. Their arrival in 1848 and the mercantile business they established were the first American inroads in this area.

Leaton distinguished himself by acquiring an old Spanish garrison, *el Fortin de San Jose* "the Little Fort of Saint Joseph." *El Fortin* was built in 1773 by Spaniards stationed at *Presidio del Norte* (present-day Ojinaga) and was abandoned in 1810. Leaton traded with friend and foe, including Apaches and Comanches who bartered stolen livestock for gunpowder, lead, and arms. Ben Leaton quickly fell out of favor with locals and officials on both sides of the border.

A favorite Leaton boast was that his fort enclosed exactly one acre. The restoration of so large an adobe structure was a major undertaking. Renovation required 77,000 adobe bricks. Craftsmen with such skills—adobe brick making and laying—were found in Mexico. Brought to Fort Leaton, they crafted the bricks and applied the stucco finish using traditional methods. Tours of Fort Leaton include 25 of the fort's 40 rooms with exhibits and programs detailing the history of the Spanish, Mexican, Texan, and American colonizers. Several picnic sites are available.

OTHER POINTS OF INTEREST

BIG BEND RANCH STATE PARK
Western entrance at Fort Leaton State Historical Park
three miles east of Presidio on FM 170

See separate listing under **BIG BEND RANCH STATE PARK.**

SHOPPING

UETA
2403 O'Reilly • 915-229-3766
Monday–Saturday 10–6 • Sunday 12–5

UETA stores can be found at most major border crossings from Brownsville to San Diego. Originally designed to target Mexican nationals with brand-name, duty-free goods, *norteamericanos* can find bargains too. A quick pass through the Presidio store uncovered Lee jeans, Victorinox Swiss Army knives, Rolex watches, Calvin Klein perfumes and colognes, and Johnny Walker scotch at prices well below retail. For some items, such as a Rolex, alcohol, or cigarettes, you'll have to cross the border to receive your purchase, declare it, and pay a duty or tax before you can bring it back to the States. For the hardened shopper this only adds to the satisfaction of uncovering a bargain.

SIDE TRIPS

COPPER CANYON
For decades, West Texans have kept for themselves and their close friends an unspoiled Mexican getaway, *las Barrancas de Cobre.* Unlike Acapulco or Cancun, commercial development won't tarnish this jewel. The only way to enjoy the six-canyon journey is by train, twisting and winding across 39 bridges and through 86 tunnels during a 400-mile journey from Chihuahua City to Los Mochis on the Gulf of California. Local travel agents are well-versed with the itinerary which can vary slightly. **ALPINE TRAVEL** (915-837-3356), in Alpine, quoted a rate of $950 per person, double occupancy, for a professionally escorted Copper Canyon trip including two nights in Chihuahua City, one night en route to the coast, and one more down on the water.

PEGUIS CANYON
About 30 miles west of Ojinaga on the Chihuahua Highway

Imagine viewing Santa Elena Canyon from the top down. That's what this venture is for. Just as the Rio Grande slices through several canyons in Big Bend National Park, the Rio Conchos carves through the Peguis Mountains west of Ojinaga. No special vehicle permit or visa is required to drive to the overlook which is less than 45 minutes outside of Ojinaga via the Chihuahua Highway (Mexico 16). You'll park at the top of a long incline at the *area de descanso* (rest stop), and hike down a paved trail to spectacular vistas of sheer canyon walls and the Conchos. From Ojinaga, the road narrows to a paved, one-lane highway with speed limits up to 80 kph (less than 50 mph). Daytime forays are recommended.

ANNUAL EVENTS

May

ONION FESTIVAL
Downtown Presidio • 915-229-3199 (Chamber of Commerce)

Millions of years of rich sedimentary deposits along the Rio Grande and the Rio Conchos have developed a soil perfect for onion growing (melons, too). Locals celebrate this gift of nature with a parade, a 5K race, volleyball and softball tournaments, an arts and crafts bazaar, *folk-lorico* dancing, and dances Friday and Saturday nights featuring entertainers like Freddy Fender.

RESTAURANTS

CAFE ROSE'S
Next to the Three Palms Inn on Business 67 • 915-229-3998
Daily • Breakfast, lunch, and dinner • $–$$ • W

Ever had an *encharito?* Rose's is your best bet to sample this sliced beef and green *chile* (mild) treat, served in a flour *tortilla* and smothered in cheese. On the lighter side, order a *chalupa: frijoles*, lettuce, tomatoes, and *guacamole* on a corn tortilla. Scrumptious homemade desserts, particularly the pecan pie.

LAS PAMPAS
O'Reilly St. • 915-299-3552
Daily • Breakfast, lunch, and dinner • $–$$

After a professional soccer career in Argentina, Brazil, and Mexico, Gualberto Laperuta settled in Presidio, where he prepares Argentine, Italian, Mexican, and American specialties. Like Texans, Argentines love a good steak; order yours *churrasco*-style and enjoy this top sirloin cut served with Gualberto's own *chimichurre*. The popular *milanesa* is the choice of chicken-fried steak fans. The *huevos rancheros* are served all day long. Las Pampas and families go together; pizza, burgers, Mexican food, and a salad bar cover most hard-to-please appetites. Beer and wine.

ACCOMMODATIONS

THREE PALMS INN

Highway 67 Business • Presidio • 915-229-3211 • $–$$

This two-story, 42-room motel is located on what used to be Presidio's principal thoroughfare which has now been circumvented by the new Highway 67. Four non-smoking units are available. Rooms include cable TV (HBO) and phones with no charge for local calls. Ojinaga is not a local call. An outdoor pool and free parking are available. Cafe Rose's is right next door. Pets OK.

SIERRA BLANCA

HUDSPETH COUNTY SEAT • 758 • (915)

Named for the imposing 6,894-foot massif northwest of town, Sierra Blanca offers more than just a welcome break between El Paso and Van Horn. The mountains, canyons, and flats that comprise Hudspeth County have been important crossroads for centuries. Native Americans venturing to and from Old Mexico regularly stopped at springs 30 miles south of town (as did Pancho Villa, Gene Tunney, and former owner H. L. Hunt).

To curb Indian attacks along the Butterfield Overland Mail route, Fort Quitman was established just before the Civil War. Abandoned for the duration of the conflict, it eventually served as headquarters for the final effort to subdue Apaches under Victorio. (No remnants exist of either Fort Quitman or Fort Hancock, a sub-post of Fort Bliss.) Indian battles at Quitman Canyon and Rattlesnake Springs were among the state's last (1880), but it was Mexican forces who killed Victorio the following year to end the struggle.

Neither Indian nor soldier participated in Hudspeth County's best known fracas: the El Paso Salt War of the 1870s. Long before there was an El Paso, Mexicans from both sides of the Rio Grande led their *caretas* (two-wheeled ox carts) through the desert to salt flats still visible at the foot of the Guadalupe Mountains and the national park, roughly 100 miles east of El Paso. After the Civil War, the battle over who should profit from this windfall corrupted El Paso politicians and businessmen, as well as the parish priest at San Elizario. In addition to numerous murders and executions, vigilantism and looting, the Salt War marked the only known surrender by Texas Rangers to a hostile force and the reactivation of Fort Bliss.

Helpful Numbers

SIERRA BLANCA EXXON FOOD MART
209 E. El Paso St. • 915-369-2341 (24 hours)

You are unofficially in the middle of nowhere when you call on this AAA approved towing service to haul your vehicle to Van Horn, El Paso, or wherever, for service.

HISTORIC PLACES

RAILROAD DEPOT/HUDSPETH COUNTY MUSEUM
P.O. Box 411 • Sierra Blanca • 79851
Wednesday afternoons from 1 to 5
Free (donations accepted) • W (ramp around back)

America's second transcontinental railroad was completed in Sierra Blanca (1881), connecting the Texas & Pacific line with the Southern Pacific. The depot that houses the museum was built by the SP a year later (1882). Look out its back door depot toward Sierra Blanca Mountain and you'll see where the tracks merge. Inside you'll learn about the state's only adobe courthouse, the history of the state's third largest county, former residents such as Lt. George Patton (posted here during World War I), and the only known bombing of an American city during World War II.

RESTAURANTS

The Best Cafe, Michael's, and **Lina's** are Sierra Blanca's only restaurants with **Lina's** taking the honors with its easy-to-find location (by the Chevron station off I-10) and its regular hours (daily from 7 a.m. to 10 p.m.). The Exxon Station in town on Business Loop I-10 is open all night and offers deli sandwiches, snacks and beverages, as well as clean tables.

ACCOMMODATIONS

($ = Under $40, $$ = $40–$75, $$$ = $75–$100, $$$$ = Over $100)

EL CAMINO MOTEL
Business Loop I-10 • 915-369-3331 • $

There are 13 units at this recently renovated single-story property. All have cable TV (HBO). Pets OK. Group discounts available.

TERLINGUA

BREWSTER COUNTY • 50 • (915)

In the timeless view of Wick Fowler, "the only place on earth where a disaster would never be noticed, the town itself being a disaster." Since those fateful days in 1967, the choice of Terlingua for World Championship Chili Cook-offs has put this abandoned mining town back on the map. The annual event held the first weekend of each November draws crowds from all over the country to revel in raucous times and fiery foods. The rest of the year, Terlingua caters to the ever booming tourism industry in south Brewster and Presidio counties, offering wayfarers a laid-back look at life that this once abandoned ghost town is now famous for and an occasional glimpse of the pioneering days of this rugged last frontier of Texas.

Cinnabar—also known as quicksilver ore—was discovered locally in the 1890s. The Terlingua mining district extended from Study Butte to Lajitas and quickly became the largest supplier of mercury in North America. The Chisos Mine at Terlingua was the big producer and the region's largest employer pushing Terlingua's population close to 2,000 at its height. After World War II, the demand for cinnabar tapered and likewise Terlingua's fortunes. Brown & Root, the Houston-based mine owner, closed the Chisos Mine for the last time in 1946 and sold the town to Rex Ivey, whose family is currently renovating this south Brewster County landmark.

TOURIST SERVICES

TERLINGUA TRADING COMPANY
P.O. Box 362 • Terlingua • 78952 • 915-371-2234

The knowledgeable staff includes folks who can recall the first chili cook-off. Call or stop by for information on Terlingua, the rest of the Big Bend, and the latest chili cook-off updates.

SPORTS AND ACTIVITIES

Rafting

BIG BEND NATIONAL PARK
See separate listing.

SHOPPING

TERLINGUA TRADING COMPANY

P.O. Box 362 • Terlingua • 79852 • 915-371-2234
Daily 8–8 • ghostown@overland.net

You'll find this establishment right in the heart of the ghost town's booming commercial district. In addition to a good selection of books and maps, a wide variety of gifts are available: art, jewelry, and other handcrafted items from the desert Southwest and old Mexico.

ANNUAL EVENTS

November

FRANK X. TOLBERT—WICK FOWLER MEMORIAL CHILI COOK-OFF

CASI CHILI COOK-OFF (CHILI APPRECIATION SOCIETY INTERNATIONAL)

First weekend of November

What began as a culinary challenge over a quarter of a century ago has mushroomed into a Texas tradition. During the early part of cook-off week, travel trailers and RVs from across America arrive in Brewster County to stake a claim before the horde descends. By the weekend, more than 7,000 contestants, spectators, peace officers, and startled tourists show up. Once upon a time, almost 10,000 packed the old ghost town, site of the original cook-offs.

Bickering led to the establishment of two contenders. The Tolbert-Fowler Cook-off is held on the east side of the ghost town behind the Terlingua General Store. The CASI Cook-off has its own site on the west side of the ghost town. For purists, the chili competitions are the heart and soul of these events. For everyone else, the top priority is showmanship. A lot of time, effort, and alcohol go into the skits, costumes, and sets for this category. Champions are crowned Saturday; showmanship in the morning and chili judging around lunch.

BE ADVISED: With so many adults acting like children, neither chili cook-off is recommended for kids or even adults averse to plenty of bare flesh, open drunkenness, and the behavior that accompanies the two. Other caveats: Terlingua is in the heart of the Chihuahuan Desert. Temperatures during the cook-off can range from freezing to sweltering. With plenty of dust and even more rocks, don't dress for success. And if you plan to stay at any area lodge, get on the waiting list now.

RESTAURANTS

($ = Under $7.50, $$ = Under $15, $$$ = $15+ plus tax & tip)

Live music is served à la carte at most Terlingua restaurants. A good number of locals are either musicians or are into music, and almost every time you sit down for dinner, someone is behind a mike singing old favorites or making up new ones. More popular weekends find out-of-town performers on stage for bigger gigs.

LA KIVA RESTAURANT AND BAR

Where Terlingua Creek crosses FM 170 • 915-371-2250
Dinner daily • Sunday brunch 11–2 • $–$$ • MC V

Fred Flintstone was well into his Olmec phase when he put this place together. The bathrooms are worth a pit stop in themselves: big brass pots for basins and urinals. Descend into the dark, cavernous dining room for grilled entrées—fish, fowl, and beef. A welcome addition is the chicken Caesar salad, joining longtime menu mainstay *el Diablo Chili*. Bar.

STARLIGHT THEATER

Terlingua Ghost Town • 915-371-2326
Dinner daily • $–$$ • Checks not drawn on Terlingua banks

This theater was built in the late 1930s for local miners. At the end of World War II, Terlingua was dismantled and the theater sat roofless for almost half a century. Reroofed in October 1990, renovated in 1991, it reopened in 1992 to rave reviews as a restaurant and a club. The latest addition is a 20' × 30' mural by Stylle Read, *The Spirit of Terlingua*, right behind the stage. Happy hour starts at five, dinner is served till 9–9:30, and the bar shuts down at midnight (1:00 a.m. on Saturdays). The nightly specials are always a good bet, and there is live entertainment almost every evening. Bar.

ACCOMMODATIONS

See **BIG BEND NATIONAL PARK** *or* **LAJITAS.**

VALENTINE

JEFF DAVIS COUNTY • 217 • (915)

Valentine is the only Texas town to be hit by two earthquakes, but it is better known for amorous reasons. The Texas & New Orleans Railroad arrived here on Valentine's Day, 1882. Come late January and early February, over 20,000 Valentine's Day cards from all 50 states and scores of foreign countries are posted to this West Texas crossroads to be postmarked with the unique Valentine cancellation. To get yours postmarked and delivered in time for February 14th, place your stamped, addressed card(s) inside a larger envelope and mail to:

VALENTINE POST OFFICE
VALENTINE, TEXAS 79854-9998
ATT: VALENTINE DAY CANCELLATION

VAN HORN

CULBERSON COUNTY • 2,930 • (915)

Only a few miles east of the Mountain Time Zone, Van Horn serves as the crossroads of West Texas. Situated on Interstate 10, it's the largest and the last city east of El Paso before Interstate 20 branches off of Interstate 10. Consequently, millions of vehicles heading west from Dallas/Fort Worth, Houston, and San Antonio pass through these arid hills en route to the west coast and back.

In addition to the extensive east-west traffic, Van Horn sits between three national parks: Guadalupe Mountains and Carlsbad Caverns to the north on Highway 54 and Big Bend to the south on Highway 90. From stagecoaches in the mid-1800s to John Madden's Greyhound each football season (*see* **CHUY'S**), travelers rest and refuel at this watering hole on the southmost overland route across the U.S. Not surprisingly, it has more motels and gas stations than you'd expect for a town of less than three thousand.

TOURIST SERVICES

VAN HORN CONVENTION CENTER AND VISITORS BUREAU
1801 W. Broadway • P.O. Box 488 • 79855 • 915-283-2682

Located on the south side of Broadway at the west end of town. Brochures and other literature on nearby points of interest like national and state parks are available, as well as a thorough visitor guide which lists accommodations and restaurants.

SIDE TRIPS

BIG BEND NATIONAL PARK

See separate listing.

CARLSBAD CAVERNS NATIONAL PARK

See separate listing.

GUADALUPE MOUNTAINS NATIONAL PARK

See separate listing.

RESTAURANTS

($ = Under $7.50, $$ = Under $15, $$$ = $15+ plus tax & tip)

CHUY'S

1200 W. Broadway • 915-283-2066 • Daily
Breakfast, lunch, and dinner • $–$$ • AE MC V • W

The Garcias have been running a first-class operation since the late 1950s. Ask anyone who is familiar with West Texas or, if you get the chance, John Madden, former head coach of the Oakland Raiders and pro football color commentator. Madden travels cross-country by bus and lists Papa Chuy's restaurant among his preferred stops. He has even gone as far as designating one of Chuy's dining rooms "Madden's Haul of Fame," and each season he admits two pros into his elite pantheon based upon their eating prowess.

Like Madden, renowned travel experts David and Karen Lee require Chuy's Lime Freeze as mandatory rations on any trip to the Big Bend. This frozen concoction takes the heat out of a scorching West Texas afternoon and is an ideal palate cleanser prior to Chuy's sizzling *fajitas* plate. Jumper cables on-site.

SMOKEHOUSE RESTAURANT AND AUTO MUSEUM

905 W. Broadway (Highway 80) • 915-283-2453
Monday–Saturday • Breakfast, lunch, and dinner
Closed Sunday • $–$$ • AE D MC V • W

As the name implies, smoked meats are the specialty. One Smokehouse Special ought to be enough for the entire table—smoked brisket, ham, and sausage served with cole slaw, beans, mashed potatoes, and homemade bread. Plenty of other menu choices include smoked turkey and bacon, steaks, and Mexican food as well as rainbow trout, a fruit plate, and the chef's salad. Restaurant owners Mitch and Glenda Van Horn display their extensive automotive collection right off the main dining room. The display changes every other week and includes cars from the 1920s through the 1960s, as well as other automobilia.

ACCOMMODATIONS

($ = Under $40, $$ = $40–$75, $$$ = $75–$100, $$$$ = Over $100)

BEST WESTERN INN OF VAN HORN

1705 W. Broadway (Highway 80)
915-283-2410 or 800-528-1234 • $

This single-story motel has 61 smoking and non-smoking units including one suite. Rooms include cable TV (HBO) and phones (no charge for local calls). Amenities include a complimentary continental breakfast, the Westerner and the Iron Rail restaurants, outdoor heated pool, gift shop, convenience store on the property, laundry room, complimentary golf, and free parking. Pets OK. AAA, AARP, corporate, and group rates are available.

PLAZA INN

200 E. Golf Course Dr. • 915-283-2804 or 800-543-8831 • $

This two-story motel has 98 smoking and non-smoking units including handicapped-access rooms. Rooms include cable TV (HBO) and phones with free local calls. Amenities include the Chaparral Restaurant, the Sportsman Lounge, an outdoor unheated pool, laundry facilities, complimentary golf, and free parking. Pets OK. AAA, AARP, and commercial discounts are available.

PANHANDLE-PLAINS

The Panhandle-Plains extends from the Oklahoma border south to the Permian Basin. *Panhandle* is a simple term and refers to the northmost twenty-six counties in Texas. *Plains,* however, includes several regions. Like any part of the Great Plains, the Texas portion was created by debris that eroded from the Rocky Mountains. Local designations are numerous.

The region around Amarillo, including parts of the Panhandle, is called the High Plains. A second area, with Lubbock as its hub, is known as the South Plains. And a third region, south of the Canadian River and north of the Pecos, has been known for centuries as the *Llano Estacado* (*see* **MUSEUM OF THE LLANO ESTACADO**). Decades after the 49ers and the Butterfield Overland Mail plied Texas west of the Pecos, Comanches, *comancheros* (traders from New Mexico), and *ciboleros* (buffalo hunters) traversed these endless grasslands.

After the defeat of the Comanches at their Palo Duro Canyon camp (1874), settlement began. Grasslands once home to huge bison herds became the largest ranches in Texas history (*see* **DALHART**). Cattlemen, cowboys, and cattle drives quickly followed. Old Mobeetie and Tascosa, ghost towns today, embodied the Wild West with their saloons, bordellos, gunfights, and boot hill cemeteries. Far more valuable resources lay underground, ones that shaped the development of this region even more than beef production. The Ogallala aquifer, immense petrochemical reserves, and most of the world's helium are found under the Panhandle-Plains. The bustle above is a tribute to pioneers of both centuries.

PANHANDLE-PLAINS

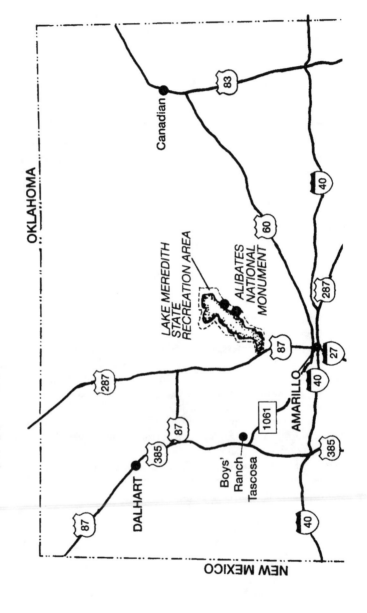

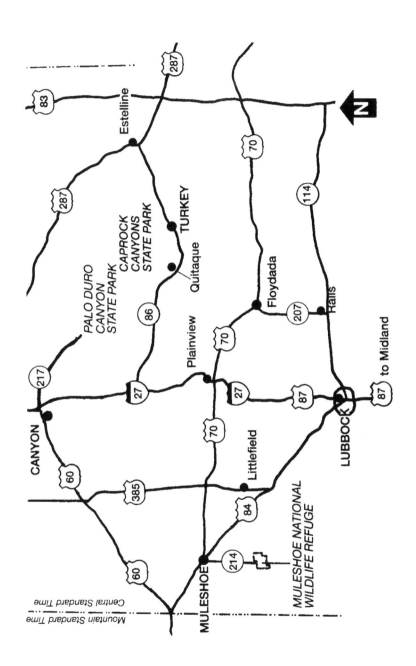

AMARILLO

POTTER AND RANDALL COUNTIES • 157,615 • (806)

Portions of West Texas, such as El Paso, were colonized over a century before the American Revolution. Others, most notably the Panhandle, saw no settlement until the end of the Red River War (1875). Within a few years, only one battle remained—to develop Amarillo. James Berry, Abilene's mastermind, settled that score by rigging the election for the county seat. Local cowboys got two lots in return for their vote, and Berry's site won.

During its first decade, Amarillo became America's largest rural shipping point for cattle. Millions of acres of ranch land on the LX, the JA, the T-Anchor, and the XIT gave rise to an industry that manifests itself in modern times at the **Amarillo Livestock Auction**, the world largest's weekly cattle auction (*see* **OTHER POINTS OF INTEREST**).

Other agricultural interests developed before the turn of the century as the multi-million-acre XIT began large-scale production of forage

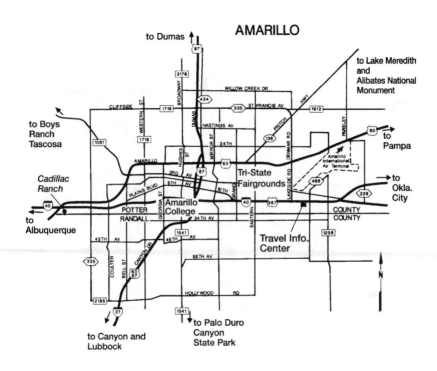

crops for cattle feed. Soon the enormous Ogallala aquifer was tapped, and millions of acres of cattle country were converted to croplands. The Panhandle Oil and Gas Field was discovered in 1916 and recognized as the world's largest by 1930 (just before oil was discovered in Arabia). Oil and gas, pipelines and refineries, carbon black and the world's largest helium field fueled Amarillo's growth. The city now serves as a regional and national crossroads and commercial center.

TOURIST SERVICES

AMARILLO CONVENTION AND VISITORS COUNCIL
1000 S. Polk • Amarillo • 79101 • 806-374-1497 or 800-692-1338
Monday–Friday 8–5 • W • www.amarillo-cvb.org

The Bivins home is the headquarters for Amarillo's tourism office. Here the staff offers the latest details on Amarillo activities.

TEXAS TRAVEL INFORMATION CENTER
I-40 East between Lakeside and Airport exits • 806-335-1441
Open daily 8–5 except New Year's and Christmas • W

The state-run info centers are staffed by trained travel counselors. Pick up a free copy of the *Texas State Travel Guide*, the best travel value in the state.

GUIDEBOOKS AND PUBLICATIONS

ACCENT WEST
$2.00 • Box 1504 • Amarillo • 79105 • 806-371-8411

This monthly offers a complete listing and accurate descriptions of area restaurants, clubs, and events.

MUSEUMS

AMARILLO MUSEUM OF ART
Amarillo College Campus • 2200 S. Van Buren • 806-371-5050
Tuesday–Friday 10–5 • Weekends 1–5 • Free • W+

Housed in a three-story facility designed by Edward Stone of Kennedy Center fame, the range of exhibits extends from antiquity to the present. The permanent collection emphasizes American moderns, including works by former Panhandle resident Georgia O'Keeffe.

AMERICAN QUARTER HORSE HERITAGE CENTER AND MUSEUM

I-40 East at Quarter Horse Drive • 806-376-5181
Summer hours: 9–5 Monday–Saturday • 12–5 Sunday
September through April: 10–5 Tuesday–Saturday
Admission • Gift shop • W+

With over three million quarter horses registered, this is the largest horse registry in the world. Designed to appeal to the novice as well as the veteran horseman, hands-on displays range from authentic starting gates to the real McCoy—genuine American quarter horses at the Demonstration Arena. In addition to the orientation show in the 70-seat Theater of America's Horse, two other video mini-theaters feature six programs and allow more select viewing of equine activities.

DON HARRINGTON DISCOVERY CENTER AND PLANETARIUM

Amarillo Medical Center • 1200 Streit • 806-355-9547
Tuesday–Saturday 10–5 • Sunday 1–5 • Free • W+
Planetarium shows daily in summer and weekends in winter
Admission • Gift shop • W+

Unless a school group is in attendance, most visitors to the Discovery Center are curious adults. Featuring temporary and permanent exhibits, the Discovery Center has several learning centers including an Exploration Gallery, the Construction Zone, and Kidscovery.

Outside by the Discovery Center parking lot is the **Helium Monument,** America's only above-ground time capsule. Erected in 1968, the first of the four columns was opened in 1993 (a 25-year wait). The other three are scheduled for 2018 (50 years), 2068 (a century), and 2968 (a millennium). The smart money says an almost fresh Collin Street Bakery fruitcake will be found in all three. Folks interested in helium, its production and uses in fields like cryogenics, press the button at the base of the monument. Right.

AIR & SPACE MUSEUM

English Field • 806-335-1812 • Hours vary

Sponsored by the Texas Aviation Historical Society, this working museum demonstrates aircraft restoration and hosts an air show annually.

HISTORIC PLACES

HARRINGTON HOUSE

1600 S. Polk St. • 806-374-5490 • April–December Tuesday and Thursday from 10 a.m.–12:30 p.m.

This 15,000-square-foot neoclassical mansion was built in 1914 by John and Pat Landergin, local ranchers. Acquired in 1940 by Don and

Sybil Harrington, visitors 14 and older are welcome to tour in groups of four or less by appointment only.

OTHER POINTS OF INTEREST

AMARILLO BOTANICAL GARDENS

**1400 Streit • 806-352-6513 • Monday–Friday 9–5
Center closes December 15–31 • Free • W**

Covering two acres, the gardens are open year-round and include an iris bed, a rose garden, and a scent garden.

CADILLAC RANCH

Just west of Amarillo's city limits

Few ranches in Texas history rival the Cadillac, where Amarillo native Stanley Marsh rides herd on ten vintage Cadillacs. Rumor has it that their angle of burial is parallel to the sides of the Great Pyramid of Cheops. If you're driving west, exit Arnot Rd. where a U-turn under the Interstate leads to the ranch. Those driving in from the west (New Mexico) should take the Hope Road/Helium Road exit (Exit 62A) and keep their eyes open. A well-worn path leads to the wrecks and perfect pictures every time.

LIVESTOCK AUCTION

**Western Stockyards • 100 Manhattan St. • 806-373-7464
Cattle auctions Tuesday at 9 a.m. except the weeks of
July 4th and Christmas**

If you think it stinks out here, remember what the locals say: it smells like money. Each year, by satellite or in person, buyers from across America close on over a quarter million cattle at the state's largest cattle auction. Tours are available daily, but call in advance for one on sale day. Mosey next door to the **Stockyard Cafe** for authentic cowboy fixings. Breakfast and lunch is on Monday through Saturday, and dinner is served Friday and Saturday nights. Prices are fair, the steaks are excellent, and MasterCard and Visa are accepted.

THOMPSON PARK

Just north of Amarillo on US 287 • Open around the clock • W

More than 600 acres of park land include a 36-hole golf course, an Olympic-sized swimming pool, Wonderland Park, and Storyland Zoo.

SPORTS AND ACTIVITIES

Amusement Parks

WONDERLAND AMUSEMENT PARK

Highway 287 north to Thompson Park
April–September weekends only • May–August daily
7 a.m. to 10 p.m. • Admission • W

The highlight is the Texas Tornado, which has been voted the best double loop, steel roller coaster in America. Other attractions include a 19-hole miniature golf course and the Rattlesnake River Raft Ride.

Chuckwagons

Each of these outfits offers a different way to see the Old West. All have toll free numbers. Call in advance for reservations and accurate prices.

BAR-H DUDE RANCH

Take US 287 south 54 miles to FM 3257 (three miles west of Clarendon) • North two miles to the Bar-H Dude Ranch on the left
806-874-2634 or 800-627-9871

Guest ranches serve up vittles, herd cattle, or perhaps put on a show. A dude ranch such as the Bar-H takes guests overnight, puts them up (in climate-controlled bunkhouses), serves meals prepared by a chuck-wagon crew, and offers a variety of daytime activities like working cattle, feeding livestock, or mending fences. If you came to play, try horseback riding, fishing, horseshoes, or relaxing poolside.

COWBOY MORNING

Take Interstate 40 east to Exit 77 • Head 27 miles south on FM 1258 to Cowboy Morning • 806-944-5562 or 800-658-2613

Originally part of the million-acre JA Ranch, the Figure 3 Ranch is run by the Christian family. Several generations ago, they helped settle the High Plains and even worked cattle for Charles Goodnight. Plan to arrive at the Figure 3 by 8:30 a.m. for the two-hour venture. Everyone piles into mule-drawn wagons to ride to the rim of Palo Duro Canyon where ranch hands serve up stunning scenery, steaming coffee, orange juice, fresh sourdough biscuits, sausage, gravy, and eggs. Steak is served at the dinner excursion where you'll sample the same panoramas enjoyed by millions of moviegoers who watched Harrison Ford and Sean Connery in *Indiana Jones and the Last Crusade*.

Golf

AMARILLO GOLF COURSE
Texas State College Campus • 806-335-1142

18-hole course

COMANCHE TRAILS GOLF COURSE
4200 South Grand • 806-378-4281

18-hole course

ROSS ROGERS GOLF COURSE
Adjacent to Thompson Park • 806-378-3086

36-hole course

Hunting

The Panhandle offers excellent bird hunting including golden pheasant, duck, and sandhill crane. Most property is privately owned, and a wide variety of native game and birds as well as exotics are available in an area covering over 300,000 acres.

Tennis

MUNICIPAL TENNIS CENTER
Austin Middle School • Elmwood and 26th • 806-378-4213

Eleven hardcourts and a pro shop with concessions and lessons.

COLLEGES AND UNIVERSITIES

AMARILLO COLLEGE
2201 S. Washington • 806-371-5000

A state and locally supported two-year institution with an enrollment of more than 5,000, the curriculum at AC ranges from vocational to academic. One of the highlights on campus is the Amarillo Arts Center (*see* **MUSEUMS**), which is part of a three-building, Edward Stone-designed complex that also includes indoor and outdoor theaters and a sculpture court. Prominent AC alumni include G. William Miller, Secretary of the Treasury under Jimmy Carter, and Ben Sargent, Pulitzer Prize-winning editorial cartoonist for the *Austin American-Statesman*.

PERFORMING ARTS

AMARILLO CIVIC CENTER
3rd and Buchanan • 806-359-5491 • W+

This 270,000-square-foot facility hosts everything from ice capades to rodeo to Broadway as well as the Amarillo Symphony and other concerts.

AMARILLO LITTLE THEATRE
2019 Civic Circle • 806-355-9991 • Admission • W

The longest continually performing little theater in the United States. Four productions are scheduled each year, including a drama, a musical, and a children's show.

AMARILLO SYMPHONY
Civic Center Music Hall • 806-376-8782 • Admission varies • W+

An Amarillo tradition since 1924. The season runs from September to April featuring half a dozen concerts, including a holiday production of *The Nutcracker* with the Lone Star Ballet.

LONE STAR BALLET
Civic Center Auditorium • 806-372-2463 • Admission varies • W+

What do those performers from the musical *TEXAS* do when summer ends? They band together and perform *The Nutcracker* with students from West Texas A&M and the Amarillo Symphony. Call for a complete schedule of performances and prices.

SHOPPING

OLD SAN JACINTO ANTIQUES AND CRAFTS ON HISTORIC ROUTE 66
6th Street between Georgia and Western • 806-374-0459
Most shops open Monday–Saturday 10–5:30 and Sunday 1–5

Not too long ago, this section of town was a rundown historic district. Only two miles west of downtown (just stay on Sixth), it has some of Amarillo's best antique shopping as well as several enjoyable watering holes and eateries including the **Garden Light Cafe** and the **Neon Grill**.

WESTGATE MALL
Interstate 40 West at Coulter or Soncy • 806-358-7221
Monday–Saturday 10–9 • Sunday 12:30–5:30

Right off I-40 on the city's western edge, Westgate has over a hundred stores and a six-screen theater. Major department stores include Sears, Dillard's, Mervyn's, Beall's, and J.C. Penney.

SIDE TRIPS

PALO DURO CANYON STATE PARK

Highway 217 • Canyon • 806-488-2227
www.tpwd.state.tx.us/park/paloduro/paloduro.htm

A scenic shortcut via South Washington Street (FM 1541) goes directly to Highway 217 and the park and shaves several miles off the usual 20-minute drive. The foolproof method is to follow I-27 south to Canyon and the Palo Duro Canyon State Park exit. See separate listing under **CANYON**.

ALIBATES FLINT QUARRIES NATIONAL MONUMENT
LAKE MEREDITH NATIONAL RECREATION AREA

40 miles northeast of Amarillo on Texas 136 • Follow signs
Superintendent • Lake Meredith National Recreation Area
P.O. Box 1460 • Fritch • 79036 • 806-857-3151
www.nps.gov/alfl/ • www.nps.gov/lamr/

The Panhandle town of Fritch serves as the headquarters for the region's most visited attraction—Lake Meredith—as well as Alibates Flint Quarries National Monument and the Lake Meredith Aquatic and Wildlife Museum. Activities on the lake include boating, waterskiing, fishing, and swimming. Boat ramps and a full service marina are available, including boat rentals. Fish for largemouth, smallmouth, and white bass, carp, catfish, white crappie, sunfish, and walleye.

Alibates Flint Quarries National Monument preserves a site of human habitation that dates back at least 12,000 years. The flint quarries were a natural draw for prehistoric man. Flint from Alibates was crafted into tools and used for trade for thousands of years until 1870. The quarries and flint mining villages can be viewed only by free guided tours. Contact the superintendent's office for details on tours, which must be ranger-led.

Run by the City of Fritch, the Lake Meredith Aquatic and Wildlife Museum has five aquariums, including the Panhandle's largest, and six dioramas featuring area wildlife.

CAL FARLEY'S BOYS RANCH
JULIAN BIVINS MUSEUM • OLD TASCOSA

Take Tascosa Road (RR 1061) 34 miles northwest from Amarillo to US 385 • The Boys Ranch entrance is two miles north off U.S. 385
806-372-2341 • Open daily from 8–5 • Free • Gift shop

Tascosa was the cowboy capital of the western Panhandle. Established in 1876 near the Canadian River by Hispanic *pastores* (shepherds), it was the seat of Oldham County as well as the judicial center for the western Panhandle's numerous unorganized counties. In addition to serving ranches like the XIT, the LIT, the LX, and the LS, Tascosa was the starting point for cattle drives to Kansas, Colorado, and Montana. Proof of the town's notoriety is its boot hill cemetery. Take your first right after entering the Boys Ranch and you'll find it atop the passable dirt to the right of the Boys Ranch Cemetery. The 20-odd occupants include plenty of gunslingers. In some cases the cause of death was accidental or even natural, but a March 26, 1886, shootout claimed four *hombres.*

Before the 1880s were up, the Fort Worth and Denver Railroad had bypassed Tascosa by a mere two miles; the town's days were numbered. Vega (24 miles south by US 385) eventually became county seat. The original Oldham county courthouse, the Panhandle's second, still stands at Boys Ranch; it houses the Bivins Museum. The world famous Boys Ranch was founded in 1939 by Mr. Farley. More than 4,000 boys ages four to eighteen have been schooled along the Canadian Breaks on this 10,000-acre ranch.

CANADIAN, TEXAS

100 miles northeast of Amarillo via US 60 east (93 miles) and US 60/83 north (7 miles) • 806-323-6234 (Chamber of Commerce)

Named for the nearby Canadian River, the county seat of Hemphill County is renowned for its autumn colors. Since the 1950s, a Fall Foliage Festival has been held in and around Canadian, Lake Marvin, and the Black Kettle National Grassland featuring driving and walking tours, a sanctioned rodeo and chili cook-off, and historic home tours. The **River Valley Pioneer Museum** (806-323-6548) houses dinosaur bones, Indian artifacts, and plenty of more recent Panhandle history.

ANNUAL EVENTS

September

TRI-STATE FAIR

Bell and 10th at the Fairgrounds • 806-376-7767
Third week of the month • Admission • Parking • W

The Panhandle is closer for many out-of-staters than their own state fairs. More than 250,000 participants and spectators visit the Tri-State Fair to compete in the livestock show, to listen to nationally-known entertainers, and to enjoy the midweek carnival.

RESTAURANTS

($ = Under $7.50, $$ = Under $15, $$$ = $15+ plus tax & tip)

For up-to-date reviews, refer to *Accent West* magazine.

BIG TEXAN STEAK RANCH

I-40 East at Lakeside Exit • 806-372-7000 or 800-657-7177
Daily • Lunch and dinner • Cr • $–$$ • W+

Tens of thousands have taken the challenge: Finish the Big Texan in less than an hour and the $50 tab is on the house. Before you place your order, consider your chances—less than 20 percent—and your portion—a 72-ounce side of beef, as well as a baked potato, a shrimp cocktail, salad, and a roll. No leaving the table and no barfing. Try instead the rattlesnake, rabbit, Rocky Mountain oysters, or a buffalo burger. Dinner shows run nightly and include musicals, cowboy poetry, a melodrama, and the opry. Bar.

LA FRONTERA

1401 S. Arthur • 806-372-4593 • Tuesday–Saturday late breakfast, lunch, and dinner • Sunday breakfast and lunch Closed Monday • $ • Cr

The old Cuellar Grocery (1939–1975) has new life now that one of Juan Cuellar's grandsons, Greg Martinez, and his wife Mary have opened *La Frontera.* Try a *burrito;* it's made with beef tips, not ground beef. Or choose from other plates that Greg himself cooks: the soft *tacos,* the *enchiladas,* the *tostadas,* and the *carne guisada* served either regular or spicy. Located just east of downtown in the heart of Amarillo's *barrio,* the kitchen uses fresh meats, horns of Colby cheese, and homemade *tortillas.* You bring the beer.

OHMS GALLERY CAFE

619 S. Tyler (Atrium Plaza) • 806-373-3233 Monday–Friday lunch • Friday–Saturday dinner Closed Sunday • $–$$ • MC V • W

A cafeteria-style eatery. Signature dishes include pork loin and chicken breast with cornbread stuffing. There are always several vegetarian dishes to choose from. Be sure to go with several friends—the kitchen has its own fudge kettle and serves slabs by the pound. Specialty teas, beer, and wine.

SCOTT'S OYSTER BAR

4150 Paramount • 806-354-9110 • Monday dinner Tuesday–Saturday lunch and dinner • Closed Sunday • $

"If you're in a big hurry, Long John Silver's is down the street." Get the picture? The Oyster Bar is a popular Amarillo night spot with favorites like boiled shrimp, fried oysters, po-boys, and oysters on the half shell. Shrimp creole, crawfish etouffée, and other specials are served regularly. Beer and wine coolers.

VAN DYKE'S

210 W. 6th just west of Polk St. • 806-373-1441 Monday–Saturday breakfast and lunch • Closed Sunday • $

It seems like forever to most natives, but it was only the late 1950s when Red Van Dyke first started serving some of the best breakfasts in the Panhandle smack dab in the heart of downtown Amarillo. Norma Murphy spent three years working for Mr. Van Dyke and has owned Van Dyke's for over a decade since then. Breakfast is the busiest part of the day (particularly Saturdays). Real ham, homemade sausage, and omelettes have made Van Dyke's an Amarillo institution. Though breakfast steals the thunder, the lunch menu has plenty of good home cooking: meatloaf, chicken-fried steak, and daily specials. Just north of the tallest building in town.

CLUBS AND BARS

HUMMER'S SPORTS CAFE

2600 Paramount • 806-353-0723 • Bar stays open until 2 a.m. except Sundays until 12 a.m. • Kitchen is open during the week until 11 p.m. • Friday & Saturday until 12 a.m. • Sunday until 10 p.m.

Unlike most sports bars—crowded with potbellied wannabees clad in coaching shorts—Hummer's attracts all ages and all physiques. Families enjoy the casual menu and laid-back atmosphere, fans head right to the photos of championship teams from years gone by, and the dozen TVs cover all sports. Over 50 different beers are served at the full bar.

ACCOMMODATIONS

($ = Under $40, $$ = $40–$75, $$$ = $75–$100, $$$$ = Over $100)
Room Tax 13%

AMARILLO HOLIDAY INN

1911 Interstate 40 at Ross Rd. • 806-372-8741 or
800-HOLIDAY • $$–$$$

This four-story hotel has 247 units including one suite and non-smoking rooms with cable TV (Showtime) and pay-per-view movies, room phones (charge for local calls), fire sprinklers, smoke detectors, and visual alert systems in all rooms. Amenities include a hotel restaurant and lounge, an indoor pool with sauna, jacuzzi, and whirlpool as well as an outdoor deck, exercise room, game room, billiards, gift shop, courtesy shuttle to Amarillo Airport, complimentary breakfast with the Best Breaks rate, free parking, and truck parking. Pets OK. Kennels available with advance notice. AAA, AARP, corporate, government, and military rates available.

BIG TEXAN MOTEL

I-40 East at Lakeside Exit • 806-372-5000 or 800-657-7177 • $–$$

Follow the billboards to the world-famous Big Texan Steak Ranch (*see* **RESTAURANTS**) and you'll be across the parking lot from this two-story motel. Inexpensive and clean, the Big Texan has 52 smoking and non-smoking rooms; all have big brass beds. Rooms include cable TV (HBO) and pay-per-view movies and phones with free local calls. Amenities include a complimentary continental breakfast, an outdoor Texas-shaped pool (closed in the winter), and plenty of free parking. Small pets are OK.

LA QUINTA—MEDICAL CENTER
I-40 West at Coulter exit • 806-352-6311 or 800-531-5900 • $$

This three-story motor inn has 129 rooms including suites and non-smoking rooms with cable TV (Showtime) and pay-per-view movies, and room phones (free local calls). Amenities include complimentary continental breakfast from 6:30 to 9:30, complimentary coffee in the lobby, a Waffle House restaurant next door, outdoor heated pool open from May through September, and free parking. Pets under 25 pounds welcome.

RADISSON INN AMARILLO AIRPORT
Interstate 40 at Lakeside Dr • 806-373-3303 or 800-333-3333
$$–$$$

A two-story hotel, the Radisson is right by the airport and has 207 smoking and non-smoking units including suites and handicap rooms. All rooms have cable TV, pay-per-view movies, and phones with free local calls. Amenities include the Steakery restaurant, the Garden Cafe, the Silver Dollar Piano Bar, the Krystal Palace Night Club, exercise facilities, an indoor atrium pool with hot tub, game room, gift shop, same-day valet laundry, laundry room, complimentary airport transportation, and free parking. No pets. AAA rates available.

Bed & Breakfasts

GALBRAITH HOUSE BED & BREAKFAST INN
1710 S. Polk St. • 806-374-0237 • $$

It's hard to imagine that a B&B could be so centrally located, but Galbraith House is about a block from the intersection of Interstate 27 and Interstate 40. The 1912 two-story prairie-style home was built for H. W. Galbraith, co-founder of the Foxworth-Galbraith Lumber Company, and was constructed with three-inch-thick doors, parquet floors, and scores of handcrafted details.

The owners, internationally renowned soprano Mary Jane Johnson and her husband David, have furnished the five bedrooms (each with private bath) much like when their family lived here. Autographed posters from Mary Jane's performances in the U.S., Canada, and Europe line the halls. Breakfast is served in the dining room or the solarium. Limited smoking area.

PARKVIEW HOUSE
1311 S. Jefferson • 806-373-9464 • $$–$$$

Parkview offers two rooms with private baths and three with shared baths. In addition, a hot tub and sauna can be enjoyed while sampling complimentary beverages. Breakfast is served in the kitchen, out in the dining room, or on the porch. Ask about children. No smoking. No pets.

CANYON

RANDALL COUNTY SEAT • 11,365 • (806)

The combination of West Texas A&M, Palo Duro Canyon State Park, and the *TEXAS* musical makes Canyon an unusual Texas town— small enough to stay friendly yet with enough diversity to be enjoyable. Canyon is known as much for its role in Texas history as for attractions like the park and the university. Quanah Parker's band of Comanches wintered in Palo Duro Canyon, and their defeat by the U.S. Cavalry under Colonel Ranald Mackenzie (1874) was the last major Indian battle in the Lone Star State. Two years later, Charles Goodnight stocked the JA Ranch with 1,600 cattle trailed south from Colorado and brought large-scale ranching to the Panhandle. Stop by the Panhandle-Plains Historical Museum to view the T-Anchor Ranch headquarters (1877). Built by Leigh Dyer, a brother-in-law of Goodnight's, it's the oldest surviving structure in the Panhandle and formed the nucleus for this High Plains university town.

TOURIST SERVICES

SAD MONKEY RAILROAD

P.O. Box 952 • Canyon • 79015 • 806-488-2222
Weekends year-round • Daily April through September • W
Admission • $2.50

The Sad Monkey is a narrow-gauge railroad and follows a 30-minute, two-mile loop to areas not accessible by cars. The tour includes a concise presentation on the park's history.

MUSEUMS

PANHANDLE-PLAINS HISTORICAL MUSEUM

West Texas A&M Campus • 806-656-2244
Monday–Saturday 9–5 (until 6 p.m. June–August)
Sundays 2–5 • Free • Gift shop • W+

Budget plenty of time for the state's oldest (1933) and largest museum. An art deco masterpiece, the main building anchors the south boundary of West Texas A&M and houses more than three million artifacts. Look above the entrance doors and note the brands of pioneer ranches. Inside, the collection is grouped into five specialties: dinosaurs, western heritage, fine art, vintage autos, and the Don Harrington Petroleum Wing which features an informative film on one of the state's greatest boomtown's, Borger. Outside, the original T-Anchor Ranch House stands reconstructed with windmill and outbuildings.

OTHER POINTS OF INTEREST

PALO DURO CANYON STATE PARK
Highway 217 • 12 miles east to Park Rd. 5 • 806-488-2227
www.tpwd.state.tx.us/park/paloduro/paloduro.htm
Daily • Entrance fee • W

Visually attractive and historically significant, the name Palo Duro is Spanish for "hard wood," a reference to the plentiful junipers in this 100-mile-long canyon. Hundreds of millions of years are exposed in the red-stained rocks, and many picturesque formations are visible within the park's 16,000 acres including the famous Lighthouse Formation. Spanish explorers camped here in 1541, so did generations of Comanches. You can tour it best by car or by taking a ride on the Sad Monkey Railroad (*see* **TOURIST SERVICES**). Picnic sites, hiking trails, mountain bike trails, riding stables, and over 100 campsites are available ranging from primitive to RV.

SIDE TRIPS

MUSEUM OF THE LLANO ESTACADO
1900 W. 8th St. • Plainview • 79072 • 806-296-4735
Take I-27 60 miles south from Canyon to Plainview
9–5 weekdays • 1–5 on weekends (March–November only)
Free • W+

If your trip south from Canyon or Amarillo includes Plainview, take a breather at this first-rate facility featuring 20th century *llano* history as well as its formation over 200 million years ago. See separate listing under **LUBBOCK**.

COLLEGES AND UNIVERSITIES

WEST TEXAS A&M UNIVERSITY
2501 Fourth Ave. • 806-656-2000

Founded in 1910, WTAMU is the only institution within 150 miles to grant bachelors and masters degrees. Enrollment is over 6,600 with three-quarters of the student body from the 26-county Panhandle region. The curriculum includes more than 140 undergraduate majors and 40 master's programs from five different colleges. Two WTAMU institutes have developed national reputations: the Dryland Agriculture Institute and the Alternative Energy Institute, the state's principal center for wind research.

PERFORMING ARTS

TEXAS MUSICAL

Pioneer Amphitheatre in Palo Duro Canyon State Park
TEXAS Tickets • Box 268 • Canyon • 79015 • 806-655-2181
Nightly except Sunday from mid-June to late August
Barbecue buffet begins at 6:00 p.m. • Admission
Performance begins at 8:30 p.m. • Admission
Free parking • Snack bar • Gift shop • No credit cards

With 30 seasons and more than two million spectators to its credit, the Official Play of the State of Texas is alive and well in Palo Duro Canyon. Acknowledged as the best attended outdoor drama in the nation, *TEXAS* was written by Pulitzer prize winner Paul Green, is set in the 1880s, and comes complete with cowboys, Indians, and early settlers. The Pioneer Amphitheater, a natural stage with its 600-foot backdrop, showcases the presentation.

RESTAURANTS

($ = Under $7.50, $$ = Under $15, $$$ = $15+ plus tax & tip)

DOS CABALLEROS

711 23rd Street • 806-655-7734 • Tuesday–Sunday
Lunch and dinner • $ • AE D V MC • W

Stop in for delicous *fajitas* (chicken or beef) or the *enchiladas*. For a taste of everything, try the combination plates, particularly #2 and #3.

COPE'S CONEY ISLAND

2201 Fourth Ave. (just west of WTAMU) • 806-655-1184
Monday–Saturday • Breakfast, lunch, and dinner
$ • Checks • W

With less than three dozen seats, this Canyon eatery defines down-home. Hope that you stop by Tuesday (all-you-can-eat fried chicken) or Saturday (all-you-can-eat fried fish). Otherwise, enjoy a club steak ($). Cope's homemade pies are a local favorite. Choose from half a dozen, fresh from the oven, including the rare opportunity to sample a slice of Jeff Davis Pie.

CLUBS AND BARS

Get out of town. This precinct is dry.

ACCOMMODATIONS

($ = Under $40, $$ = $40–$75, $$$ = $75–$100, $$$$ = Over $100)

BED & BREAKFASTS

HISTORICAL HUDSPETH HOUSE

1905 4th Ave. • $$ • Cr • 806-655-9800

Dave and Sally Haynie have brought new life to Mary Hudspeth's famed home. Miss Hudspeth, longtime faculty member and a former dean at West Texas Normal College, was a prominent Canyon hostess who set a celebrated table. Among the invitees was Georgia O'Keeffe, one of West Texas Normal's early instructors. The two-story Victorian has five rooms, three with private baths. Seven fireplaces, a jacuzzi, spacious common areas, and the Georgia O'Keeffe Dining Room round out the 1909 home. A full breakfast is served either in the dining room or in guest rooms; other meals are available by reservation. Well-behaved children are welcome.

DALHART

DALLAM COUNTY SEAT • 6,246 • (806)

Dalhart's history includes chapters on the largest ranch in Texas— the XIT, the largest state capitol in America—in Austin, and the largest free barbecue in the world—the XIT Reunion each August. Most of the rest of the year, residents tend their crops, graze their cattle, and cater to truckers and tourists crossing Texas to and from New Mexico, Colorado, and Oklahoma.

MUSEUMS

XIT MUSEUM

108 E. Fifth • 806-249-5646 (Chamber of Commerce)
Tuesday through Saturday 2–5 • 9–5 during the XIT Reunion
Closed December 24th through January 2nd • Free • W

A visit to the XIT Museum is an opportunity to learn about the largest ranch in Texas history. At its height, the 3,000,000-acre XIT Ranch had nine divisions, 94 fenced pastures, 335 water wells, and 500 windmills. The XIT came about because the cash-poor state, worn thin by Reconstruction, swapped three million acres of the public domain for construction of the present state capitol. Bailey, Castro, Cochran, Dallam, Deaf Smith, Hartley, Hockley, Lamb, Oldham, and Parmer counties—ten in all—combined to form this tract, hence the name XIT (ten in Texas). The deal was a bargain for the state, whose vast holdings were slightly diminished at a value more than twice the market rate of 50¢ an acre.

OTHER POINTS OF INTEREST

EMPTY SADDLE MONUMENT
Highways 87 North and 285 on the north side of town

Traditionally, a riderless horse symbolizes a fallen soldier. This monument honors deceased XIT cowboys and was erected to memorialize one widow's wish that her husband not be forgotten.

ANNUAL EVENTS

August

XIT RODEO AND REUNION
Rita Blanca Park • 806-249-5646 • First Thursday, Friday, and Saturday • Admission to rodeo and dances

The world's largest amateur rodeo is combined with the world's largest barbecue to celebrate the largest ranch in Texas history (*see* **MUSEUMS**). A Reunion Parade, a children's rodeo, Pony Express races, and the XIT Arts and Crafts Show are also held.

LUBBOCK

LUBBOCK COUNTY SEAT • 192,704 • (806)

Here's a simple geography lesson that can save lives. Most Texans (and plenty of other fine folks) know that if the Lone Star State were a pan, then the top 26 counties would form its handle. What people don't realize is the price you can pay for mistakenly including Lubbock County and Lubbock, Texas, in that grouping. It is true that Lubbock is situated on the southern reaches of the Great Plains, which also includes the Panhandle. However, the Panhandle does not extend as far south as Lubbock County, and Lubbock is proudly known as the Hub City of the Plains, not the Panhandle.

LUBBOCK

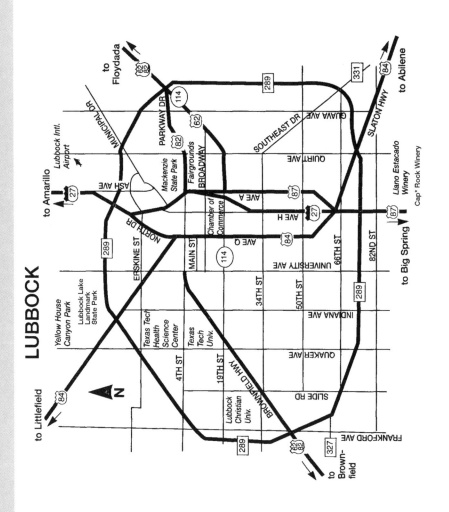

Lubbock was named for Thomas Lubbock, who commanded Terry's Texas Rangers. Situated atop the huge Ogalalla aquifer, the Lubbock area quickly evolved into one of America's foremost farming regions. Tiny O'Donnell, Texas, home to Dan Blocker of *Bonanza* fame, was the world's leading cotton baler in 1961. Over 20 percent of America's cotton is produced locally, and the Lubbock area leads Texas in grapes under cultivation. Though agribusiness is an enormous part of the local economy, Lubbock is a diverse city offering educational opportunities like Texas Tech University and Lubbock Christian University and some of the best medical care between Dallas and the west coast, with half a dozen hospitals and research centers.

TOURIST SERVICES

LUBBOCK CONVENTION AND VISITORS BUREAU

1301 Broadway Suite 200 • Lubbock • 79401
806-747-5232 or 800-692-4035 • www.lubbocklegends.com
Weekdays 8–5 • W

Brochures and information on area activities and attractions are available at this visitors center.

CITIBUS TROLLEYS

Daily throughout downtown • 806-767-2380 (routes and times) • W

Lubbock has one of the better urban acronyms for this transit system, COLT, which stands for City of Lubbock Trolley. You've probably seen these superbly crafted brass and mahogany vehicles in Austin, Brownsville, or San Antonio, and Lubbock's trolleys have the same function: short, highly touristed routes in the heart of downtown.

GUIDEBOOKS AND PUBLICATIONS

LUBBOCK TRAVEL GUIDE

Lubbock Convention & Visitors Bureau
806-747-5232 or 800-692-4035

Give the folks at the CVB a call, and they'll be glad to send out a handy 16-page publication featuring where and when to go, what to do for fun and food, and where to stay.

MUSEUMS

FINE ARTS CENTER

2600 Avenue P • 806-767-2686
Monday–Friday 9–5 • Saturday 10–4 • Free

Visual arts such as painting, photography, and sculpture are displayed on a rotating basis. Cultural programs ranging from dance to music are also regularly presented.

MUSEUM OF TEXAS TECH UNIVERSITY

4th and Indiana • 806-742-2490
Tuesday–Saturday 10–5 • Thursday until 8:30
Sunday 1–5 • Free admission to main museum

The collections of the Museum of Texas Tech University include more than 1,500,000 objects. The full extent of the Museum is apparent when you consider that it also includes the adjacent **Moody Planetarium**, the **Ranching Heritage Center** next door, and educational and research programs at the **Lubbock Lake Landmark**, as well as the **Natural Science Research Laboratory**. Self-guided tours of the main museum, the Ranching Heritage Center, and the Lubbock Lake Landmark are available, as well as guided tours at the Lubbock Lake Landmark and daily shows at the Moody Planetarium.

LUBBOCK LAKE LANDMARK STATE HISTORICAL PARK

Off Loop 289 on the northwest edge of Lubbock • 806-765-0737
Tuesday–Saturday 9–5 • Sunday 1–5 • Admission
www.tpwd.state.tx.us/park/lubbock/lubbock.htm

This 307-acre park is the only known continually inhabited site in the South Plains region over the past 12,000 years. Life on the South Plains from prehistoric times up to its settlement is presented via self-guided and guided tours.

MOODY PLANETARIUM

4th and Indiana • 806-742-2490 • Shows begin at 2 p.m.
Tuesday–Friday • 2 and 3:30 on weekends
Admission: Adult $1, children 50¢

Daily programs and special outer space exhibits are featured in the Stardome located between the Museum of Texas Tech University and the Ranching Heritage Center.

RANCHING HERITAGE CENTER

4th and Indiana • 806-742-2498 • Monday–Saturday 10–5
Sunday 2–5 • Free • W+

Historic structures dating back to the Republic of Texas have been relocated to Lubbock to form this monument to ranching in the Lone Star state. Stop by the Orientation Building and pick up a guide to the 33 buildings that have been moved to this 14-acre site next to the Museum of Texas Tech.

A sampling of what you'll find outside includes the *El Capote* Cabin (ca. 1838), the Waggoner Ranch Commissary (1870), and King Ranch Cattle Shipping Pens (1934), ranch offices, carriage houses, bunkhouses, a milk and meat house, even a locomotive. Note the two-story, white limestone *Las Escarbadas,* one of the XIT Ranch's nine division headquarters.

SCIENCE SPECTRUM

2579 South Loop 289 between Indiana & University • 806-745-2525
Monday–Friday 10:00–5:30 • Saturday 10–6 • Sunday 1–5:30
Admission: Seniors $4.50, adults $5.50, children $4.50

Technology and science are this museum's focus with topics like light, sound, and energy explored for visitors young and old. A hands-on approach is taken, giving kids the opportunity to work with computers and make their own bubbles, as well as view over 200 demonstrations, films, and exhibits available. Special attention is given to preschoolers. An excellent stop in conjunction with a visit to neighboring Omnimax Theatre. (*see* **OTHER POINTS OF INTEREST**).

SOUTHWEST COLLECTION

Texas Tech University • 806-742-3749
Monday–Friday 9–5 • Tuesday 9–7 • Saturday 9–1

The research center's collection and the scholars who study it are concerned with the historical aspect of the Southwest and its cultures. The Southwest Collection contains a rare cache of manuscripts, books, maps, and other materials pertinent to the American Southwest.

HISTORIC PLACES

LUBBOCK LAKE LANDMARK STATE HISTORICAL PARK

Take US 84 to Loop 289 • 806-765-0737

Operated by the Texas Parks & Wildlife Department, this archaeological site evidences man and animal dating back approximately 12,000 years. The Museum of Texas Tech University also operates a Learning Center. Other activities include self-guided tours, a one-mile archaeological trail, a four-mile nature trail through the 366-acre park, and picnic areas.

OTHER POINTS OF INTEREST

BUDDY HOLLY STATUE AND WALK OF FAME

8th and Avenue Q at Civic Center entrance • 806-747-2236

Bigger than life and above the crowd stands this bronze Buddy Holly—minus his band, the Crickets, who were back in New York when he perished in an Iowa plane crash with Ritchy Valens and the Big Bopper. Other West Texans from the music and entertainment world honored here include Bob Wills, Waylon Jennings, Joe Ely, Tanya Tucker, Mac Davis, Bob "the Bopper" Murphy, and Wink's own Roy Orbison.

More of the spirit of Buddy Holly can be found at the **LUBBOCK CITY CEMETERY**, where Buddy and his parents are interred. Though it's listed on 34th Street, don't expect to drive straight from the downtown area east on 34th and get there. You'll have better luck by finding 19th Street, heading east through Yellowhouse Canyon Lakes Park, and taking a right (south) on Quirt Road. Just before you start up the huge overpass that spans the railroad tracks, take a left on 34th. The cemetery is straight ahead. Pass through the gates and immediately fork right. Their headstones are on the left across from the tire ruts. Buddy's marker is bolted down. Note the different spelling of the Holley name. On Buddy's first record contract, his name was listed incorrectly and was printed on record labels minus the "e."

MACKENZIE PARK

Enter from Avenue A or East Broadway • Free • 806-765-6679

In addition to Joyland Amusement Park and Meadowbrook Golf Course (*see* **SPORTS AND ACTIVITIES**), Mackenzie Park is the home of one of America's last prairie dog colonies—Prairie Dog Town.

MUNICIPAL GARDEN AND ART CENTER

4215 University Avenue • 806-767-3724

Tour the gardens and consider attending or participating in one of the many lectures or workshops.

OMNIMAX THEATRE

2579 S. Loop 289 between Indiana & University • 806-745-6299
Admission: Adults $6, seniors $5

The projector in this facility stands over six feet tall and weighs two thousand pounds. The image that emerges is so crisp (and so large) that the screen is actually a dome with a diameter of 80 feet. Ten clusters of speakers—72 in all—are positioned to master the six-track sound. Combined admission with the Science Spectrum is available.

SPORTS AND ACTIVITIES

Amusement Parks

JOYLAND AMUSEMENT PARK

Mackenzie Park • 806-763-2719
March 15–September 15: Saturday–Sunday 2–10
June through Labor Day: weekdays until 7 p.m. • Admission

With over 20 rides, Joyland caters to families. Bumper cars, merry-go-rounds, and skyrides are all included in the single admission price with snacks, fast food, and drinks also available.

TEXAS WATER RAMPAGE

Brownfield Highway • 806-796-0701
June–August: Sunday–Friday 12–7 • Saturday 11–7
May and October weekends only • Admission
Plenty of ways to get wet: a wave pool, slides, and an adult pool. For
the landlubbers who tag along, there is a children's activity center,
horseshoes, go-carts, and volleyball.

Basketball

TEXAS TECH RED RAIDERS AND LADY RAIDERS

United Spirit Arena • Admission • W+

The Texas Tech basketball program—men's and women's—has attracted some well-deserved attention including the 1993 NCAA women's
championship with a decisive victory in the Final 4 over Ohio State.

Football

TEXAS TECH RED RAIDERS

Jones Stadium • Texas Tech University Campus at University and
4th • 806-742-3341 or 800-GOBIG12 • Admission • W+

A lot of West Texans call the Red Raiders their team. In addition to
grudge matches against Big 12 rivals Texas and Texas A&M, Tech typically schedules grueling non-conference opponents.

Golf

MEADOWBROOK GOLF COURSE

Mackenzie Park • 806-765-6679

PINE VALLEY GOLF COURSE

111th & Indiana • 806-748-1448

SHADOW HILLS GOLF COURSE

6002 3rd • 806-793-9700

TREASURE ISLAND GOLF CENTER

501 Frankford • 806-795-9311

Tennis

LUBBOCK MUNICIPAL TENNIS CENTER
3030 66th at Indiana • 806-767-3727 • Open daily • Fee

Twelve outdoor lighted hard courts and a pro shop. Reasonably priced lessons are available by the hour and half-hour.

COLLEGES AND UNIVERSITIES

LUBBOCK CHRISTIAN UNIVERSITY
5601 19th St. • 806-792-3221 • W

An independent liberal arts school with 35 degree programs, LCU was founded in 1957 and is affiliated with the Church of Christ. Enrollment on the 120-acre campus is over 1,000, and numerous sporting and theatrical events are open to the public.

TEXAS TECH UNIVERSITY
University and Broadway • 806-742-2011 • W

It's hard to think of Lubbock without including Texas Tech. The fifth largest university in Texas is situated on an 1,837-acre campus in the heart of downtown Lubbock. Texas Technological College opened in 1925, and was designated a university by the legislature in 1969. Economically, the expenditures of the 25,000 students and the employee payroll combine to make the university a substantial factor in the South Plains economy, but Tech's impact is obvious in many other ways. Red Raider athletics are big news, Texas Tech's museums, archives, and collections are highly respected, and South Plains residents regularly enjoy Tech's cultural events. Noteworthy programs include the Advanced Technological Learning Center, the Seismological Observatory, and commitment to fostering grape growing and wine production atop the caprock formation.

PERFORMING ARTS

BALLET LUBBOCK
Civic Center Theater • 806-785-3090

Contact the ticket office for performances in addition to the annual production of *The Nutcracker* with the Lubbock Symphony.

CACTUS THEATER
1812 Buddy Holly Ave. • 806-747-7047

Right in the middle of the Lubbock's historic Depot District, the Cactus features live music reviews of the '50s, '60s, and '70s, and is popular with locals and visitors alike.

LUBBOCK SYMPHONY ORCHESTRA

1500 Broadway, Suite 1117 • 806-762-1688
Call for program, dates, prices, and venue

From its first performance nearly half a century ago, the Lubbock Symphony has progressed from a volunteer organization to one recognized and rated by the American Symphony Orchestra League. Performances range from outdoor concerts on the Fourth of July to an annual performance of *The Nutcracker* in conjunction with Ballet Lubbock at the Civic Center.

TEXAS TECH UNIVERSITY THEATER

University Theater Building • 806-742-3601 • Admission • W

Site of several productions each semester by Tech players.

SHOPPING

ANTIQUE MALL OF LUBBOCK

Three miles west of Loop 289 at 7907 W. 19th St.
806-796-2166 • Daily 10–6 • W

With more than 50 booths and 24,000 square feet of display space, the Antique Mall is Lubbock's largest and is limited to just antiques and collectibles. Arts and crafts are not exhibited. Antique and reproduction signage, jukeboxes, glassware, and furniture are featured at different vendors. Weekends are busiest. Cokes and coffee available up front.

BUFFALO BEANO COMPANY

801 University Avenue • 806-762-8553 or 800-788-2326
Monday–Saturday 10–6 • Sunday 1–5

The list of hand-held contraptions available at Buffalo Beano is amazing: boomerangs, darts, and frisbees in addition to one-of-a-kind, all-leather "Texas Ripstop" kites. Probably the only leather kites on the market (no one else has stepped forward to fight for the honor), they are handcrafted, numbered, and actually do fly. Others in stock include indoor kites, sport kites, dual control stunt kites, and a full range of single-line kites—boxes, deltas, diamonds, and parafoils (*see* **ANNUAL EVENTS**).

SOUTH PLAINS MALL

6002 Slide Rd. • 806-792-4653

Monday–Saturday 10–9 • Sunday 1–6

Lubbock approaches major metropolitan status with this immense mall, the largest in the region. Anchored by national giants Sears, J.C. Penney, Mervyn's, and Dillard's, smaller shops include Eddie Bauer, the Gap, and Victoria's Secret.

SIDE TRIPS

BUFFALO SPRINGS LAKE RECREATIONAL AREA

50th Street (turns into FM 835) five miles southeast of Lubbock
806-747-3353 • Admission: Adults $1.50, children 75¢ • W

Buffalo Springs Lake sits in Yellowhouse Canyon on a fork of the Brazos River—the same Brazos River that runs clear across Texas through Waco down to the Gulf of Mexico. Spring-fed and big enough for any water sport, this county park offers full and electric hookups, tent camping, archery, fishing, hiking, picnicking, volleyball, and a new beach area with waterslides. Buffalo Springs also hosts its own triathlon. There is an Audubon Society Nature Trail, as well as nationally famous horseshoe pits. On the lake, take a sightseeing tour, rent a paddleboat, go tubing, or put your water skis on. With its own marina and two concrete launching pads, any craft can be accommodated. As a finishing touch, there is a restaurant by the lake.

CAP*ROCK WINERY

Less than a mile east of US 87 south of Lubbock on Woodrow Rd
806-863-2704 or 800-546-9463 • Monday-Saturday 10–5
Sunday 12–5

Cap*Rock Winery is one of the most picturesque wineries nationwide, and its mission-style architecture is worth a look even if you're not a wine connoisseur. Once inside, Cap*Rock treats visitors lavishly with its gorgeous tasting room and tours of its state-of-the-art production facility.

HERITAGE FARM

Ten miles west on Hwy 84 to Shallowater
Exit FM 179 • 806-832-4294

Stop in on Elleine and Dana Woodward and step back half a century to a typical West Texas farm. Complete with barn, windmill, and a two-hole crapper, you kind of expect to bump into Auntie Em on the porch.

LLANO ESTACADO WINERY

3 miles east of Hwy 87 south of Lubbock on FM 1585
806-745-2258 or 800-634-3854 • Tours and tastings
Monday–Saturday 10–5 • Sunday 12–5

Perhaps the state's most prestigious winery, Llano Estacado has a well-deserved reputation for excellence. With only ten acres under cultivation at the winery itself, Llano purchases all of its grapes from within a 60-mile radius. These South Plains grapes and Llano's winemaking skills produce *vinos* that have garnered a host of awards.

MUSEUM OF THE LLANO ESTACADO

1900 W. 8th St. • Plainview • 79072 • 806-296-4735
Take I-27 50 miles north from Lubbock to the 5th Street Exit in
Plainview • Drive east (right) to Quincy St. and take a left
The museum is just north of W. 8th Street • 9–5 on weekdays
1–5 on weekends (March–November only) • Free • W+

The Museum of the Llano Estacado stands adjacent to the campus of
Wayland Baptist University. The centuries-old term *Llano Estacado*
describes the plain south of the Canadian River and north of the Pecos
River. The museum collection includes geologic, biologic, and historic
exhibits pertaining to this rich region. Artifacts range from a 20,000- to
25,000-year-old Imperial mammoth skull and tusks to the uniform and
equipment of Buffalo Soldiers. Also on display are many items from
Native American cultures like Pueblo and Comanche Indians, as well as
from *ciboleros* (buffalo hunters) who hunted the herds to near extinction
while satisfying fashion-conscious American markets.

PHEASANT RIDGE WINERY

Two miles east and one mile south of New Deal off of I-27 and
FM 1729 • 806-885-3843 • Tours by appointment only

Unlike Cap*Rock and Llano Estacado, Pheasant Ridge buys no
grapes and uses only those produced at the winery. This European-style
operation is much less commercialized to the point that it doesn't have
a tasting room. A tour of Pheasant Ridge offers visitors a hands-on trek
through the vineyards, including discussion of the varietals, wine production, and the rich soil of the South Plains.

ANNUAL EVENTS

February

TASTE OF LUBBOCK

Call 806-797-6150 for venue, events, and admission

A Taste of Lubbock marries the cooking of dozens of members of the
Lubbock Restaurant Association with wines from over 20 different
Texas Wine and Grape Growers. Attend the second serving. The
restaurateurs serve and the vintners pour til the lights go out. For the
aficionado, lectures and seminars on wine characteristics and pairing
food and wine are also offered.

EASTER EGG HUNT

Buffalo Springs Lake • 806-747-3353

The Easter Bunny really has taken to Buffalo Springs Lake. Over the last
few years, he's cached more than twenty thousand eggs at a time along the
shore of this south Lubbock oasis for area kids (and ones passing through).

April

BUFFALO BEANO KITE FLY AND FRISBEE FLING

Berl Huffman Soccer Complex • 806-762-8553 or 800-788-2326
Last Sunday of the month

This extravaganza includes Sport Kite Conference competitions and several different frisbee categories: adult, canine, and kids. The *rokkaku* event is based on traditional Japanese kite fighting.

September

LITTLEFIELD DENIM FESTIVAL

40 miles west of Lubbock via Highway 84 to Littlefield
The week following Labor Day • 806-385-5331
(Littlefield Chamber)

The self-proclaimed Denim Capital of America mushrooms from 7,400 residents to almost 50,000 during this week-long event. Many show up to enjoy the free street dance hosted by Littlefield native Waylon Jennings but a host of other activities are always slated (call the Chamber for a complete list). A few include Waylon's West Texas Bar-B-Que Cook-Off (a sanctioned event), a radio-controlled airplane fly-in, sewing and photo contests, and tours of the American Cotton Growers plant.

NATIONAL COWBOY SYMPOSIUM AND CELEBRATION

Lubbock Memorial Civic Center • 1501 6th St. • 806-795-2455
Admission: Adults $5, children $2.50 • Meals & events extra

A full-blown, four-day fandango dedicated to exploring and extolling life on the range. Artisans, cowboys, and scholars gather to demonstrate, ruminate, and pontificate on matters close to their hearts. About twenty different wagons vie in the chuckwagon cook-off, and there are ones for chili and brisket, too. Each night features a different entertainment program. Additional events are held at the South Plains Fairgrounds, including a cutting horse competition, team roping, team penning, trick roping, and sheepdog demonstrations. Call the Ranching Heritage Association (806-795-2455) for dates, times, and details.

September/October

PANHANDLE SOUTH PLAINS FAIR

Fair Park • 105 E. Broadway • 806-763-2833
Last week of September

Even with the horse and livestock shows, flower festival, and other activities, this is not just a carnival. Each year, the Fair brings in top-dollar talent to highlight the event. Mickey Gilley, Charlie Pride, Barbara Mandrell, Reba McEntire, Marty Robbins, and Mel Tillis have all performed. Call for schedule and prices.

October

FLOYDADA PUNKIN DAYS

Less than an hour east via US 82 and Hwy 207 to Floydada
Weekend closest to Halloween • 800-288-3619
(Floydada Chamber of Commerce)

More than a million pumpkins are harvested each fall in fields surrounding Floydada, America's Pumpkin Capital, and, once the crop is
in, locals celebrate with two days of activities and contests. Try your
hand at pumpkin carving, cow-patty bingo, Pumpkin Pie Relays, a
wheelbarrow race, and a not-too-serious Pumpkin Queen Contest, or
enjoy plenty of pumpkin pie, pumpkin ice cream, pumpkin cake, and
other pumpkin products.

RESTAURANTS

($ = Under $7.50, $$ = Under $15, $$$ = $15+ plus tax & tip)

COUNTY LINE

FM 2641 west of I-27 N. and the airport • 806-763-6001
Daily dinner • $–$$ • AE MC V • W call ahead

Patrons argue over favorite entrées, but everyone enjoys the Escondi-
do Canyon views at County Line. Though à la carte dinners are available, most order platters and get the extra homemade potato salad, cole
slaw, and beans. County Line is not all beef and pork (though the ribs
are outstanding). Try the grilled chicken, smoked chicken or turkey.
Call ahead to avoid a lengthy wait. Bar.

FOX AND HOUND ENGLISH PUB AND GRILLE

4210 82nd • 806-791-1526
Daily lunch and dinner • $–$$ • Cr. • W+

Don't be fooled by the name; there's plenty of food at the Fox and
Hound that wouldn't qualify as English including pastas, salads, soups,
and sandwiches. Head over to the bar, where over a dozen beers are on
tap, and you might find yourself enjoying a Guinness. Bar.

GRAPEVINE CAFÉ AND WINE BAR

2407-B 19th • 806-744-8246
Daily lunch • Dinner Tuesday–Sunday • $–$$ • D MC V

The Lubbock area is home to a hefty percentage of the Lone Star
State's better known vineyards and wineries. Not surprisingly, an establishment like the Grapevine makes the most of such a home court
advantage (and serves some pretty good grub, as well).

CLUBS AND BARS

LONE STAR OYSTER BAR

3040 34th Street and Flint • 806-796-0101

Though you can order a dozen oysters on the half shell or boiled shrimp, most locals come to the original Oyster Bar to enjoy the happy hour from 4 to 7 p.m. Young professionals hang around until dinner, and the Tech crowd starts to show up after 10 p.m. Thursday, Friday, and Saturday nights are a zoo. Bar.

MIDNIGHT RODEO

7301 S. University Ave. at Loop 289 • 806-745-2813
Cover varies • 21 and over only

This country and western club offers a comfortable, upscale atmosphere full of sofas, nice furniture, and a signature circular dance floor. A DJ spins records most nights, but top talent—like Jerry Jeff Walker, David Alan Coe, and Brooks & Dunn—is brought in at least once a month. Rock & rollers and Top 40 fans head to a separate back room. The award-winning fajita buffet is Sunday from 7 to 9 p.m. for a paltry $2 cover. Bar.

ACCOMMODATIONS

($ = Under $40, $$ = $40–$75, $$$ = $75–$100, $$$$ = Over $100)
Room Tax 13%

BARCELONA COURT

5215 S. Loop 289 • 806-794-5353 or 800-222-1122 • $$

Located adjacent to South Plains Mall, this three-story all-suite hotel has 161 two-room units and non-smoking suites with cable TV and room phones (charge for local calls). Amenities include complimentary cooked-to-order breakfast, complimentary afternoon cocktails, room service from the Olive Garden, indoor pool, jacuzzi, exercise room, game room, gift shop, barber shop, beauty salon, laundry, courtesy shuttle to airport and shopping, guest memberships available at local club for tennis and racquetball, and free parking. No pets and no tipping allowed.

HOLIDAY INN CIVIC CENTER

801 Avenue Q • 806-763-1200 or 800-HOLIDAY • $$–$$$

Adjacent to the Lubbock Memorial Civic Center, this six-story Holiday Inn has 295 rooms including suites and non-smoking rooms with cable TV (Showtime) and pay-per-view movies, room phones (charge for local calls), and fire sprinklers and smoke detectors in all rooms. Amenities include the Greenery restaurant, the Brass Banjo Dance Club, a heated indoor pool with sauna and whirlpool, game room, complimentary airport shuttle, complimentary breakfast with Best Breaks rate, and free parking. Pets OK. AAA, AARP, corporate, government, and military rates offered.

LA QUINTA INN CIVIC CENTER

601 Avenue Q • 806-763-9441 or 800-531-5900 • $$

This two-story motor inn across from Texas Tech and next to the Civic Center has 137 units including suites and non-smoking rooms with cable TV (Showtime), room phones (no charge for local calls), microwaves upon request, and fire alarms for the hearing impaired in all rooms. Denny's is right next door, and amenities include a complimentary continental breakfast, complimentary coffee in the lobby, an outdoor pool, and free parking. Small pets are allowed. AAA, Sam's Wholesale Club, and government rates available.

FOUR POINTS HOTEL BY SHERATON

505 Avenue Q • 806-747-0171 or 800-325-3535 • $$$

This six-story hotel is right by the Civic Center and has 145 units including suites and non-smoking rooms with cable TV and pay-per-view movies, room phones (charge for local calls), coffee makers, and fire sprinklers in all rooms. Amenities include Vintages Restaurant, the Atrium Lounge, heated indoor pool, fitness center privileges at a health club, courtesy shuttle to the airport, complimentary breakfast, complimentary newspaper, and free parking. No pets. A variety of discount rates are available.

MULESHOE

BAILEY COUNTY SEAT • 4,571 • (806)

The town was named for the muleshoe brand of one of the many ranches carved from the famed XIT Ranch (*see* **DALHART**) and is still a High Plains hub. For more information contact the **Muleshoe Chamber of Commerce** at 806-272-4248 or write to P.O. Box 356, Muleshoe, Texas 79347.

OTHER POINTS OF INTEREST

NATIONAL MULE MEMORIAL
Downtown at the intersection of US 70/84 and Main Street

This fiberglass testimonial to an American trailblazer stands fifteen hands tall and has been a Muleshoe monument since 1965.

SIDE TRIPS

MULESHOE NATIONAL WILDLIFE REFUGE
20 miles south of Muleshoe on Texas 214 • 806-946-3341
Monday–Friday 8–4:30 • Free • W

No state in the Union hosts a wider variety of birds than Texas, and one of the most important flyways extends from Canada to Mexico through the Panhandle. The Muleshoe National Wildlife Refuge was established for these migratory birds, particularly waterfowl, and is the oldest in the state (1935). The 5,809-acre preserve is mainly native gramma grasses and shrubs surrounded by caliche rock outcroppings, but sorghum, wheat, and rainwater lakes (a rarity on the High Plains) attract thousands of duck, geese, and sandhill cranes during the winter months. The small visitor center is open during the week only. Photography, not hunting, is permitted. Notable year-round residents include a prairie dog colony along the entrance road.

TURKEY

HALL COUNTY SEAT • 2,348 • (806)

Combine western dance music and big band jazz—sometimes called swing—and the offshoot is western swing. In a career spanning five decades, Turkey's own Bob Wills and his Texas Playboys were western swing at its finest. Born in East Texas, Wills grew up in Turkey. He quit his chair at Ham's Barber Shop in 1929, moved to Fort Worth, and two years later put together the best known band in Texas political history: the Light Crust Doughboys who later propelled W. Lee "Pappy" O'Daniel into the governor's mansion and eventually a Senate seat. It was only after Wills and the Doughboys went their separate ways that he put together his most signature band, the Playboys (1933).

The town of Turkey and thousands of Bob's fans pay homage to the King of Western Swing the last weekend of April, but there's plenty to see and do year-round now that nearby Caprock Canyons State Park has opened a 64-mile Rail-Trail addition.

SIDE TRIPS

CAPROCK CANYONS STATE PARK

Superintendent • Box 204 • Quitaque • 79255 • 806-455-1492
Hwy 86 14 miles west to Quitaque and FM 1065 three miles north

Situated on the eastern edge of the High Plains, Caprock Canyons is one of the best multi-use parks in the state. It's roughly 100 miles northeast of Lubbock and 100 miles southeast of Amarillo. Nearly 14,000 acres of activities, animals, and vistas are located at the main park site. Lake Theo has a designated swimming area, a playground, a fishing pier, and plenty of hungry bass, catfish, crappie, and perch.

Campers can choose from primitive, tent, sheltered, or equestrian camps. Eighteen miles of hiking and equestrian trails exist at the main park, but head to the recently opened 64-mile Caprock Canyons State Park Rail-Trail for plenty more.

Built as the Fort Worth and Denver South Plains Railroad in 1927–28, it achieved record profits during its heyday before the advent of the modern highway system. Burlington-Northern closed the line in 1989, and with the assistance of the Rails-to-Trails Conservancy it was donated to the Texas Parks & Wildlife Department. Recently opened as the Rail-Trail, it extends from Estelline (east of Turkey on Highway 86) to South Plains (20-plus miles southwest of the state park). This new right-of-way offers hikers, mountain bikers, and trail riders access to the second longest trail in Texas and is the nation's fourth longest rail conversion.

ANNUAL EVENTS

April

BOB WILLS DAY

Last Saturday of April

People always had a great time when Bob Wills brought them together, and this day is no exception. With its parade, arts and crafts show, fiddlers contest, and outdoor concert, Turkey takes off. A special treat is the dance. Of course, breakfast is served afterward. As much as you'll do and see this weekend, don't forget to stop in at the Bob Wills Museum at Sixth and Lyons featuring music and memorabilia relating to Wills and his Texas Playboys. Keep in mind that Bob Wills Day organizers book the Hotel Turkey for the entire weekend.

BED & BREAKFASTS

HOTEL TURKEY
Alexander and 3rd • 806-423-1151 or 800-657-7110 • $$

This two-story brick building was built in 1927 and has been open for business without exception every day since. The State of Texas recognizes the hotel as a Living Museum, in that all furnishings and furniture are of museum quality and are used daily. Each of the twenty bedrooms is appointed with antiques, linens, and other unique furnishings. Four rooms share baths (all have sinks).

Owners Jane and Scott Johnson serve a full American breakfast including flapjacks and breakfast meats, along with their trademark sweet potato pancakes, fresh fruit, pastries, cereal, toast, orange juice, and coffee. Special diets and dinner service can be accommodated with advance notice.

Out back, an arbor shades the summer breakfast service and leads to a duck pond and petting barnyard including llamas, miniature goats, a pot-bellied pig—and Gobbler, a black steed who pulls a 1918 Amish surrey. Swimming and tennis are available on the property, and the Hotel Turkey is adjacent to the 64-mile Rail-Trail which offers hiking, biking, and horseback riding. Group rates available.

WEST TEXAS

The Edwards Plateau sits at the center of Texas. Its eastern, eroded edge is known as the Hill Country and enjoys plentiful streams, occasional rivers, and almost 30 inches of rain a year. Follow the setting sun, and crops give way to cowboys as rainfall drops and creek beds run dry. This is where West Texas begins—on the western reaches of the Edwards Plateau and along the prairie to the north.

Closer to the Gulf Coast than either the Trans-Pecos or the Panhandle-Plains, West Texas wasn't easier to settle nor was it settled earlier. Credit the Comanches for the slow start. For over a century, America's greatest horsemen hunted, inhabited, and traversed the Edwards Plateau and the Hill Country as well as the Big Bend and the Plains. Technology and the times ended their reign: The combination of the Colt revolver and the close of the Civil War focused too much firepower and too many soldiers on the outmatched natives.

Note the diverse biologic and geologic zones, including the Permian Basin, the Chihuahuan Desert, and the Edwards Plateau. Local economies fluctuate with changes in geography and geology and include most of America's wool and mohair production and the nation's largest inland petrochemical complex. As with any portion of Texas, federal installations are abundant and include three Air Force bases—Dyess, Goodfellow, and Laughlin—and a B-1B Bomber Wing.

WEST TEXAS

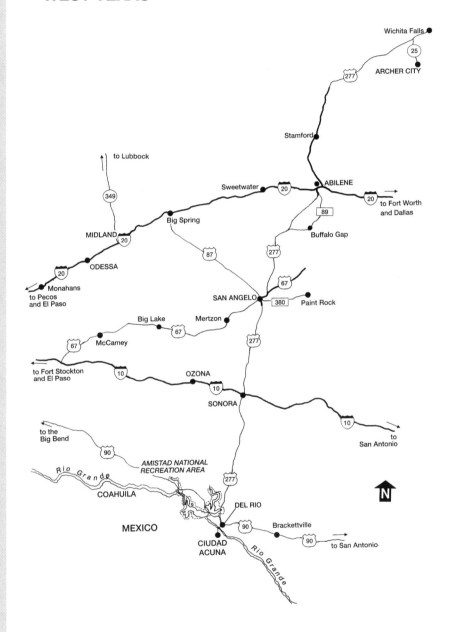

ABILENE

TAYLOR COUNTY SEAT • 106,654 • (915)

In 1880, the county seat of Taylor County, named to honor two brothers who fell at the Alamo, was the prosperous community of Buffalo Gap. Abilene was a city in Kansas. The present site of Abilene, Texas, was Milepost 407 on the telegraph route from Marshall to El Paso. The future of Buffalo Gap was derailed (and its historic nature preserved) when area ranchers finally convinced the Texas & Pacific Railroad to set up a shipping point for their cattle operations north and east of the rolling hills around Buffalo Gap. Not even an intersection, Abilene was a true railroad town with the first post office as well as the railroad's ticket office housed in boxcars. James T. Berry organized the sale of the original townsite, which became the county seat and the commercial center for Taylor County.

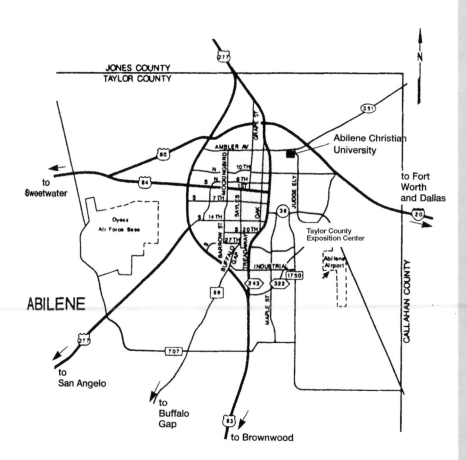

Buffalo Gap is doing fine these days (*see* **SIDE TRIPS**), and so is Abilene whose greatest resource is and has always been the ingenuity and drive of its citizens. The city is home to three institutions of higher learning and a United States Air Force base. Extensive community support has also resulted in the preservation of civic monuments like the Paramount Theatre and the T&P Depot, as well as the creation of cultural centers, museums, and annual events that make this city and its neighbors well worth a visit.

TOURIST SERVICES

ABILENE CONVENTION AND VISITORS BUREAU
T&P Railroad Depot • 800-727-7704 • www.abilene.com
Weekdays 8:30–5 • Saturdays 10–2 • W+

Housed in the renovated Texas & Pacific Depot, the Convention and Visitors Council offers brochures and coupons from area hotels, motels, restaurants, attractions, and Abilene promotional items.

MUSEUMS

THE GRACE MUSEUM
102 Cypress Street • 915-673-4587 • Thursday 10–8:30
Sunday 1–5 • Closed Monday • All others 10–5 • Admission

The classic Mission Revival styling of the Texas & Pacific Depot, the Elks Building, and the Grace Hotel (1909) manifest Abilene's rise. This portion of the downtown district served as Abilene's hub for decades, with the Grace Hotel the site of countless volumes of local fact and fiction. Located across from the T&P Depot, the Grace has been converted into the home of three of Abilene's cultural institutions and has again become a focal point for Abilene. All follow the same schedule and fee structure.

The Art Museum displays exhibitions from many sources, in addition to the museum's permanent collection of paintings by American regionalists from 1900 to 1950.

The Historical Museum focuses on Abilene in the twentieth century. Period rooms from pre-World War I, the Roaring Twenties, and post-World War II are presented along with a recreated hotel room from the Grace circa 1928.

The Children's Museum encourages kids and adults to do exactly what museums abhor: touch the merchandise. Kids two and older are welcome.

HISTORIC PLACES

In addition to the Paramount, Abilene has several distinct historic districts: the **Parramore** district north of North Sixth Street and west of

Hickory Street; **Sayles Boulevard,** with its distinctive landscaped esplanade; the **Abilene State Epileptic Colony,** once the largest in Texas; and the **Commercial** district centered on the Texas & Pacific Depot and the Grace Hotel (now the Grace Cultural Center). Contact the City's Planning Department at 915-676-6237 for a list of historic properties.

PARAMOUNT THEATRE

352 Cypress St. • Business hours daily 1–5 • 915-676-9620
Call for event schedule and prices

Before the rise of TV and long before the advent of VCRs, there were movie houses where America went for entertainment. The Paramount was built in 1930 under the auspices of the Paramount Motion Picture Company for more than $400,000. Restored in 1985, nothing on HBO can quite compare to this jewel with its two grand staircases, floor-to-mezzanine arched columns, and glass chandeliers.

OTHER POINTS OF INTEREST

ABILENE ZOO AND DISCOVERY CENTER

State Highway 36 at Loop 322 in Nelson Park • 915-676-6085
Memorial Day–Labor Day: 9–5 weekdays and 9–7 weekends
9–5 all other times • Closed Thanksgiving, Christmas, New Year's
Admission: Adults $3, seniors/children $2 • Gift shop • Picnic area

Abilene's top attraction is also the only zoo between Fort Worth and El Paso. The zoo's design enables different animals to live together in groups similar to their natural habitats. Spread over 13 acres, more than 500 species of mammals, reptiles, amphibians, and invertebrates are represented in a unique comparison of animal and plant life from the American Southwest with their counterparts from the African *veldt* (plains).

LINEAR AIR PARK AT DYESS AIR FORCE BASE

Open during daylight hours • Free • 915-696-0212

Ranging from Korea to Vietnam, nearly 30 different craft are on display at the Air Park. Though Dyess is a closed base with restricted access, a temporary pass is available at the main gate. Dyess is the home of the B-1B's sole crew training center, an Air Command Wing of B-1B bombers, a KC-135 Stratotanker squadron, and an Air Mobility Command Wing with two squadrons of C-130 Hercules transport planes. Start your visit at the Dyess Visitor Center for an overview of the base.

SPORTS AND ACTIVITIES

Golf

MAXWELL GOLF COURSE
South 32nd St. • 915-692-2737

SHADY OAKS
3542 County Road 268 • Baird • 915-854-1757

WILLOW CREEK GOLF CENTER
1166 Ben Richey Dr. • 915-691-0909

Outdoor Activities

ABILENE STATE PARK
Park Rd. 32, 15 miles southeast of Abilene off FM 89
Park Superintendent • Route 1 • Tuscola • 79562 • 915-572-3204
Pool open Memorial Day through Labor Day from 12 to 9
Admission: $3 per vehicle or 50¢ per pedestrian or cyclist

This recreational area is a welcome wet spot near semi-arid Abilene. Swim in the spring-fed pool, hike nature trails, picnic under pecan trees, or spend the night—campsites and screened shelters are available.

Tennis

ROSE PARK TENNIS CENTER
South 7th and Mockingbird • 915-676-6292
Monday–Thursday 9–8 • Friday 9–5 • Weekends 1–5

All 13 hardcourts have lights, but only six stay lit after the pro shop closes. Fees are $2 per person per 90-minute session. Pro shop with stringing, concessions, and lessons available.

COLLEGES AND UNIVERSITIES

ABILENE CHRISTIAN UNIVERSITY
1600 Campus Court • 915-674-2000 • W+ but not all areas

Founded in 1906, granted senior college status in 1919 and university status in 1969, ACU has an enrollment of about 4,000 students and includes graduate programs. Exchange programs with Hardin-Simmons and McMurry expand the broad curriculum, and campus facilities present a wide variety of athletic, theatrical, and cultural programs. Affiliated with the Church of Christ, the 208-acre campus is located right in the heart of town and is also home to Prairie Dogs, Abilene's minor league baseball team.

HARDIN-SIMMONS UNIVERSITY

2200 Hickory • 915-670-1000 • W+ but not all areas

Founded in 1891 and affiliated with the Southern Baptist Church, Hardin-Simmons has an enrollment of approximately 2,000 and is an active member of the Abilene community. Performances at the Van Ellis Theatre like *The Man Who Came to Dinner* and *The Taming of the Shrew*, concerts at the Woodward-Dellis Recital Hall, and regular art exhibits keep a steady stream of visitors on the 40-acre campus.

McMURRY UNIVERSITY

Sayles and 14th • 915-691-6200 • W+ but not all areas

A third institution of higher learning in Abilene, McMurry also has a church affiliation, the United Methodist Church. McMurry offers associate's degrees as well as bachelor's, and McMurry's athletic teams compete in the TIAA versus other non-scholarship schools like Tarleton and Sul Ross.

PERFORMING ARTS

ABILENE CIVIC CENTER

1100 N. 6th • 915-676-6211

Rodeos and big concerts head to the Taylor County Exposition Center. The Civic Center hosts events like the Taste of Abilene, auto shows, conventions, arts and crafts fairs, gun and knife shows, and performances by the Abilene Philharmonic. Several gift shows and the Abilene Tree Lighting Ceremony are scheduled in November.

ABILENE COMMUNITY THEATER

801 S. Mockingbird Lane • 915-673-6271 for schedule and tickets

Productions have included *Funny Money, Father of the Bride, The Lion in Winter, A Few Good Men,* and *Little Shop of Horrors.*

ABILENE PHILHARMONIC ORCHESTRA

Civic Center • 915-677-6710 for schedule and tickets

The concert season runs from September through April with programs ranging from classical to pop to patriotic.

ABILENE REPERTORY THEATRE

801 N. Mockingbird • 915-672-9991 for schedule and tickets

Recent performances include *One Flew Over the Cuckoo's Nest, On Golden Pond,* and *The Tempest.*

PARAMOUNT THEATRE

352 Cypress St. • Business hours daily 1–5 • 915-676-9620

The Paramount, also listed under **HISTORIC PLACES**, regularly runs American and foreign classics. Christmas favorites are scheduled in December. The theatre is also home to the Paramount Performing Arts Series, which has a long tradition of productions like *Me and My Girl* and *Salute to a Century*.

TAYLOR COUNTY EXPOSITION CENTER

Texas Highway 36 • 915-677-4376

The site of the Western Heritage Classic, the Taylor County Live-stock Show, the West Texas Fair, the Farm and Ranch Show, barrel racing, cutting shows and clinics, team ropings, and the Abilene Aviators pro hockey team.

SHOPPING

ART REED CUSTOM SADDLES

361 S. 11th • 915-677-4572 • W

Right down the street from James Leddy Boots, Art Reed's reputation as a first-rate saddlemaker goes back three decades. Reed's saddlery is a rarity because his saddle trees are crafted at the shop. Most saddle shops buy the trees these days (and some don't even make the saddle). Tack and chaps along with other hand-tooled leather items are also available.

JAMES LEDDY BOOTS

1602 N. Treadaway • 915-677-7811

In a state full of bootmakers, James Leddy stands tall. Custom-made boots, matching belts, and billfolds can set a dandy (or a lady) back thousands of dollars. This shop is not just for show. Repairs and boots for working hands keep work benches busy.

MALL OF ABILENE

4310 Buffalo Gap Rd. • 915-698-4351 • W

In addition to Sears, Dillard's, J.C. Penney, and 100 other stores, the Mall of Abilene schedules a variety of programs like antique, art, bridal, and home shows. Six-screen cinema.

SIDE TRIPS

BUFFALO GAP HISTORIC VILLAGE

FM 89 (Buffalo Gap Rd.) 14 miles southwest of Abilene
915-572-3365 • Summer hours 10–6 daily • Winter hours 10–5
weekends only • Admission: Adults $4, seniors $3, children $2

This complex of 19 buildings, many over a century old, preserves pioneer structures from the earliest days of Taylor County. The town got its name from migrating herds of buffalo that used to pass through nearby Callahan Divide. Buffalo Gap lost out when cattlemen lured the Texas & Pacific Railroad to Abilene. It gradually became the historical curiosity it is today, with half the population of more than a century ago. The original county courthouse and jail are here, as is the oldest log cabin in the area and one of the oldest churches in the region, the Buffalo Gap Chapel. The self-guided tour includes a brief video and a visit to the Buffalo Gap Historic Museum.

FORT PHANTOM HILL

FM 600 14 miles north of Abilene
915-676-2556 (Visitors Bureau) • Free

Privately owned, the ruins are well maintained and graciously shared with the public. Though never officially named, this garrison was founded (1851) along with Forts Belknap, Chadbourne, and McKavett to protect 49ers en route to West Texas and California. The post never stood a chance because timber was scarce, reliable water was never discovered, and, worst of all, the companies assigned to corral the Comanches were infantry units. Almost no contact was ever made with these superb horsemen, and the post was abandoned in 1854. The charred ruins were used as a changing station on the Butterfield Overland Mail Route (1858), as a post for the Texas Rangers and the Confederates during the Civil War, and as a sub-post of Fort Griffin during the Indian Wars (1871–1872).

ANNUAL EVENTS

March

SWEETWATER JAYCEES RATTLESNAKE ROUNDUP

Nolan County Coliseum • Sweetwater • 915-235-5488
40 miles west of Abilene on Interstate 20 • Admission • W

Thousands of wild rattlesnakes are stalked and caught, milked for their venom, cleaned for their skins, and served up for vittles at the largest rattlesnake roundup in Texas. Ranch outings, plenty of rattlesnake snacks, a

10-K run, and a variety of contests fill this March weekend. Sweetwater is also home to Lake Sweetwater and several public golf courses.

April

CELEBRATE ABILENE!

Downtown • Sweetwater • 915-676-2556 (Visitors Bureau)

Springtime and warmer weather are welcomed locally with this art festival set in the historic heart of old Abilene.

May

WESTERN HERITAGE CLASSIC

Taylor County Exposition Center • 915-677-4376
Second weekend

Tickets to each night's ranch rodeo also include admission to the dance and breakfast that follow. During the day, enjoy the world's largest bit and spur show, held at the Expo Center. Other activities include sheep dog trials, cowboy horse races, readings by the Cowboy Poets Society, and a chuckwagon cook-off.

July

TEXAS COWBOY REUNION

Stamford Rodeo and Reunion Grounds • Stamford
38 miles north of Abilene on US 277 • Fourth of July weekend

Stamford hosts a rodeo and reunion known far and wide. Things get going bright and early with the slack roping contests followed by the Cowboy Reunion parade and a memorial service for deceased members of the Texas Cowboy Oldtimers Association. By the time lunch rolls around, the cook-offs are underway. There's one for chuckwagons and another for brisket, as well as a fiddler's contest and a spur and bit show. Barbecue lunches and dinners are served, and the rodeo begins nightly at 8 p.m. followed by the dance.

RESTAURANTS

($ = Under $7.50, $$ = Under $15, $$$ = $15+ plus tax & tip)

CASA HERRERA

4109 Ridgemont Dr. • 915-692-7065 • Monday–Saturday
Lunch and dinner • Sunday lunch only • $–$$ • AE MC V • W

After almost twenty years, Casa Herrera has a new location and the same delicious food. Their new Santa Fe style (down to the saltillo tiles) hasn't changed the popular luncheon buffet featuring spicy *enchiladas rancheras* on flour tortillas, cheese and beef enchiladas, tacos, beans and rice. Always a treat off the salad bar is the cabbage, lemon, and vinegar salad—the perfect complement to any Mexican plate. Order the excellent *chile rellenos* at dinner. Bar.

HICKORY STREET CAFE

644 Hickory • 915-675-0465
Monday–Friday • Lunch • $ • MC V • W call ahead

This tea room is located in one of Abilene's many historic homes and also features a Victorian gift shop upstairs. The cafe is on the first floor and is popular with the downtown crowd, as well as for birthday parties and luncheons. Enjoy the chicken salad that comes with a wonderful zucchini bread. Other good bets include the quiche and the soup *du jour*. Plenty of homemade chocolate dessert items.

JOE ALLEN'S PIT BAR-B-QUE

1233 S. Treadaway • 915-672-6082 • Monday–Saturday
Lunch and dinner • $–$$$ • AE MC V • W

When was the last time you ordered steak by the inch? At Joe Allen's, you not only choose how well you want your beef mesquite-grilled but you also decide the thickness of your cut of beef. Inch to inch-and-a-quarter ribeyes are the house favorite ($$), but cuts can be pared down to three-quarters of an inch ($$) or up to two inches ($$$) at your request. Plenty of mesquite also goes into smoking and grilling Joe Allen's brisket, sausage, ham, chicken, and pork ribs. Beer and wine.

PERINI RANCH STEAK HOUSE

FM 89 seven-tenths of a mile southwest of Buffalo Gap
915-572-3339 • Wednesday–Thursday dinner • Friday–Sunday
lunch and dinner • $–$$ • MC V • W

When in Buffalo Gap, stop by the Perini Ranch for an order of delicious pork ribs and a side of Zuccini Perini or Mexican hominy. Wrap things up with their bread pudding, made with sourdough bread and with pecans instead of raisins. Most entrées are cooked over a mesquite fire, and in addition to ribs they serve plenty of steaks, chicken, and fish. Summer nights are spent out on the patio listening or dancing to live country and western music. Bar.

TURNERHILL'S HOUSE OF BARBECUE

1881 N. Treadaway • 915-675-0401 • Monday–Saturday
Lunch and dinner • $ • AE D MC V • W

Turnerhill's picnic-style service is as popular as it is filling. Prices are inexpensive and vary with the choice of meats, including pit-smoked brisket. Plates come with your choice of vegetable and salad. For a tasty change, try the fried catfish that is battered with a special seasoning. If you have room for dessert, get the old-fashioned butter roll. Beer and wine.

CLUBS AND BARS

PONDEROSA BALLROOM

3881 Vine • 915-698-2102 • Daily • 7 p.m. to midnight (1 a.m. on Saturday nights)

The patrons and the bands come from across West Texas to this Abilene institution. The Ponderosa is home to country & western music and those who like to play it, dance to it, and listen to it. No gimmicks, no bucking broncs, just plenty of dance floor. A DJ spins country classics Monday through Thursday nights (no cover). Weekends have live music with four and five-dollar cover charges. Special events may cost more. From famous (Ray Price, B.J. Thomas, Moe Bandy, and Radney Foster) to favorites (Jody Nix and the Texas Cowboys, from Big Spring; Southern Cross, from Coleman; and Perfect Stranger, from Palestine), the Ponderosa is what a Texas dance hall is all about. Bar.

ACCOMMODATIONS

($ = Under $40, $$ = $40–$75, $$$ = $75–$100, $$$$ = Over $100) Room Tax 13%

EMBASSY SUITES HOTEL

4250 Ridgemont Drive • 915-698-1234 or 800-362-2779 • $$–$$$

This property has only suites—170 of them. The standard suite includes a separate living room and bedroom, satellite TV, microwave, coffee maker, and free local calls. In addition, a full breakfast is included daily as well as a complimentary two-hour manager's reception. Connections to and from the airport are available. For relaxation, they have a heated indoor pool, jacuzzi, sauna, and steam bath, as well as live entertainment in the lounge of Remington's Steakhouse.

HOLIDAY INN EXPRESS

Highway 351 at Interstate 20 • 915-673-5271 or 800-465-4329 • $–$$

Winner of a 1992 Quality of Excellence service award within the Holiday Inn organization, this hotel is better than average with some nice amenities. Most of the usual applies: complimentary continental breakfast, free local phone calls, satellite TV, outdoor pool, and free coffee and newspapers in the lobby. A nice plus is the 12 p.m. check-in/check-out time. A full-service restaurant is not located on the premises.

LA QUINTA INN
3501 West Lake Rd. • 915-676-1676 or 800-531-5900 • $$

This two-story inn next to Interstate 20 at FM 600 has 106 rooms, including non-smoking rooms with cable TV (Showtime), pay-per-view movies, and room phones (free local calls). Amenities include complimentary continental breakfast, complimentary coffee in the lobby, an adjacent Denny's restaurant that's open 24 hours, an outdoor unheated pool open April through October, and free parking. One pet per room is allowed, and it must weigh less than 25 pounds. Discounted rates available include AAA, AARP, Sam's Wholesale Club, and active military personnel.

Bed & Breakfasts

BOLIN'S PRAIRIE HOUSE BED & BREAKFAST
508 Mulberry • 915-675-5855 • $–$$

Abilene is barely a century old, and this renovated 1902 Frank Lloyd Wright prairie-style has seen most of those years. Four bedrooms share two baths, and everyone shares breakfast in the dining room (special menus available). It's right next to downtown; if you're coming in from Interstate 20, take the Grape Street Exit, head north to North 5th, and go east one block to Mulberry. Children over 12. No smoking. No pets.

ARCHER CITY

ARCHER COUNTY SEAT • 1,748 • (940)

If Archer City looks familiar, you either grew up here or watched the film *The Last Picture Show* (1972) written by Archer City native Larry McMurtry. A better way to catch up on this part-time local's work is at his book store, the **Blue Pig Book Shop.**

SHOPPING

BLUE PIG BOOK SHOP
216 S. Center (a block past the courthouse on Hwy 79)
940-574-4245 Tuesday–Saturday 10–5

Housed in five different buildings along Center Street, over 100,000 books are displayed in the former settings of the Archer County Housing Authority, a car dealership, and the Archer County Tax Office. Phone orders from Houston, Dallas, and across the Southwest are the main source of sales. Most books are antiquarian—rare, out-of-print, or hard-to-find. Prices range from as little as five dollars to thousands per volume. The Blue Pig's specialty is Americana; it also has strong Texana and Southwest sections. New books are limited to McMurtry's and occasional author signings.

RESTAURANTS

($ = Under $7.50, $$ = Under $15, $$$ = $15+ plus tax & tip)

THE COTTAGE TEA AND ANTIQUES
105 N. Ash • 940-574-4016
Lunch Monday–Friday • Private parties by appointment • $

Soups, sandwiches, teas, and coffees were the intent, but the locals won't let Harold and Bertie Beekman stop there. Favorites include marinated chicken breast, Yankee pot roast, chicken and dumplings, and meatloaf. Whatever your order, enjoy a serving of Bertie's chocolate meringue pie.

ACCOMMODATIONS

($ = Under $40, $$ = $40–$75, $$$ = $75–$100, $$$$ = Over $100)

SPUR HOTEL
110 N. Center • 915-574-2501 • $$$

With 11 rooms and a complimentary continental breakfast, the Spur has more in common with a bed-and-breakfast than a hotel. Built in the late 1920s and renovated in 1990–1991, numerous design accents make the Spur a wonderful stop: the Texas sandstone fireplace; the solid mesquite mantle; Afghani, Iraqi, and Native American rugs; and refinished antiques. Unlike a B&B, however, each room has its own bath, central heat, and air. No pets.

DEL RIO AND ACUÑA

VAL VERDE COUNTY SEAT • 30,705 • (830)

STATE OF COAHUILA • 120,000 • (011 52 877)

Del Rio, the largest city between San Antonio and El Paso, was initially named San Felipe del Rio (St. Phillip of the River). Some say it was named by Spanish explorers after their monarch, King Phillip— while others say it was named by Spanish missionaries who arrived here on St. Phillip's Day in the early 1600s. Either way, the name survived more than two centuries until the 1880s when the Post Office suggest-

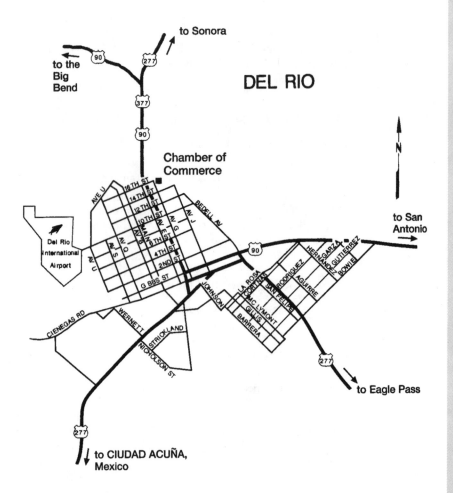

to Sonora

to the
Big
Bend

DEL RIO

Chamber of
Commerce

to San
Antonio

Del Rio
International
Airport

to Eagle Pass

to CIUDAD ACUÑA,
Mexico

ed shortening it to Del Rio to avoid confusion with another town named San Felipe de Austin.

There are some 400 archaeological sites in Val Verde County, many giving evidence to the presence of Indians in this area thousands of years ago. For example, pictographs painted on the wall of area caves have been dated back some 8,000 years.

Like most towns in semi-arid regions, Del Rio came into being because it was an oasis. The San Felipe Springs, just off US 90 East, gush forth from a subterranean river at a rate of more than 90 million gallons a day. In the early days, the springs were an important watering stop on the historic Chihuahua Road that connected Mexico's Chihuahua City with the bustling Texas port of Indianola. Later, they also served as a watering stop for stage coaches on the San Antonio to San

Diego trail. But the first real settlement grew up here after the Civil War when a group of ranchers moved in and dug an irrigation system based on the springs.

Although irrigated farming is important, farmers also discovered that sheep and goats could thrive on the sparse vegetation in the surrounding hills. Today, Del Rio claims to be the wool and mohair capital of the world. While other Texas cities, like San Angelo, dispute that claim, there's no doubt that Val Verde County is among the top producers in the state of sheep, lamb, wool, and mohair.

An outstanding feature of downtown Del Rio is the number of native limestone buildings. These were constructed by Italian stonemasons who came to build the infant city after the construction of Fort Clark at Brackettville and the stone embankments for the Galveston, Harrisburg and San Antonio Railroad that reached Del Rio in 1882. Some of the Italians also planted vineyards and built a winery that is now called the Val Verde Winery, the oldest winery in Texas.

To the northwest is Amistad Lake, an international reservoir that is located partially in Texas and partially in Mexico. About three miles south, across the Rio Grande, is the Mexican city of Acuña with a population of roughly 120,000.

TOURIST SERVICES

DEL RIO CHAMBER OF COMMERCE
1915 Avenue F • Del Rio • 78840 • Behind the Civic Center
830-775-3551 • W

Among things you can get here are a free city map, a walking tour brochure, and information on going into Mexico.

AMISTAD TOURS
US 90 West • HCR 3, Box 44 • Del Rio • 78840
830-775-6484 or 800-525-3386

They provide boat tours of Amistad Lake and the Pecos and Rio Grande Rivers on launches. Sights include the Indian pictographs on the canyon walls, the dam, and the high bridges. Most tours last about four hours. They also offer land tours of Del Rio and Ciudad Acuña and into Mexico.

MUSEUMS

FIREHOUSE ART GALLERY
120 E. Garfield • 830-775-0888 • Monday–Friday 8:30–5:30
Saturday 10–4 in November and December • Free • W (side door)

Traveling art exhibitions in a variety of media are usually rotated about once a month. In May, there's the annual juried "Western Art

Show and Sale." The building is a 1932 structure that served as Del Rio's city hall and fire station. The gallery is in the old City Hall area with the rest of the building occupied by the gallery's parent organization, the Del Rio Council for the Arts. In November and December, the gallery becomes a Christmas shop with art and handcrafted items for sale.

WHITEHEAD MEMORIAL MUSEUM

1308 S. Main at Wallen • 830-774-7568
Tuesday–Saturday 9–11:30 and 1–4:30 • Adults $1, children 50¢ • W

In 1962, the old Perry Mercantile Building, dating from the 1870s and once the largest store between San Antonio and El Paso, was given to the city for a museum by the Whiteheads, a local ranching family. Since that time, the museum has grown to include nine buildings on several landscaped acres. The entrance to the grounds is through the Hacienda. In addition to the small visitor center and gift shop, this building houses the Chapel, which is dedicated to the memory of the Spaniards who brought Christianity to the region.

The Perry Store is now an exhibition area for pioneer history. The Hal Patton Office, built in 1905, features both African-American history and the story of the Seminole Scouts (*see* **SIDE TRIPS**).

A replica of the Jersey Lilly, the saloon/court operated by the famous Judge Roy Bean, is also on the grounds and behind it are the graves of the Judge and his son, Sam. The original Jersey Lilly saloon is located in Langtry, about 60 miles west of Del Rio, and was named by Bean after his theater idol, English actress Lillie Langtry. It was in the Jersey Lilly that Bean dispensed his own brand of justice that made him a legend as "the Law West of the Pecos."

Other buildings on the grounds include the Log Cabin, which was built by local Boy Scouts in 1924 and contains exhibits about the early settlers; the Barn, which houses exhibits about prehistoric man and the Indians who lived in the area; and the most recent addition, the Cadena Nativity Scene, which depicts Bethlehem on the night of Christ's birth. For this Nativity scene, over 600 figurines and more than 1,200 items were assembled to form this 32-foot-long exhibit.

HISTORIC PLACES

A brochure guide to Historic Del Rio is available from the Chamber of Commerce. This includes a walking tour of the downtown Courthouse Square area, as well as a map locating the historic buildings in the rest of the city.

COURTHOUSE SQUARE AREA

The oldest building here is the Old Jail, on the northeast corner of the Square, which was built in 1885. Nearby, at 400 Pecan, is the Courthouse, built in 1887, which is listed in the National Register of Historic Places. The old Sacred Heart Church (1892) is at 310 Mills.

The original French stained glass windows from this church are now in the new church immediately north.

OTHER AREAS OF THE CITY

There are a number of other historic buildings scattered throughout the city. The ones listed here were all built in the late nineteenth century: Tardy-Borroum Home (1883), 703 Losoya; Brodbent-Hamilton Home (1895), 404 Spring; Chris Qualia Home (1898), 901 S. Main; Tagliabue Home (1881), 609 Pecan; Taylor-Rivers House (1870), 100 Hudson, built by one of the founders of Del Rio and now the oldest existing house in town; Mason-Foster House (1887), 123 Hudson; and the Val Verde Winery (1883), 139 Hudson (*see* **OTHER POINTS OF INTEREST**).

OTHER POINTS OF INTEREST

AMISTAD NATIONAL RECREATION AREA

Take US 90 west about 10 miles to the entrances • 830-775-7491 www.nps.gov/amis/ • Open at all times • No admission Camping and boat use fees • W

The eagle is a symbol of both the United States and Mexico, so it's appropriate that seven-foot-high bronze U.S. and Mexican eagles stand at the border between the two countries in the center of the joint U.S.-Mexican Amistad Dam across the Rio Grande. It was at this site that the presidents of the two countries, Richard Nixon and Gustavo Diaz Ordaz, dedicated the dam on September 8, 1969. You can drive into Mexico across the toll-free road atop the six-mile long dam from 10 a.m. to 4 p.m. daily. A visitor center, near the customs station on the dam, is operated daily from 10 a.m. to 6 p.m. during the summer by the National Park Service.

The dam impounds an international lake that reaches 74 miles up the Rio Grande, 25 miles up the Devil's River, and 14 miles up the Pecos River with more than 67,000 water surface acres (44,000 acres are in Texas) and 850 miles of shoreline (540 miles in Texas).

More than a million visitors come to the U.S. recreation area every year. There are facilities for boating and houseboating (rentals available), swimming, waterskiing and other water sports, fishing, limited hunting, nature study, primitive camping, and picnicking. Park facilities are mostly on the east end of the lake; the Pecos River Area (44 miles west of Del Rio), however, has a boat ramp and picnic tables.

You can fish on both sides of the international boundary that runs through the lake, and there is no closed season, but a Texas fishing license is required in U.S. waters and a Mexican license in Mexican waters. Check with the park headquarters or the Chamber of Commerce for places where you can get these licenses on the American side. The Chamber can also provide a list of fishing guides. The phenomenal visibility of the water in fall, winter, and spring makes this lake a choice place for scuba shops across the state to bring their students for check-out dives. There are also several commercial campgrounds along the shoreline.

On the Mexican side are a swimming beach, picnic facilities, and a marina with launching ramp. However, the president of Mexico has announced "top priority" plans to build a $50 million resort on the lake including a "five-star" resort hotel and a golf course.

In addition to a map/brochure of the area, the National Park Service offers a brochure outlining a self-guided tour of the major attractions in the Pecos River District including the Indian pictographs at the Panther and Parida Caves. For information, contact Superintendent, Amistad National Recreation Area, P.O. Box 420367, Del Rio, Texas 78842-0367.

BRINKLEY MANSION

512 Qualia Drive • Not open to the public

During the Depression, Dr. John R. Brinkley built this mansion with the profits from his controversial goat gland implants for men that were supposed to restore youthful vigor. To sell his services, he built radio station XERF across the border in Acuña. At that time, this station had 500,000 watts of output—which could reach radio sets as far away as Canada—making it one of the most powerful radio stations in the world.

CIUDAD ACUÑA

Take Garfield Ave. (Spur 239) west three miles to the International Bridge • Area Code 011-52-877

This city of about 120,000 is named for Manuel Acuña, a romantic poet of the Mexican Revolution. The central plaza, called **Plaza Benjamin Canales** after another revolutionary hero, is worth a visit. On this tree-lined plaza is the *Palacio Municipal* (City Hall). In 1960, Presidents Eisenhower and Lopez Mateo addressed the people from its balcony when they met to conclude the agreement to build Amistad Dam. Most of the tourist shopping is near the bridge, especially along Avenida Hidalgo. The shops here offer a variety of Mexican handicrafts, gifts, souvenirs, and curios. Most shopkeepers speak English and deal in American dollars. As in many tourist shops, there's a lot of junk for sale, but there are also genuine bargains if you know what you're looking for and what it would cost in the States.

There are also several restaurants and nightclubs in Acuña that are popular with American visitors. You can drive your car over, but if you do it's suggested you pick up Mexican auto insurance at one of the insurance agencies in Del Rio (*See* **Driving in Mexico** in the Introduction). If you don't wish to drive, you can park near the bridge and walk across (it's about ¾ mile to the shopping area) or take a taxi or bus. You can also pick up the bus to Acuña in downtown Del Rio. Del Rio and Ciudad Acuña jointly celebrate Fiesta de Amistad in October each year.

LAUGHLIN AIR FORCE BASE

US 90 six miles east of Del Rio • 830-298-5201 (Public Affairs)

An Air Force jet pilot training base, tours are available for groups only. You can call, however, and if there is a tour group scheduled and there's space, you may be able to join it.

VAL VERDE WINERY

100 Qualia Drive • Monday–Saturday 9–5 • Free tour
830-775-9714

This is the oldest winery in Texas. Started in 1883 by Frank Qualia, an immigrant from Milan, Italy, it is still operated by the Qualia family more than 100 years later. For years it was the only licensed winery in the state. The tour takes about 20 minutes and covers all the steps in winemaking from growing the grapes to bottling. You will see the vineyard (look for the geese that are used for weeding), storage vats, aging room, and other facilities. Eight different wines are produced here, including the *Lenoir* that was the first wine produced by the winery in the 1880s, and all are usually available for tasting (and sale) during the tour. Diagonally across the street at 100 Hudson is the Taylor-Rivers Home (1870), the oldest existing house in Del Rio, and further down Hudson at 512 is the Brinkley Mansion.

SPORTS AND ACTIVITIES

Fishing

AMISTAD NATIONAL RECREATIONAL AREA

See separate listing.

Golf

SAN FELIPE COUNTRY CLUB GOLF COURSE

US 90 E at San Felipe Springs Rd. • 830-775-3953
Nine-hole course • Weekdays $15 • Weekends $22

Houseboating

LAKE AMISTAD RESORT AND MARINA

US 90 W at Diablo East Recreation Area • 830-774-4157

Houseboats are available for rent at this Amistad National Recreation Area concession. Each one accommodates up to ten people and is equipped with bunk beds, stove, oven, refrigerator and ice chest, barbecue grill, cooking and eating utensils, and a shower. You must provide your own bedding, linens, towels, and food. No special boat license is required, but you must take instruction on the safe operation of the boat and its equipment from the concessionaire before setting out. From June 8 to September 2, rates run from about $220 for one night to $1,095 for seven nights. From September 3 through June 7, rates run from about $135 for one night to $665 for seven nights. There is also a damage deposit required, and you pay for your own gas.

Hunting

Limited free hunting is available at Amistad National Recreational Area (see **OTHER POINTS OF INTEREST**). A listing of member ranches offering hunting is available from the Chamber of Commerce. The following is an example of one of these.

DOLAN CREEK RANCHES
P.O. Box 420069 • Del Rio • 78842 • 830-775-3129 or 830-775-6163

Hunters are picked up at local motels and led on guided hunts for white-tailed deer and wild turkey. A three-day hunting package runs about $1,400. This includes some meals and a good chance of coming out with a buck, two does, and a turkey.

PERFORMING ARTS

PAUL POAG THEATRE
746 S. Main • 830-774-3277 • Admission varies • W call ahead

This 1940s-era movie theater has been renovated by the Del Rio Council of the Arts and turned into a 726-seat performing arts theater with a proscenium stage. The calendar includes popular musicals, mysteries, and comedies performed by the local community theater group, as well as the community concert and entertainment series which brings in outside talent.

SHOPPING

(To call from Del Rio to Acuña dial 011-52-877 and the following listed five-digit numbers.)

LA RUEDA (THE WHEEL)
215 Hidalgo East • Ciudad Acuña • 2-1260

The wagon wheel that hangs over the shop entrance is old, but inside much of the stock is modern Mexican designer clothes for women (priced from about $50 to $200), and designer jewelry.

LA VILLITA SHOPPING CENTER
2400 Avenue F • Del Rio • Daily

Shops include Dollar Crafts, the 50% Off Store, Eden's Flower Shop, and several restaurants.

LANDO CURIOS
290 Hidalgo • Ciudad Acuña • 2-1269

Mexican crafts, liquor, jewelry, and brass items are just a few of the things you'll find here. Free parking with purchase.

PANCHO'S MARKET
299 Hidalgo East • Ciudad Acuña • 2-0466

If you get weary of shopping this store for leather goods, liquor, jewelry, clothes, and other items, you can take a break in Pancho's Lounge in the rear. They also advertise prompt curb service.

PLAZA DEL SOL MALL
2205 Avenue F (US 90) near Garner • Del Rio • 830-774-3634 • W

Beall's, K-Mart, and J.C. Penney anchor this small mall that includes a three-screen cinema, a cafeteria, and a couple dozen stores and fast food shops.

ROSS EMPORIUM
800 S. Main St. • Del Rio • 830-774-0962

This turn-of-the-century drugstore has been converted into an old-fashioned soda fountain complete with sodas, sundaes, and coffee drinks including cappucino. A gift shop full of collectibles also offers a surprising array of coffee beans.

SIDE TRIPS

ALAMO VILLAGE MOVIELAND
Take US 90 29 miles east to Brackettville • Take a left on RR 674 and proceed seven miles north • 830-563-2580

Site of John Wayne's epic film *The Alamo*. This western version of the San Antonio original still stands, battered and bruised, as it was at the end of the filming when the battle was over. There is also an Old West town that is used quite frequently as a set for movies and commercials. Lunch, souvenirs, and a wide variety of entertainment are always on hand.

SEMINOLE CANYON STATE HISTORICAL PARK
(*see* LANGTRY).

ANNUAL EVENTS

May

GEORGE PAUL MEMORIAL BULL RIDING COMPETITION

Val Verde County Fairgrounds • 2001 N. Main
830-775-3551 (Chamber of Commerce) • First weekend for the
competition with other events the preceding week • $8–$15 • W

Top-ranked bull riders are matched against top-ranked bulls in a competition that offers one of the biggest bull-riding purses in the world.

October

FIESTA DE AMISTAD

Downtown Del Rio • 830-775-3551 (Chamber of Commerce)
Week nearest October 24th • Most events are free

This bi-national fiesta commemorates the visit of Presidents Eisenhower and Lopez Mateo to Del Rio and Ciudad Acuña on October 24, 1960. A highlight of the fiesta is the International Parade from Del Rio to Ciudad Acuña—reportedly the only parade in the world that starts in one country and ends in another. Other activities during the week include a Battle of the Bands, the Miss Del Rio and *Senorita Amistad* pageants to choose the American and Mexican ladies who will reign over the Fiesta, the *Abrazo* ("friendship embrace") Ceremony, an open house and air show at Laughlin Air Force Base, an arts and crafts show, a bicycle race, and a 10K International Run. The grand finale is a PRCA Pro Rodeo.

RESTAURANTS

($ = Under $7.50, $$ = Under $15, $$$ = $15+ plus tax & tip)

ASADERO LA POSTA

348 Allende • Ciudad Acuña • 2-2327
Daily • Breakfast, lunch, and dinner • $–$$ • MC V

Roasted and grilled steaks, beef ribs, and other meats are the house specialty in this cozy, brick-walled restaurant. A special *fajita* plate with onions, *quesadilla*, and *guacamole* goes for about $5. Organ music on Friday and Saturday nights. Bar.

CRIPPLE CREEK SALOON

US 90 about one mile west of the "Y" with US 277/377
830-775-0153 • Monday–Saturday • Dinner • $$ • MC V • W

Outside the log cabin style building there's a small animal farm to entertain the kids. Inside, while owner George Aubrey plays barrel house piano and occasionally leads sing-alongs, the kitchen dishes up entrées that include a variety of mesquite-grilled steaks, swordfish steaks, and chicken, plus prime rib, lobster, shrimp, king crab, catfish, frog legs, and quail. Bar.

CROSBY'S

195 Hidalgo • Ciudad Acuña • 2-2020 • Daily
Breakfast, lunch, and dinner • $$ • MC V • W

It started back in the 1930s and, even though the owners have changed, it's still going strong and holding on to its reputation of being one of the best places to eat in Acuña. Inside the etched glass entrance, old photos from the Mexican Revolution and masks from Oaxaca decorate the walls. The menu includes both continental and Mexican entrées ranging from *cabrito* and *fajitas* to seafood, quail, and a house specialty: Portuguese Chicken. Bar and piano bar.

LANDO'S RESTAURANT AND BAR

270 Hidalgo • Ciudad Acuña • 2-1205
Daily • Lunch and dinner • Reservations recommended
on weekends • $$ • MC V • W • Secure parking

The walls are covered with elegant wallpaper, the ceiling is mirrored, and there's a chandelier to round out the plush atmosphere. The menu features both Mexican and Continental entrées. Disco Thursday through Saturday nights. Bar.

LA PALAPA DE LANDO'S

1190 S. Guerrero Blvd. • Ciudad Acuña • 2-3982
Daily • Lunch and dinner • $ • MC V • W • Secure parking

While the downtown Lando's is elegant and cozy, this walled restaurant is bright and wide open. Dining on the patio is a big attraction. The menu offers a variety of Mexican dishes, including *tampiquena* and broiled steaks. A little out of the way, it's still not hard to get to. Two blocks past the bridge, turn left on Iturbide, go nine blocks to Guerrero and turn left again—or take a taxi. Bar.

MEMO'S

804 E. Losoya • Del Rio • 830-775-8104
Monday–Saturday • Lunch and dinner • Sunday dinner only
Reservations suggested for Tuesday night jam sessions
$–$$ • Cr • W

One of the people in the many celebrity photos that line the walls of this Mexican restaurant is always Moises (Blondie) Calderon. Blondie (whose hair is now black but was blonde when he was young) runs the family restaurant when he's in town. He's also the bandleader and piano player for country & western singer Ray Price, which makes him a celebrity in his own right. When he's not on the road, Blondie and his local band play and have jam sessions on Tuesday nights. The food? Well, the family has been serving up Tex-Mex and American dishes since 1936, so it must be pleasing the customers. The menu runs from *chalupas, tacos, enchiladas,* and *fajitas* to T-bone and chicken-fried steaks. The dining room overlooks the San Felipe Creek. Bar.

ACCOMMODATIONS

($ = Under $40, $$ = $40–$75, $$$ = $75–$100, $$$$ = Over $100)
Room Tax 13%

AMISTAD LODGE

US 90 W near Amistad Lake, ½ mile east of Diablo East Marina
HCR 3, Box 29 • Del Rio 78840 • 830-775-8591 • $ • W

Overlooking the lake, some of the 40 rooms include kitchenettes. Children under 12 stay free in room with parents. Cable TV. Room phones (local calls free). Restaurant, room service, lounge open seven nights. Outdoor pool. Free airport transportation. Boat parking. Fish cleaning house. Texas and Mexican fishing licenses for sale. Pets OK.

BEST WESTERN INN OF DEL RIO

810 Avenue F (US 90 W) • 830-775-7511 or
800-528-1234 • $$ • W

This two-story Best Western has 62 rooms including six non-smoking. Cable TV with HBO. Room phones (local calls free). Outdoor pool and whirlpool. Free airport transportation. Free coffee in lobby, free cocktail hour, and free full breakfast. Self-service laundry and same-day dry cleaning. Boat parking. Pets OK (charge of $3/day). Senior discount.

HOTEL SAN ANTONIO

Hidalgo St. • Ciudad Acuña • 2-5535 or 2-5108 • $–$$

With a total of 65 units in two wings, the Hotel San Antonio is located on the right-hand side of the fourth block of Hidalgo Street. Amenities include a hotel restaurant, the Amadeus Video Bar, and private parking behind the hotel.

LA QUINTA INN

2005 Avenue F (US 90 W) • 830-775-7591 or 800-621-2915 $-$$ • W+

The two-story inn has 101 units that include one suite ($$$$) and 11 non-smoking rooms. Children under 18 stay free in the same room with their parents. Cable TV featuring the Movie Channel and free local phones. Restaurant, room service, and lounge open Monday–Saturday. Outdoor pool. Free airport transportation. Free coffee in lobby in morning. Self-service laundry and same-day dry cleaning. Boat parking. No pets. Senior discount.

LAGUNA DIABLO RESORT

Sanders Point Rd. on Devil's River Arm of Lake Amistad 830-774-2422 • $$-$$$ • W

The 10 units in this resort consist of six two-bedroom and four one-bedroom apartments with full kitchen, bath, and living and dining area. Two-night minimum for reservations. Call or write for directions to this hideaway on the lake. No pets.

RAMADA INN

2101 Ave. F (US 90 W) • 830-775-1511 or 800-272-6232 $$-$$$$ • W

A two-story Ramada with 127 units including one suite with jacuzzi ($$$$) and 27 non-smoking rooms. Children under 18 stay free in room with parents. Cable TV with HBO and VCR rentals. Room phones (local calls free). Restaurant, room service, lounge open seven nights with occasional entertainment on weekends. Outdoor heated pool and whirlpool, exercise room. Free transportation to airport and bridge. Self-service laundry and same-day dry cleaning. Boat parking. Pets OK (pet deposit required). Package plans available, senior discount, and weekend rates.

MIDLAND

MIDLAND COUNTY SEAT • 97,000 • (915)

You'll find Midland halfway between Fort Worth and El Paso. Midway was its chosen name, but the postal service turned down the request. (To this day, Midway is still in Madison County, not far from North Zulch.) For almost half a century, this stopping point along the Comanche Trail prospered as a regional shipping center for area ranches. Then, the oil well now known as Santa Rita No. 1 blew in at 6:00 a.m. on May 27, 1923, and the immense petroleum reserves that became known as the Permian Basin were discovered. Though Midland wasn't the site of much drilling initially, it became the headquarters for many of the locally owned companies that drilled or serviced the petroleum industry as well as regional headquarters for the majors.

From the town's perspective, oil brought a new way of life. This region developed into America's largest inland petrochemical complex, and royalties from state leases bankrolled the Permanent University Fund, i.e., the University of Texas and Texas A&M University systems. For a city of just under 100,000, Midland has the trappings of a much larger community, including a symphony, a professional baseball team, and Midland College, along with numerous museums and attractions.

TOURIST SERVICES

MIDLAND INTERNATIONAL AIRPORT INFORMATION BOOTH
915-560-2200

This is a good first stop after you debark into the new $35 million terminal that opened in early 1999. While at the airport, have a look at the Pliska Aircraft. It's hanging from the ceiling of the main terminal now but was one of the first flying machines in the Lone Star State over 90 years ago.

MIDLAND CONVENTION AND VISITORS BUREAU
109 N. Main • 915-683-3381 or 800-624-6435 • W
www.visitmidlandtx.com

Midland emphasizes its convenient access to an immense region of West Texas and New Mexico. The Midland CVB offers plenty of advice and information on local attractions, as well as destinations like the Big Bend, the Davis Mountains, and Carlsbad Caverns.

MUSEUMS

AMERICAN AIRPOWER HERITAGE MUSEUM
Midland International Airport • 915-563-1000
www.avdigest.com/aahm/aahm.html
Monday–Saturday 9–5 • Sunday and holidays 12–5
Adults $6, seniors and teens $5, children $4 • W+

Specializing in World War II aircraft, the Ghost Squadron boasts war birds from the U.S. Army Air Force, the Royal Air Force, the Imperial Japanese Navy, and the Luftwaffe. The planes are rotated quarterly and fly to nearly 100 different squadrons and wings internationally. Almost all gather in Midland each October for the CAF AIRSHO (see **ANNUAL**

EVENTS). Many of the planes are rare or unique including "FIFI," the last of the great B-29 Superfortresses. Also displayed are uniforms, weapons, armament, and other equipment. The museum also has a research library and archives featuring oral histories, photographs, and films.

FREDDA TURNER DURHAM CHILDREN'S MUSEUM

1705 W. Missouri • 915-683-2882
Tuesday–Saturday 10–5 • Sunday 2–5 • Free • W

Experience five interactive exhibits for teaching kids (and adults) about the world around us. The Lowe Learning Center features a bank of computers which make learning fun.

MIDLAND COUNTY HISTORICAL MUSEUM

310 W. Missouri Ave. • 915-688-8947
Monday, Wednesday, Friday, Saturday 2–5 • Free • W

From prehistoric Midland Man to modern times, the history of Midland and Midland County is on display in the basement of the Midland County Library in hundreds of photographs, artifacts, and files.

MUSEUM OF THE SOUTHWEST

1705 W. Missouri • 915-683-2882 • www.museumsw.com
Tuesday–Saturday 10–5 • Sunday 2–5 • Free • W

An entire city block, this 1934 mansion contains both permanent and rotating collections of Southwestern art and archaeologic artifacts as well as the Hogan collection, a permanent exhibit of works by the founding members of the Taos Society of Artists. Both the Fredda Turner Durham Children's Museum and the Marian Blakemore Planetarium are on the premises.

PERMIAN BASIN PETROLEUM MUSEUM

1500 I-20 West • 915-683-4403 • www.petroleummuseum.org
Monday–Saturday 9–5 • Sunday 2–5
Adults $5 • Seniors/students $4 • Children $3 • W

This museum features the main ingredient in the making of Midland—oil. Special effects enable visitors to feel the force of bringing a well in, to walk under an ancient sea, and to stroll through Boomtown. From the early days of wildcatting to modern technology, explanations, diagrams, and exhibits convey the essence of the oil patch, including the world's largest collection of antique oil field equipment.

OTHER POINTS OF INTEREST

MARIAN BLAKEMORE PLANETARIUM

1705 W. Missouri • 915-683-2882 • Call for schedule
of public shows • Adults $3 • Children $2 • W+

An assortment of materials from NASA are displayed. In addition to
the public shows offered each week, groups, clubs, and organizations
can call in advance to schedule private ones. Monthly stargazing is also
offered next door at Haley Park. Call for the most up-to-date schedule.

NITA STEWART HALEY LIBRARY

1805 W. Indiana Avenue • 915-682-5785 • www.haileylibrary.com
Monday–Friday • 9–5 • Free • W

This independent research facility houses nearly 30,000 items in collections of books, photographs, maps, and interviews. Researchers and
scholars from across the nation study early range cattle history and
frontier settlement. The permanent collection of Western art features
bronzes and paintings by many of the masters along with saddles, spurs,
firearms, and other items.

SPORTS AND ACTIVITIES

Athletic Clubs

RESULTS

225 Corporate Drive • 915-682-0813
Daily • Guest fee for non-members

Results offers a full fitness program for visitors. Facilities include four
indoor lighted tennis courts and eight outdoor ones, eight racquetball
courts, an indoor Olympic-size lap pool, a jogging track around the
pool, a sand volleyball pit, free weights, nautilus, and daily aerobic
classes. Other features include a nursery, saunas, a steam room, a snack
bar, and a restaurant that serves lunch during the week.

Baseball

MIDLAND ROCKHOUNDS

3600 N. Fairgrounds Rd. • 915-683-4251
Call for schedule and ticket information

A member of the Oakland A's organization, the Rockhounds play in
the Texas League against Western Division foes El Paso, San Antonio,
and Wichita, as well as interdivision rivals from Jackson, Shreveport,
Arkansas, and Tulsa. The guys playing today just might turn out to be

baseball legends like Fernando Valenzuala, Darryl Strawberry, and Bert Blyleven—all of whom played locally.

Golf

HOGAN PARK 36-HOLE PUBLIC GOLF COURSE
3600 N. Fairgrounds Rd. • 915-685-7360
Weekdays: $11.50; Weekends: $16.50.

COLLEGES AND UNIVERSITIES

MIDLAND COLLEGE
3600 N. Garfield • 915-685-4500 • W+ but not all areas
www.midland.cc.tx.us/
Founded in 1969, Midland College offers a two-year degree plan and has more than 4,000 students enrolled. Majors are available in numerous disciplines ranging from accounting to welding technology on the 100-acre campus. A member of the NJCAA, the college fields a variety of men's and women's teams.

PERFORMING ARTS

CENTENNIAL PLAZA AND AMPHITHEATER
105 N. Main • 915-683-3381
With its cascading water fountain and water wall, Centennial Plaza offers welcome and wet relief from the West Texas sun. A 300-seat amphitheater hosts a variety of different performances, and just a stroll away is a bronze plaque commemorating the rescue of Jessica McClure from an abandoned water well in October 1987.

MIDLAND/ODESSA SYMPHONY & CHORALE
3100 LaForce Blvd. • 915-563-0921
Call for schedule and ticketing • www.mosc.org
The largest orchestra in West Texas, the Symphony is home of the Lindsayan String Quartet and the Lone Star Brass Quintet. The symphony performs classical, Pops, and chamber concerts during the September to May season.

SIDE TRIPS

BIG SPRING, TEXAS
40 miles east on Interstate 20 • 915-263-7641 (Big Spring Chamber of Commerce)
An important watering hole throughout the centuries for Comanches, Forty-Niners, and the railroad, the location of the town's namesake

big spring is now a 479-acre city park. Big Spring also boasts 370-acre
Big Spring State Park (915-263-4931 or www.tpwd.state.tx.us/park/
bigsprin/bigsprin.htm). Take the Business 20 exit eastbound from I-20
and turn right on FM 700 for plenty of picnic sites, a prairie dog town,
and nature walks on Scenic Mountain, site of century old rock carvings.

ANNUAL EVENTS

October

CONFEDERATE AIR FORCE AIRSHO
Midland International Airport • 915-563-1000
Admission • Parking fee • W+

Step back in time to the Battle of Britain or Pearl Harbor on December 7, 1941, as hundreds of vintage aircraft from the Ghost Squadron of
the Confederate Air Force relive some of history's greatest moments.
More than 100 planes comprise the CAF collection of flyable World
War II planes, and many of them are on hand for this two-day event
including the world's only remaining flyable Boeing B-29 Superfortress
and replicas of Japanese fighters. Flying demonstrations get underway
at noon, but gates are open from 7:30 a.m. until 5:00 p.m.

RESTAURANTS

($ = Under $7.50, $$ = Under $15, $$$ = $15+ plus tax & tip)

American

WALL STREET BAR AND GRILL
115 W. Wall St. • 915-684-8686 • Sunday–Friday lunch and dinner
Saturday dinner only • Cr • W • $$

For many Midlanders and certainly the downtown crowd, Wall
Street is as good as Midland gets. Originally a saddle shop (1916), it
still boasts the original pressed-tin ceiling and an 1867 Brunswick bar.
On the high-tech side, diehard tape watchers can peruse up-to-the-
minute quotes from the floor of the New York Stock Exchange above
the entrance. The house salad is mandatory—by itself, at lunch with
the soup *du jour*, or with an entrée selection. The filet and charbroiled
shrimp ($$) marries two Wall Street specialties, or try the salmon *Mexicana*. First grilled, it's served topped with *pico de gallo*. Charbroiled,
Jamaican, and a honey dijon chicken are menu mainstays. If your timing
is right and your shoes are scuffed, stop in next door at the **Lone Star
Barber Shop** for a shine. Bar.

Italian

LUIGI'S

111 N. Big Spring • 915-683-6363 • Monday–Friday lunch and
dinner • Saturday dinner only • Cr • W • $$

Good *trattoria* cooking in the middle of West Texas? Stranger things
have happened. The *antipasto* salad is a good start. The large salad is a
meal in itself, while the small one makes for good beginnings. Entrée
suggestions? The eggplant *parmigiana*. It never misses. Families devour
pizza (available in whole or half sizes), sandwiches, or items off the
smaller appetite menu. Everything is available to go. Moderately priced
wine list. Bar.

VENEZIA

20 Plaza Center • Intersection of Wadley and Garfield
915-687-0900 • Monday–Friday lunch and dinner
Saturday dinner only • Closed Sunday • Cr • W

Definitely worth the time spent to find its out-of-the-way location.
Off by itself in the southeast corner of a neighborhood shopping cen-
ter, the upscale ambience is deceptive. Prices are moderate, service is
excellent, and the food is better. The pepper steak is the best in town.
Several small details make dining at Venezia complete. Get the *bruschet-
ta* (garlic bread with olive oil), indulge in the cheese soup, and end the
meal with the rum cake. Beer and a good wine list.

Mexican

ABUELO'S

4610 N. Garfield • 915-685-3335 • Daily
Lunch and dinner • $–$$ • Cr • W

Most of the entrées at Abuelo's were first sampled in Mexico and
brought back to Midland. *Alambre de camaron* features bacon-wrapped
jumbo shrimp, accented with a slice of jalapeño, charbroiled, and
served with a hint of Monterrey Jack cheese. Need a Mexican fix?
Abuelo's Grande Combination comes with a beef enchilada, a cheese
enchilada, a beef chile relleno, a taco, a tamale, and a small side of guacamole. *Papas con chile* served with all entrees. Bar.

LA BODEGA

2700 N. Big Spring • 915-684-5594
Daily lunch and dinner • Cr • W

Top shelf margaritas. Start with an order of stuffed jalapeños or the
nachos. For dinner try the chile rellenos, the chicken fajitas, and Midland's best jalapeño burger. Bar.

ACCOMMODATIONS

($ = Under $40, $$ = $40–$75, $$$ = $75–$100, $$$$ = Over $100)
Room Tax 13%

LA QUINTA

4130 W. Wall • 915-697-9900 or 800-687-6667 • $$ • W

This two-story La Quinta, located about six miles from the Midland airport, has 147 units including non-smoking rooms with cable TV (HBO), pay-per-view movies, and room phones (free local calls). Amenities include a complimentary continental breakfast from 6:30 to 10 a.m., complimentary coffee in the lobby, coffee makers in each room, a nearby Kettle restaurant, outdoor unheated pool open from May to September, and free parking. Small pets, 25 pounds or less, are welcome too. AAA, AARP, government, and military rates available.

DAYS INN

1003 S. Midkiff • 915-697-3155 or 800-329-7466 • $$

This three-story, all-suite property has 82 units including mini one- and two-bedroom suites with non-smoking ones available. Cable TV (HBO), pay-per-view movies, room phones (charge for local calls), a full-sized refrigerator, and a complete kitchen are included.

Amenities include complimentary continental breakfast, outdoor heated pool, and free parking. Smaller pets are welcome, but the hotel requires a refundable $100 deposit. AAA and AARP rates are available, and better rates are offered on weekends.

MIDLAND HILTON AND TOWERS

117 W. Wall at Loraine • 800-445-8667 or
915-683-6131 • $$–$$$

This 22-story Hilton is located right in the center of downtown Midland, has 249 units including suites and non-smoking rooms, and completed a $3 million renovation in 1999. Each room comes with pay-per-view movies and two room phones (free local calls). Amenities include complimentary continental breakfast for weekend guests with the Bounce Back package, two hotel restaurants—the Santa Fe Cafe and the Santa Fe Grill, an outdoor pool, jacuzzi, fitness center, flower shop, gift shop, valet laundry service, complimentary 24-hour shuttle to the Midland Airport, valet, and free parking. No pets. Government rates available to federal and state employees only.

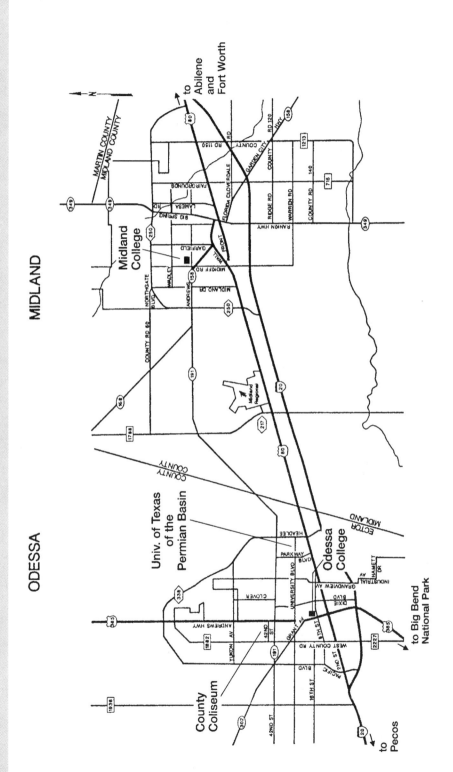

ODESSA   MIDLAND

ODESSA

ECTOR COUNTY SEAT • 97,500 • (915)

Founded as a railroad stop for the Texas & Pacific Railroad (1881), the similarity of the Odessa area to the Russian steppes led to the city's being named for a port city on the Black Sea. It wasn't until oil was struck in Ector County (1926) that Odessa took off. Production spread to the farthest reaches of the Permian Basin and made this area the world's largest inland petrochemical complex. Homage to this age of the great oil boom is found throughout Odessa. There is, for instance, the Permian Playhouse and Permian High School—along with the Permian Basin Oil Show, which is held every other year.

TOURIST SERVICES

ODESSA CONVENTION AND VISITORS BUREAU

P.O. Box 3626 • Odessa • 79760
915-333-7178 or 800-780-4678 • www.ci.odessa.tx.us/

Visitor packets, moving packets, and plenty of other information is available at the second floor office of the Odessa CVB, located at 700 N. Grant.

MUSEUMS

PRESIDENTIAL MUSEUM

622 N. Lee (7th and Lee) • 915-332-7123
Tuesday–Saturday 10–5 • Adults $2 • W+

Documents, campaign memorabilia, photographs, and original cartoons covering the Presidency from Washington to Clinton are on display at the only museum in the United States that focuses on the Chief Executive. In addition, other permanent exhibits include the Dishong Collection of First Lady Dolls, which documents colorful designs seen at inaugural balls through the centuries.

WHITE-POOL HOUSE

112 E. Murphy • 915-333-4072
Hours vary • Call for schedule and/or appointment
Free (donations accepted) • W downstairs only

Lured to Odessa by Texas & Pacific ads promoting cheap dirt and a bright future, the Charles White family relocated from Indiana to Ector

County and acquired this tract in 1887. The house, Odessa's oldest structure, was up within a year, and the Whites stayed through 1906. Acquired by Oso Pool in 1923, it stayed in the Pool family until 1978 when it was donated to the county.

OTHER POINTS OF INTEREST

ELLEN NOËL ART MUSEUM OF THE PERMIAN BASIN
4909 E. University • 915-368-7222
Tuesday–Saturday 10–5 • Sunday 2–5 • Donations accepted • W+

Grand Striptease by Giacomo Manzu stands in front of the Art Institute, a facility that emphasizes visual arts and integrates other art forms such as music with imaginative exhibits. Each exhibition is presented for about a month, and ranges from sculpture, painting, or photography to quilting and juried shows. Lectures, workshops, videos, and other activities are scheduled in conjunction with exhibits.

ODESSA METEOR CRATER
10 miles west of Odessa via Business 20

Approximately 550 feet in diameter, the second largest crater in the nation is the result of a barrage of meteors that crashed to earth 20,000 to 30,000 years ago. Self-guided tour.

WORLD'S LARGEST JACKRABBIT
Corner of Sam Houston and 8th

From the same mutant gene pool as Paisano Pete in Fort Stockton (the world's largest roadrunner), this bunny stands ten feet tall and doesn't flinch at oncoming pickup trucks.

SPORTS AND ACTIVITIES

Amusement Parks

HERO'S WATER WONDERLAND ENTERTAINMENT COMPLEX
12300 E. Business Loop 20 • 915-563-1933
Open early May to Labor Day

Over 20 acres of water slides, wading pools, tubing, and other activities. A 36-hole miniature golf course and a driving range adjoin the park (separate fee). Concession stands serve drinks and snacks, and a cafeteria-style restaurant serves lunch.

Hockey

ODESSA JACKALOPES

Ector County Coliseum • Andrews Highway and 42nd Street
October–March season • 915-552-PUCK

No longer a mythic creature, the Jackalope is alive and well in Odessa where fans choose from a 35-game schedule featuring Western Professional Hockey League play.

COLLEGES AND UNIVERSITIES

ODESSA COLLEGE

201 W. University • 915-335-6400 • W+ but not all areas
www.ocbbs.odessa.edu/public/oc/index.html

In addition to highly competitive athletic squads, Odessa College is best known as the home of the Globe of the Great Southwest Theater (*see* PERFORMING ARTS). OC was founded in 1946 and has an enrollment of about 5,000. Students, visitors, and locals often frequent the many cultural, athletic, and educational events on the 87-acre campus.

UNIVERSITY OF TEXAS OF THE PERMIAN BASIN

4901 E. University • 915-367-2011
W+ but not all areas • www.utpb.edu

One of the youngest components of the immense University of Texas system was authorized by the Texas Legislature in 1969 as a two-year upper division and graduate school. Home of the Center for Energy and Economic Development, UTPB recently expanded to a four-year university (1991). UT Permian Basin has an enrollment of more than 2,300 students and offers bachelors and masters degrees in the arts, business administration, and science.

PERFORMING ARTS

ECTOR COUNTY COLISEUM

42nd and Andrews Highway • 915-366-3541

If there's going to be a crowd—rock & roll, country & western bands, *tejano,* or large shows—chances are it's at the coliseum, which also serves as home to the Odessa Jackalopes of the Western Professional Hockey League.

GLOBE OF THE GREAT SOUTHWEST THEATRE

Odessa College • 2308 Shakespeare Rd. • 915-332-1586 • W+

A replica of the London original, the octagonal Globe of the Great Southwest seats 410 and hosts the annual Shakespeare Festival, numerous other theater productions, a Renaissance Madrigal Feast, and live country & western revues courtesy of the Odessa Brand New Opree. Tours are available but please call in advance.

MIDLAND/ODESSA SYMPHONY & CHORALE

3100 LaForce Blvd. • 915-563-0921
Call for schedule and ticketing

The largest orchestra in West Texas is based out of both of the Permian Basin's leading communities. Regular performances by the Symphony and Chorale, the Lindsayan String Quartet, and the Lone Star Brass Quintet are scheduled.

PERMIAN PLAYHOUSE

310 W. 42nd St. • 915-362-2329 • Admission varies • W

For over 40 years, the playhouse has been the stage for dance, drama, music, and mysteries. Productions by children and young adults are also featured, and the Playhouse offers young people the opportunity to explore the world on-stage through the Kaleidoscope Company. Located near the Ector County Coliseum.

SIDE TRIPS

MONAHANS SANDHILLS STATE PARK

Interstate 20, 20 miles west of Odessa at exit 86 • 915-943-2092
www.tpwd.state.tx.us/park/monahans/monahans.htm
Daily • $2 per person • W+ but not all areas

An enormous dune field more than 200 miles wide stretches from southeast New Mexico into West Texas. Over 3,000 acres of it form this state park right off the Interstate. Where did it come from? New Mexico. During the dry spell that followed the last Ice Age, winds blew portions of the dune field into Texas. Learn more at the interpretive center. Other activities at the park include wildlife viewing and sandsurfing. Boards and disks can be rented. For overnight excursions, showers, restrooms, and trailer sites with hookups are available.

ANNUAL EVENTS

January

THE SANDHILLS STOCK SHOW AND RODEO

Ector County Coliseum • 915-366-3541
First week • Admission • W+

This event is the first rodeo of the year on the PRCA calendar and the only stock show dedicated strictly to the Hereford breed. Cowboys and cowgirls compete for top prizes during the weeklong event, which also features a Quarter Horse show, Tex-Mex barrel race, and several rodeo dances.

September

PERMIAN BASIN FAIR AND EXPOSITION
Ector County Coliseum Fairgrounds • 915-550-3232

A wide variety of entertainment, activities, and competition can be found out at the Ector County Fairgrounds during this nine-day event.

October

CONFEDERATE AIR FORCE AIRSHO
Midland International Airport • 915-563-1000 • Admission • W+
See separate listing under **MIDLAND.**

RESTAURANTS

($ = Under $7.50, $$ = Under $15, $$$ = $15+ plus tax & tip)

BARN DOOR & PECOS DEPOT BAR
2140 N. Grant • 915-337-4142
Monday–Saturday • Lunch and dinner • $–$$$ • AE MC V

This local favorite sits in the old Pecos City Depot, purchased from the Panhandle-Santa Fe Railway when the station closed in 1972. Decorated with turn-of-the-century antiques and artifacts, the centerpiece is a 20-foot mahogany, maple, and cherrywood bar. Ribeyes, sirloins, tenderloins, and T-Bones are grilled over charcoal, and the prime rib is served in seven-ounce, ten-ounce, and 15-ounce cuts. Other menu items include seafood, poultry, and Mexican food. Bar.

BIG DADDY'S CATFISH AND CHICKEN
1121 E. 42nd St. • 915-363-8010
Tuesday–Sunday • Lunch Dinner • $–$$

Unique atmosphere and a terrific staff make this fish, fowl, and rib joint a local favorite. Non-smoking, smoking, and private party seating available. Live entertainment Wednesday nights. Bar.

DOS AMIGOS
47th and Golder • 915-368-7556
Tuesday–Saturday • Lunch Dinner • $–$$ • AE MC V • W

Located right across from the Ector County Coliseum, Dos Amigos draws a crowd of regulars because of the good food, great setting, and the Sunday bullriding. Green chicken enchiladas, the fajita plate, and nightly specials make this a popular dinner spot. The Tuesday night special is a 10-ounce ribeye served with a baked potato and salad. Cook it yourself over a bed of mesquite coals. Thursday night is seafood—loads of oysters, shrimp, lobster, or catfish at inexpensive prices. The big draw from March to November is the bullriding competition, held every other Sunday. For more than a decade, amateurs and professional cowboys have vied for honors, including a $5,000 added purse at the season finale Stan Ham Memorial Bull Ride and Bullfight. Beer and wine.

ACCOMMODATIONS

($ = Under $40, $$ = $40–$75, $$$ = $75–$100, $$$$ = Over $100)
Room Tax 13%

LA QUINTA INN

5001 E. Business Highway 20
915-333-2820 or 800-531-5900 • $$

This two-story inn has 122 smoking and non-smoking rooms with cable TV (Showtime), pay-per-view movies, and room phones (free local calls). Amenities include complimentary continental breakfast from 6:30 to 10 a.m., free coffee in the lobby, an adjacent Denny's and nearby Harrigans restaurant, an unheated outdoor pool open from April 15 to September 15, courtesy car from the Midland Airport, and free parking. Pets under 25 pounds welcome. AAA, AARP, government and military rates available.

RADISSON ODESSA

5200 University at Loop 338 • 915-368-5885 or
800-333-3333 • $$-$$$

This eight-story hotel is close to UTPB and the Ellen Noël Art Museum. It has 94 units, including six suites and non-smoking rooms featuring cable TV (HBO) and room phones (charge for local calls). Amenities include Legends restaurant on-site, Spirits bar and lounge, an outdoor pool and jacuzzi, and gift shop. The Radisson also offers same-day valet laundry service, complimentary van service to and from the Midland Airport, complimentary guest privileges at Neal's Fitness Center one mile west of the hotel, and free parking. A variety of different rates are offered based upon availability. Ask about bed-and-breakfast packages.

OZONA

CROCKETT COUNTY SEAT • 3,500 • (915)

Billing itself as "the Biggest Little Town in the World," Ozona exudes a charm that comes from its historic past and fortunate circumstances. Ozona is one of the few towns in Texas that has an entire county to itself, but it wasn't always a loner. Crockett County was formed in 1875, and a spirited race for the county seat pitted Ozona against

Emerald for that honor. Ozona was declared the winner in 1891. Emerald's citizens and merchants packed up and relocated to Ozona.

As the older of the two communities, Emerald's legacy was welcome, and today Emerald House, Crockett County's oldest home, stands in Ozona's Memorial Fair Park east of town. Sheep and cattle ruled until oil and gas were discovered. Take a moment to drive Ozona's genteel boulevard, tree-lined and half a mile long, with its shady boughs and stately homes. For more information on the biggest little town in the Lone Star State, contact the **Ozona Chamber of Commerce** (915-392-3737).

OTHER POINTS OF INTEREST

DAVID CROCKETT MONUMENT
Town Square

Of all the defenders of the Alamo, none were more numerous than those from the Volunteer State and none more conspicuous than former U.S. Congressman David Crockett, namesake of Crockett County.

SIDE TRIPS

FORT LANCASTER
Go west 30 miles on I-10 to exit 343 • Go east 8 miles on US 290
www.tpwd.state.tx.us/park/fortlanc/fortlanc.htm
Wednesday–Sunday 8–5 • Free • W

Fort Lancaster was garrisoned by companies of the 1st Infantry in 1855. Its purpose was to protect the Government Road from San Antonio to El Paso linking Forts Clark, Hudson, Lancaster, and Stockton. It quickly became an impressive installation with 25 permanent buildings and a complement of 72 men and four officers. With the onset of the Civil War, however, orders were issued to abandon the post. It was never regarrisoned. Visitors can view exhibits covering the post's archaeology and history, walk the short self-guided trail around the ruins, and even picnic at the old fort.

ACCOMMODATIONS

($ = Under $40, $$ = $40–$75, $$$ = $75–$100, $$$$ = Over $100)

CIRCLE BAR 76 MOTEL
Interstate 10 at Exit 372 (Taylor Box Rd.) • 915-392-2637 • $$

The Circle Bar 76 complex is a world unto itself. Situated six miles east of Ozona, out in the middle of nowhere, stands the motel, an RV park, a restaurant that is open around the clock, a convenience store, a gas station, and even a garage with a mechanic. All rooms in the two-story motel are smoking units and come with cable TV (HBO) and phones (free local calls to Ozona).

In addition to the solitary location, most visitors remember the indoor garden area which the rooms surround. Complete with its own pool, jacuzzi, and sauna, it's a pleasant change from most motels and a big surprise to most guests. Other pluses include complimentary coffee in the lobby, laundry facilities, and free parking. No pets. AAA, AARP, corporate, and military rates are available.

SAN ANGELO

TOM GREEN COUNTY SEAT • 84,474 • (915)

If San Antonio's Riverwalk is getting a bit too crowded for your tastes, head to San Angelo. Slowly and surely, this former frontier fort has become one of the state's most livable cities, as well as a genuine tourist destination full of historical landmarks, beautiful botanical gardens, one-of-a-kind shops, and a landscaped, multi-use, four-mile River Walk.

The establishment of Fort Concho (1867) led to the development of modern San Angelo. This post, south of the confluence of the North and Main Concho rivers, gave rise to Santa Angela on the river's north bank. By the late 1880s, Santa Angela had become San Angelo, the Comanches were no longer a menace, and the railroad had arrived.

Uncle Sam abandoned Fort Concho, but the city of 2,500 had developed strong roots in the Concho Valley as an agricultural hub and commercial center. Plenty of cattle graze on area ranches, but wool and mohair is big business. The weekly Producer's Livestock Auction is America's largest sheep auction and the second biggest cattle market in Texas (after Amarillo).

Local craftsmen cater to these trades by producing some of the best-known saddles, boots, and accessories in the state. Others work with the Concho Pearl to make jewelry. Produced by freshwater mussels in the streams and lakes that surround San Angelo, this pink or purple pearl has been prized for centuries. Like San Angelo, it's a rare find.

TOURIST SERVICES

SAN ANGELO CONVENTION & VISITORS BUREAU

500 Rio Concho Drive • 76903 • 915-653-1206 or 800-375-1206
Monday–Friday 8:30–5:00 • www.sanangelo-tex.com

The Visitors Bureau has put together several informative brochures to the San Angelo area that make a stop or a call worth the extra effort. Pick up the *Visitors Guide*, which describes the city itself, and the *Historical Walking Tour of Downtown San Angelo*, which details the oldest portion of town (not including Fort Concho).

SAN ANGELO

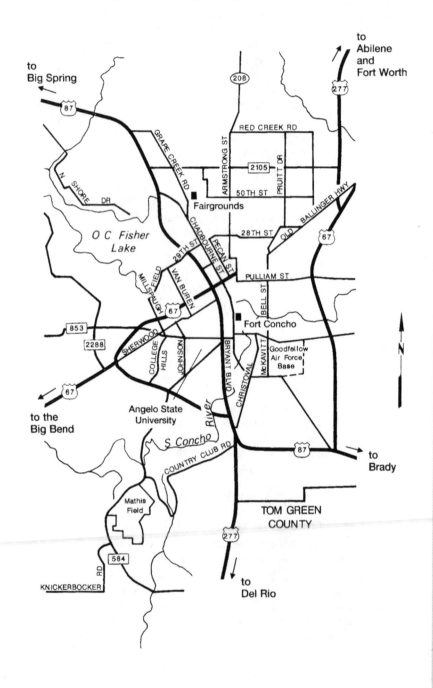

MUSEUMS

CHILDREN'S ART MUSEUM

36 Twohig on the first floor of the Cactus Hotel • 915-659-4391
Tuesday–Friday 1–6 • Saturday 10–5 • Sunday 1–5
$2 admission • Gift shop • W+

The newest museum in San Angelo is actually an arm of the well-established Museum of Fine Arts (*see below*). Housed in the historic Cactus Hotel, the Children's Art Museum features rotating exhibits that offer kids an imaginative and interactive learning experience. Adults are also welcome.

FORT CONCHO NATIONAL HISTORIC LANDMARK

213 E. Avenue D • 915-657-4441 or 915-657-4444
Tuesday–Saturday 10–5 • Sunday 1-5 • Adults $1.50,
students $1.25

Founded in late 1867, the fort was the focus of the region for almost a quarter of a century. At its height, it quartered eight companies, i.e., roughly 400 men and 50 officers. After the west was won, the Army deactivated the post (1889), but the fort lived on as civilian housing and through a variety of commercial uses.

Beginning in the late 1920s, efforts to preserve the fort began. The City of San Angelo now holds title to Fort Concho, which was designated a National Historic Landmark in 1961. Among its innovative uses is as a public school and as a meeting place for groups, special events, and even conventions.

The post hospital building not only houses the Robert Wood Johnson Museum of Frontier Medicine but also the Fort Concho Elementary School library. Across the yard, fourth graders sit beneath portraits of Grant, Lincoln, and Washington and learn lessons from primers used over a century ago.

The Fort Concho Museum emphasizes the frontier Indian Wars and the heritage of Tom Green County with photos, maps, sabers, personal effects, cannons, and even military wagons and mule teams. Each building houses a different exhibit, and loyal San Angeloans help to make the fort come alive as they realistically portray infantryman, cavalry soldiers, laundresses, and officers' wives.

SAN ANGELO MUSEUM OF FINE ARTS

Along the banks of the Concho River next to Fort Concho
915-658-4084 • Tuesday–Saturday 10–4 • Sunday 1–4
Admission • W+

The museum displays rotating exhibits ranging from local and area history to photography; painting, drawing, ceramics, and textiles.

DANNER MUSEUM OF TELEPHONY

Officers' Quarters #4 at Fort Concho • 915-653-0756
Tuesday–Saturday 10–5 • Sunday 1–5

Hundreds of antique phones and switchboards are displayed in four rooms of this renovated Fort Concho Officers' Quarters. Many date back to the nineteenth century including one of Alexander Graham Bell's original telephones and a Kellogg single-position manual magneto switchboard.

ROBERT WOOD JOHNSON MUSEUM OF FRONTIER MEDICINE

Post Hospital at Fort Concho • 915-657-4444
Tuesday–Saturday 10–5 • Sunday 1–5 • W

Housed in the old Post Hospital, the museum surveys nineteenth century medicine by exhibiting the surgical tools and equipment of frontier surgeons and physicians.

MISS HATTIE'S PARLOR AND MUSEUM

18 E. Concho Street • 915-658-3735
Monday–Saturday • $2 admission

This renovated bordello was a thriving San Angelo enterprise until its demise in 1946. One of the better anecdotes about Miss Hattie's was the tunnel that linked the San Angelo National Bank (now Caraway's) with her thriving enterprise. Used by the more circumspect clients, it was a banking service rarely mentioned in the annals of high finance. Miss Hattie's also had an elaborate network of escape routes, warning bells, and flashing lights for the inevitable raids by Texas Rangers or sheriff's deputies.

Complete with original furnishings, Miss Hattie's is a delightful stop in the middle of historic downtown San Angelo. Tours are offered twice daily, in the morning and in the afternoon. **Miss Hattie's Parlor,** specializing in lingerie, bath accessories, and other unique gifts, occupies the first floor of the building and serves as headquarters for tickets and tours.

HISTORIC PLACES

CONCHO STREET

Once upon a time, San Angelo was known as Santa Angela and Concho was Santa Angela's first street. Much of the charm and stylish design is evident in the nineteenth-century buildings that line Block One and are full of antiques, collectibles, fashions, gifts, saddles, and spurs. Some, like Miss Hattie's, are preserved intact. Others, like Caraway's (*see* **CLUBS AND BARS**), have been creatively adapted to modern uses. Pick up a copy of *A Historical Walking Tour of Downtown San*

Angelo at the San Angelo Convention & Visitors Bureau for thumbnail sketches of over 30 buildings, including many on Concho Street.

OTHER POINTS OF INTEREST

RIVER WALK
Downtown along the banks of the Concho River

Much as it brought settlers to San Angelo over a century ago, the Concho River draws locals and tourists to its banks. The city has taken to heart the preservation of this important artery and, through the River Beautification Project, has revitalized over four miles in and around the downtown district. The most recent addition enhances the Celebration Bridge area: a beautiful bronze mermaid known as the *Pearl of the Conchos.*

Scores of improvements like fountains, benches, picnic tables, see-saws, and swings are all within walking distance of downtown, as is Santa Fe Park and Golf Course. For a quick look at the River Walk, drive along winding West River Drive. The jogging-walking trail readily accommodates strolls of any length. Once summer comes round, people flock to events on or near the River Walk and River Plaza, including the River Raft Races and Fiesta del Concho in June, and the popular Fourth of July concert by the San Angelo Symphony.

CIVIC LEAGUE PARK
Bounded by Pecos, Beauregard, and Park streets

Both the Municipal Rose Garden and the International Water Lily Collection are worth visiting in themselves. Together, they form an unforgettable oasis just west of downtown San Angelo on the far bank of the Concho River. Terraced gardens and gurgling fountains are surrounded by acres of prime picnicking, historic turn-of-the-century houses, and St. Paul Presbyterian Church. Another reason to visit: Where else can you mingle with Cary Grant, Judy Garland, Queen Elizabeth, Princess Margaret, and hundreds of other famous and not-so-famous roses? Visit from March through September to view the water lily collection which features day and night blooming varietals.

ANGELO STATE UNIVERSITY PLANETARIUM
Nursing-Physical Science Building • 915-942-2188 or 915-942-2136 • Programs Thursday at 8 p.m. and Saturday at 2 p.m. • Adults $3, students/seniors/military $1.50 • W+

One of the largest in Texas and one of the most advanced in America, this planetarium utilizes laser discs to dazzle visitors with its multi-image capability. The combination of fantastic sights and stereo sounds makes travel to far-off galaxies or membership on an Apollo or Voyager mission an essential part of any visit to San Angelo. Open to the public during the school year, portions of the planetarium can be leased for private functions.

PRODUCER'S LIVESTOCK AUCTION

Auction Barn • 1131 N. Bell • 915-653-3371

Site of the nation's largest sheep auction each Tuesday. The cattle auction is held Thursdays and is among the largest in Texas.

GOODFELLOW AIR FORCE BASE

Fort McKavett Road • 915-657-3876 (Public Affairs)

San Angelo's largest employer. Intelligence training for all four branches of the armed services is provided at Goodfellow. A recent addition is the fire training facility that came on line in 1993. The Public Affairs Office handles tours.

LAKE NASWORTHY

Six miles from town on Knickerbocker Road (FM 584)
915-944-3812

Bounded by residences and lake houses, located within the city proper, and owned by the city, Nasworthy is the oldest of San Angelo's reservoirs. Sunny summer days, weekends, and holidays are busiest with ski boats, ski doos, and bass boats crowding the lake. Nasworthy's level stays constant by regulating water flow from Twin Buttes Reservoir.

On shore, the **San Angelo Nature Center** (915-942-0121) offers natural science programs and a natural history museum featuring a library, and a xeriscape garden, along with special events.

LAKE E.V. SPENCE

40 miles north of San Angelo via Highways 208 and 158

The first reservoir along the lengthy Colorado River, fishermen prefer out-of-the-way E.V. Spence because of better pickings and smaller crowds.

LAKE O.H. IVIE

40 miles east of San Angelo via FM 765 and FM 2134

Slightly larger than Lake E.V. Spence, this more distant lake is also owned by the Colorado River Municipal Water District and is at the confluence of the Colorado and Concho rivers. Marinas and recreational facilities are under construction.

O.C. FISHER RESERVOIR

Three miles northwest of town via Mercedes Street • 915-949-4757

O.C. Fisher dams the North Concho River and prevents any future floods by a river that has twice ravaged the city. In addition to good fishing, facilities for camping, boating, swimming, horseback riding, bicycling, jogging, and hiking are available.

TWIN BUTTES RESERVOIR
Five miles west of town via US Highway 67 • 915-944-3812

Whereas O.C. Fisher dams the North Concho, Twin Buttes dams the Middle and South forks of the Concho. The reservoir is actually two lakes connected by an equalization channel. Most activities—fishing, swimming, and camping—take place around the easier-to-reach north body of water.

SPORTS AND ACTIVITIES

Fishing

There is more fishing around San Angelo than anywhere else in West Texas. Some of these lakes are even within the city limits (*see* **OTHER POINTS OF INTEREST**). Choose **Nasworthy** for largemouth and white bass, channel, blue, and flathead catfish, white crappie, freshwater red drum, and redfish. Head to **O.C. Fisher** for largemouth bass, white crappie, white bass, channel, blue, and flathead catfish, and walleye. **Twin Buttes** offers largemouth and smallmouth bass, white bass, crappie, channel, blue, and flathead catfish. Drive out to **E.V. Spence** for largemouth, smallmouth, striped, and white bass, crappie, channel, blue, and flathead catfish. **O.H. Ivie** has largemouth and white bass, crappie, channel, blue, and flathead catfish, and walleye.

Golf

LAKESIDE GOLF COURSE
Mathis Field • 915-949-2069

Nine-hole course. Weekdays and weekends: $3.25

RIVERSIDE GOLF COURSE
900 W. 29th • 915-653-6130

Eighteen-hole course. Weekdays: $9; Weekends: $12

SANTA FE GOLF COURSE
Santa Fe Park • 915-657-4485

Nine-hole course. Weekdays: $6; Weekends: $7.50

Hunting

Tom Green County offers excellent white-tailed deer, pronghorn antelope, javelina, turkey, and quail hunting. The turkey hunting is some of the best in the state. Contact the visitor bureau at 800-375-1206 for details on hunting leases and outfitters.

COLLEGES AND UNIVERSITIES

ANGELO STATE UNIVERSITY
2601 W. Avenue N. • 915-942-2211

Recognized as one of the top 10 "Up and Coming" regional universities in America, as well as one of the top three state-supported regional universities in Texas (*U.S. News and World Report*), ASU joins with three other institutions to form the Texas State University System: Sam Houston (Huntsville), Stephen F. Austin (Nacogdoches), and Sul Ross (Alpine).

With an enrollment of slightly more than 6,000, Angelo State offers 44 baccalaureate and 19 master degree programs. Situated north of Red Arroyo and close to the Concho River, new buildings and recent renovations dot the attractive campus that is ideal for strolls, constitutionals, and jogs of any length. A distinctive aspect to the ASU experience is the Carr Academic Scholarship Program, whose grants make high-quality education more affordable for nearly 900 undergraduates and graduate students.

On-campus activities include the University Planetarium (*see* **OTHER POINTS OF INTEREST**) and the home stands of numerous ASU Ram teams. Women's volleyball produces consistent Lone Star Conference champions while the ASU football team boasts the winningest record among Texas senior colleges during the 1980s (73-35-1) and an NAIA national championship (1978). Now an NCAA Division II member, the Rams have earned a spot in the top 20 rankings each year since the mid-1980s.

PERFORMING ARTS

The San Angelo Cultural Affairs Council sponsors a 24-hour telephone hotline featuring updates on the arts: 915-653-6793.

RIVER STAGE
By the Celebration Bridge • 915-657-4451 (Rec Dept.)

What seems like all of San Angelo can often be found along the banks of the Concho for a concert, melodrama, or musical at the River Stage. This outdoor facility showcases San Angelo's River Walk, and stands before open seats on blankets and occasionally under the stars.

SAN ANGELO CITY AUDITORIUM
West College Avenue at City Hall • 915-653-9577

The site of performances by the San Angelo Symphony and by the San Angelo Civic Ballet including an annual *The Nutcracker*.

SAN ANGELO COLISEUM

43rd and Coliseum Dr. • 915-653-9577 • W+ but not all areas

Home of the annual San Angelo Stock Show and Rodeo, the Coliseum is also a popular venue for events like the San Angelo Symphony Pops Concert and performances by entertainers like George Strait, Reba McEntire, T. Graham Brown, and Garth Brooks.

SAN ANGELO SYMPHONY

111 W. Twohig Avenue • 915-658-5877

Performances by the symphony are frequently in conjunction with the Ballet and the Chorale. The symphony also presents the prestigious Hemphill-Wells Sorantin Competition.

SHOPPING

LEGENDS JEWELERS

18 E. Concho St. • 915-653-2902
Monday–Saturday 9:30 a.m. to 5:15 p.m.

The true home of the Concho Pearl is the lakes and streams around San Angelo, but this downtown shop has the best selection of native pearls in San Angelo. From pink to purple, in earrings, necklaces, rings, and studs, these freshwater pearls are elegantly set in tasteful designs. Many other jewelry items are also available.

CHICKEN FARM ART CENTER

2505 Martin Luther King Blvd. • 915-653-4936
Tuesday–Saturday 10–5 • W variable

You don't have to shop to enjoy this converted chicken farm. The art center now houses studios for local artists and artisans and also has a gallery, a bronze casting foundry, and learning facilities. Media include blacksmithing, metalsmithing, woodwork, fine and folk art, stained glass, pottery, weaving, sculpture, and painting. The gallery is open to the public, and much of the creative process (including the foundry) can be viewed.

R.E. DONAHO SADDLE SHOP

8 East Concho • 915-655-3270

Founded in the same location over a century ago, Donaho's was originally established as the Concho Saddle Shop in 1890 and is renowned for crafting the legendary Concho Saddle. Owner Rector Story is the son-in-law of the late Bob Donaho and has been behind the counter since 1938. If your mount doesn't need a new saddle, consider a Donaho belt, billfold, purse, or notebook.

EGGEMEYER'S GENERAL STORE

35 East Concho • 915-655-1166
Monday–Saturday 10–5:30 • Closed Sunday

Many patrons remember the old location next to Miss Hattie's, and the recent move across the street has only improved the cozy atmosphere, the delicious smells, and the many gift items. Designers like James Avery and Jeep Collins are featured next to spiral-sliced hams, Texas honey, jams, jellies, and gourmet coffees. Enjoy a nickel cup of coffee as you browse among the many children's items: games, toys, dolls, soldiers, and books. Eggemeyer's almost bursts with seasonal items around Easter, Halloween, Thanksgiving, and Christmas.

RUSTY FRANKLIN HANDMADE BOOT CO.

3275 Arden Road • 915-653-2668
Monday–Friday 8:30 A.M. to 5:00 P.M. (later if you call)

Rusty Franklin hails from the great bootmaking tradition of his grandfather M. L. Leddy. A good portion of Rusty's 40-plus years has been spent working at a Leddy shop and, since 1986, at his own. Working cowboys, ranchers, and others looking for a rugged, comfortable boot buy Rusty's either off the shelf (prices start at $350) or custom made (starting at $425). After Rusty's cousin Rod sizes you up, allow 60 to 120 days for delivery on a custom pair. John Connally did. So did Henry Kissinger, Marcel Marceau, and Tommy Lee Jones. On a local note, prosecutors linked all three defendants in the Agscam case—Mort Mertz, Wally McGowan, and Mo Morrow—by their Rusty Franklin boots. If you can't stop by, call for a brochure.

J. WILDE'S

15 E. Concho • 915-655-0878 • Monday–Saturday 10:30–5:30

You may already know the J. Wilde label from clothes and accessories at the Apparel and Gift Markets in Dallas. This downtown San Angelo store is the home of those creative designs and a colorful stop on any trip. Clothes, furnishings, decorator fabrics, and accessories are piled on floors and furniture throughout this wonderful shop right in the heart of Concho Street. Retail isn't the only trade. The J. Wilde touch has brightened homes and offices across Texas.

SIDE TRIPS

PAINT ROCK PICTOGRAPHS

30 miles east of San Angelo on RR 380 and one mile northwest of the town of Paint Rock on U.S. 83 • 915-732-4376 or 915-732-4418
Call for an appointment • Admission: Adults $6, children $3

Freshwater springs and abundant game made this area a perennial camp for generations of native Americans. Comanche, Apache, Jumano, and Tonkawa decorated this one-eighth of a mile stretch of limestone cliffs with images of their enemies, their gods, their council meetings, and early Spanish missions at this nationally renowned site. Guides offer insightful explanations to the pictographs (rock paintings) whenever possible and also discuss painting techniques, Indian and settler history, and the commitment of the Sims and Campbell families to preserving this American treasure.

Budget roughly two hours per tour unless you take the longer barge trip up the Concho River on summer weekends. All tours are guided and need to be scheduled through Paint Rock Excursions. Groups meet and depart from the Paint Rock Excursions office on US 83 in the town of Paint Rock. If you arrive early, have a look at the handsome Concho County Courthouse (1886), which was partially constructed with limestone from the cliff location.

Paint Rock is prime wool and mohair country, and **Ingrid's Custom Hand-Woven Rugs** (800-752-8004) offers an excellent selection of inexpensively priced items. On your way back to San Angelo, consider stopping in at the **Lowake Steak House** (*see* RESTAURANTS).

US 67 WEST

From the Red River to the Rio Grande, US 67 meanders over 700 miles from the Arkansas state line clear to Chihuahua. Though sparsely populated, the 160-mile portion west of San Angelo to Fort Stockton covers some of the most historic sites in Texas history.

Twenty-four miles west of San Angelo, **Mertzon** is the county seat of Irion County. Generations of Kickapoo, Comanche, and Apache hunted these rolling hills and gurgling streams. Over a century has passed since a five-hour battle with Kickapoo tribesmen left 22 Confederates and Texans dead and 19 wounded at nearby Dove Creek (1865). Slow down to go antique shopping at the Treasure Chest (directly across from the C&W convenience store on the right as you come into town), to buy native plants from Steve and Valerie Lewis (up the block from the First National Bank of Mertzon on your left), or to stock your larder at Nicholson's Meat Company on US 67 with teriyaki, jalapeño, or regular beef jerky and beef sticks. Irion County's first courthouse (1899) and cemetery are a pleasant two-mile detour to **Sherwood**, a mile back toward San Angelo and another mile west on RR 72.

Seventy miles west of San Angelo stands the largest dry lake in Texas, 1½ miles south of **Big Lake**. The famous oil well **Santa Rita No. 1** lies 13 miles farther west (83 miles from San Angelo) surrounded by acres of pump jacks and scores of No Trespassing signs. This discovery well rivals Spindletop and Daisy Bradford No. 3 in Texas lore.

Plenty of signs and historical markers highlight the hallowed ground that brought in the Big Lake Field, led to the development of the Permian Basin (the world's largest inland petrochemical complex), and made the University of Texas and the Texas A&M systems among the nation's wealthiest. Long ago, the original rig was dismantled and reassembled in Austin at the corner of Trinity and Martin Luther King, Jr.

McCamey is almost 120 miles west of San Angelo; **Girvin** is a dozen miles farther. Zane Grey aficionados know this country by heart: **Castle Gap** and the ford at **Horsehead Crossing,** milestones in American history, are local landmarks. For thousands of nineteenth century pioneers, Castle Gap was the Western equivalent of Daniel Boone's Wilderness Road through the Cumberland Gap.

Forty-niners, the Butterfield Overland Mail, and trail driver Charles Goodnight are a few of the many who followed this native American trail through the distinctive mesa formation and down to the Pecos River, site of Horsehead Crossing. This ford across the treacherous Pecos was littered with the skulls and skeletons of hundreds of horses (and cattle) stolen in Mexico by Comanche raiders, herded across miles of dry desert only to die at the river's edge, too parched to stop drinking.

Learn more about both sites and obtain specific directions to Horsehead Crossing (Castle Gap is on private property) at the **Mendoza Trail Museum** in McCamey at Santa Fe Park, Tuesday through Friday from 1:00 to 5:30 p.m. Also available at Santa Fe Park are free RV parking, picnicking, and camping courtesy of the McCamey Chamber of Commerce.

ANNUAL EVENTS

April

SABERS, SADDLES, & SPURS
Fort Concho National Historic Landmark • 915-657-4441

Beginning with the opening ceremony, which is led by living history riders from Fort Concho, this event is an equine enthusiast's dream. Riding demonstrations and special drills are staged by the San Angelo Saddle Club and the Tom Green County Sheriff's Posse. Some of the events that fill the rest of the day include period drills by the Fort Concho Cavalry, cowboy polo, skill riding, and sidesaddle riding. The American Horse and Cavalry Review ends with a grand closing ceremony featuring show jumpers, Tennessee Walkers, and Paso Finos.

POLO IN THE PARK
Hoolihan Acres • One mile east of Mertzon on US 67
915-949-4837 • Last Sunday of the month • Admission • W

Journey out to Mertzon for an afternoon fundraiser to benefit Sonrisas, a therapeutic riding program. Polo matches feature local, professional, and celebrity polo players. An awards ceremony, auction, and party follow.

June

FIESTA DEL CONCHO

Fort Concho and along the Concho River • 915-657-4441
Third weekend of the month • Admission varies • W

Concho River activities include river barge rides and the river parade Saturday night. In and around San Angelo enjoy western dances, arts and crafts, plenty of music, and Frontier Day at Fort Concho (an event in itself).

December

CHRISTMAS AT OLD FORT CONCHO

Fort Concho National Historic Landmark
First weekend of the month • Admission

Lasting all weekend, this event features more than just hundreds of booths and tasty concessions. Fort Concho serves as the backdrop while entertainers and volunteers perform traditional holiday stories and reenact nineteenth-century military and civilian life. Different buildings host different themes like Victorian House, Czech Christmas House, German House, and Mexican/Southwest House. Cowboy poets, campfires, cavalry demonstrations, and wagon rides run all week long during this unique San Angelo tradition. A shuttle bus runs from the San Angelo Convention Center parking lot for Fort Concho every 20 minutes Friday, Saturday, and Sunday.

RESTAURANTS

($ = Under $7.50, $$ = Under $15, $$$ = $15+ plus tax & tip)

No mention of dining in San Angelo is complete without paying homage to John Zentner (1899–1994). The son of a German immigrant, he was raised near Rowena and went on to found restaurants as far south as Del Rio and north to Abilene. Without peer in West Texas, his signature was superb cuts of beef served in Texas-sized portions. His legacy is a string of renowned steak houses, including two of the state's best known—the Lowake Inn and the Lowake Steak House. Even well into his nineties, he was a part of the daily operation of Zentner's Daughter Steak House on Knickerbocker Road.

CHINA GARDEN

4217 College Hills Blvd. at Loop 306 • 915-949-2838
Daily • Lunch and dinner • $–$$ • Cr • W+

Ask any San Angeloan about China Garden and he'll mention favorites like Willow Beef, the shrimp plates, and the Pu Pu Platter. By far the most popular choice for lunch is the buffet during the week ($) and on Sunday ($$). From the bar, consider a Suffering Bastard but beware the Tiki Punch. It's as potent as it is easy to down. Bar.

DUN BAR EAST RESTAURANT

1728 Pulliam • 915-655-8780 • Daily
Breakfast, lunch, and dinner • $–$$ • AE D MC V • W

Staffed by hard-charging waitresses serving generous portions hot from the kitchen, the Dun Bar East is nothing fancy and that's probably why it's packed from dawn to dusk. High marks for the T-Bone and the filet. Sandwiches and burgers for the kids. Onion rings and/or an order of hot rolls is mandatory. Beer and wine.

LOWAKE STEAK HOUSE

Take Highway 67 (the Ballinger Highway) 27 miles north through Miles • Just before Rowena, turn right on FM 381 and go 6 miles Lowake • 915-442-2301 • Tuesday–Sunday lunch and dinner $–$$ • MC V

Seafood, chicken, and sandwiches are listed on the menu but most patrons skip the small talk and order beef: T-Bones, ribeyes, filets, clubs, and "K.C. for 7"—an enormous serving of Kansas City sirloins. Pass on the french fries and order a baked potato. Even better, get the onion rings. All entrées come with a trip to the salad bar and plenty of Texas toast. Beer and wine coolers.

MEJOR QUE NADA

1911 S. Bryant Blvd. • 915-655-3553 • Monday–Saturday Lunch and dinner • $–$$ • AE D MC V • W

What began as breakfast burritos several years ago has turned into San Angelo's most popular Mexican restaurant with all the style, presentation, and service one expects in San Antonio but not the high prices. Savor the fajitas, the steak *à la mexicana,* and any of the delicious enchiladas—beef, cheese, chicken, or shrimp. Mejor Que Nada is worth a visit just for their house margarita, made with Grand Marnier and Cuervo Gold. Bar.

TASTE OF ITALY

3520 Knickerbocker Rd. • 915-944-3290 • Daily except Sunday Lunch and dinner • $–$$ • AE D MC V

Contrary to popular opinion, good Italian cooking can be found in the Concho Valley. At Taste of Italy, veal and chicken are the forte. The *parmigiana,* the *piccata,* and the *marsala* are equally popular. Skip your normal bar order and consider the extensive wine cellar stocked with chardonnays, merlots, cabernets, and Italian varietals. Bar.

ZENTNER'S DAUGHTER STEAK HOUSE

1901 Knickerbocker Rd. • 915-949-2821 • Daily
Lunch and dinner • $–$$ • AE D DC MC V • W

With locations in San Angelo (right across from Bobcat Stadium) and Abilene, Zentner's Daughter Steak Houses are testimony to the Zentner tradition. The K.C. Steak for Two easily feeds four ($$$). Two tenderloins are required to serve an order of Tenders ($$), the tenderloin on the eye of the T-Bone. And the one-pound burgers ($) are ground from trimmings off the loins butchered by the restaurant's staff. Bar.

ZENTNER'S STEAK HOUSE

2715 Sherwood Way • 915-942-8631
Daily • Lunch and dinner • $–$$ • Cr

Open the door to Zentner's and you're greeted by autographed photos of Garth Brooks, Randy Travis, Alan Jackson, the Judds, and Reba McEntire. Founded by one of the many Zentners in the restaurant industry, Zentner's features excellent cuts of beef and an award-winning chicken-fried steak. Bar.

ACCOMMODATIONS

($ = Under $40, $$ = $40–$75, $$$ = $75–$100, $$$$ = Over $100)
Room Tax 13%

LA QUINTA INN

2307 Loop 306 • 915-949-0515 or 800-531-5900 • $$

This two-story inn located a mile west of Angelo State University has 170 units, including suites and non-smoking rooms with cable TV (Showtime) and room phones (free local calls). Amenities include complimentary continental breakfast from 6:30 to 10 a.m., free coffee in the lobby, and an adjacent Cafe La Quinta that also provides room service. Right off Loop 306 at the Knickerbocker exit, half a dozen different restaurants are within a couple of miles. On the premises are an outdoor unheated pool and hot tub, a laundry room, a 24-hour courtesy shuttle to and from Mathis Airport, and free parking. Smaller pets, under 25 pounds, welcome. AAA, AARP, government and military rates available.

OLE COACH MOTOR INN

4205 S. Bryant • 915-653-6966 or 800-227-6456 • $

Two stories, this property has 82 smoking and non-smoking units. Rooms include cable TV (HBO) and phones with no charge for local calls. Amenities include complimentary coffee in the lobby, the Coachmen Club, an outdoor unheated pool, and free parking. Pets under 20 pounds OK. AAA, AARP, corporate, government, military rates available.

RAMADA INN
2502 Loop 306 • 915-944-2578 or 800-272-6232 • $$

This two-story red brick Ramada sits off Loop 306 at the Knickerbocker exit. The 101 rooms including suites and non-smoking rooms have cable TV and room phones (free local calls). Amenities include the Little River Cafe and Club, an outdoor heated pool and hot tub, an exercise room, courtesy van to Mathis Airport (limited hours), and free parking. No pets.

SONORA

SUTTON COUNTY SEAT • 3,320 • (915)

A prosperous town at the western edge of the Edwards Plateau, Sonora serves as a hub for wool and mohair producers and for natural gas exploration and production. Established near plentiful Indian springs in the late nineteenth century, Sutton County is also the site of one of America's best caving experiences and draws visitors from around the globe to tour the Caverns of Sonora.

TOURIST SERVICES

SONORA CHAMBER OF COMMERCE
706 Southwest Crockett • Sonora • 76950 • 915-387-2880

Besides plenty of information and assistance, the chamber is your best contact for white-tailed deer hunting in this area.

HISTORIC PLACES

SUTTON COUNTY COURTHOUSE
Water Avenue and Oak Street • 915-387-2711 • W

Noted Texas architect Oscar Ruffini designed the Sutton County Courthouse which was completed in 1891. The heart of Sutton County is still the courthouse square. As you park on its south side, note the markers recognizing families who pioneered this wilderness in the late 1800s and early 1900s. Information on a self-guided walking tour is available in the courthouse and includes the restored Santa Fe Depot, the Miers Home Museum (1889), and a marker for the Frisco Trailway, a one-of-a-kind right-of-way owned by the Fort Worth and Rio Grande

Railroad that extended 100 miles from Sonora to Brady. This right-of-way, 250 feet wide, was the world's longest fenced cattle trail until trucking became more economical.

SHOPPING

OL' SONORA TRADING COMPANY
Exit 400 off I-10 • South one block • 915-387-5507 or 800-852-2784

Sutton County is located in the heart of the largest mohair producing area in America. Stretching from San Antonio to Fort Stockton, this belt accounts for 92 percent of America's mohair—the fine, silky fiber sheared from Angora goats. Ol' Sonora Trading Company stocks an assortment of attractive mohair sweaters, jackets, throws, blankets, and even socks featuring this lightweight, durable fiber—warmer than wool at a third of the weight.

SIDE TRIPS

CAVERNS OF SONORA
Exit 392 off of I-10 seven miles west of Sonora and follow the signs along FM 1989 south approximately eight miles • 915-387-6507
Open daily except Christmas • Admission varies per tour
Snack Bar • Picnic Area • Gift shop

The best description of this geological landmark comes from Bill Stephenson, a former president of the American Speleogical Society, who says "this is the most indescribably beautiful cavern in the world. Its beauty can't possibly be exaggerated—even by Texans." What makes the Caverns of Sonora so remarkable is the number and quality of helictites. More have been identified at the Caverns of Sonora than in all caverns worldwide. Helictites emerge from cave walls to form loops, horseshoes, and elk's horns, and the most distinct form is the butterfly formation.

Several tours of the caverns are offered. The Crystal Palace Tour is a 45-minute walk, the Horseshoe Lake Tour takes about an hour and 15 minutes, and both are combined in the Adventure Package which runs 2½ hours. Special photographic and geological tours are available by reservation only. The temperature in the Caverns is a steady 71 degrees, and the humidity is 98 percent. Members of your party can also follow the above-ground Nature Trail that traces the subterranean tours on paths hundreds of feet above the caverns.

RESTAURANTS

($ = Under $7.50, $$ = Under $15, $$$ = $15+ plus tax & tip)

COMMERCIAL CAFE

**167 SW Plum • 915-387-9928 • Monday–Saturday
Lunch and dinner • $ • Out-of-town checks with driver's
license • BYOB**

For three generations and nearly three-quarters of a century, the Commercial Cafe has been a Sonora landmark. Lemuel Lopez, the cafe's proprietor and mayor of Sonora, maintains that the cheese enchiladas are as good today as when his grandparents served them. One reason why is because the red sauce is still made without chile powder. Though Mexican plates are the specialty, the chicken-fried steak is a treat. Located in the heart of town and away from the interstate, take the Highway 277 exit (#400) to the first stop light, then a right onto Main Street, the first left (Glasscock), and go two blocks to Plum. If you're planning on enjoying a cold one with your meal, stop at one of the convenience stores on your way there. No alcohol is served.

SUTTON COUNTY STEAKHOUSE

**I-10 Exit 400 • 915-387-3833 • Monday–Saturday breakfast, lunch,
and dinner • Sunday breakfast lunch • $–$$ • AE MC V • W**

Service is prompt, portions are large, prices are reasonable. Try the steak bits. Cubed and then cooked to order, they're delicious. Most entrées come with a monstrous baked potato, soup or salad bar. Bar.

ACCOMMODATIONS

($ = Under $40, $$ = $40–$75, $$$ = $75–$100, $$$$ = Over $100)

DEVIL'S RIVER INN

I-10 Exit 400 • 915-387-3516 • $$

This two-story motel sits right beside I-10 and right next to the Sutton County Steakhouse. With 99 rooms including non-smoking ones, it has cable TV (HBO) and free local calls. Amenities include free coffee, an outdoor unheated pool, and laundry. Pets OK. AAA and AARP discounts available.

INDEX

ABOUT THE AUTHOR

Eric O'Keefe is editor-at-large for *Cowboys & Indians*, the premier magazine of the American West. His Texas travels, from the shores of South Padre Island to the high plains of the Panhandle, have formed the basis for numerous guidebooks and writing assignments. A graduate of Rice University, O'Keefe's high school years were spent in Alpine, the heart of the Big Bend/Davis Mountains region.